D1526545

ROBERT CHURCHILL'S
GAME SHOOTING

Other Titles by Countrysport Press

BEST GUNS *by Michael McIntosh*

THE BIG BORE RIFLE: The Book of Fine Magazine & Double Rifles .375-.700 Caliber *by Michael McIntosh*

CALL OF THE QUAIL: A Tribute to the Gentleman Game Bird

EASTERN UPLAND SHOOTING *by Dr. Charles C. Norris*

THE GRAND PASSAGE: A Chronicle of North American Waterfowling

"MR. BUCK": The Autobiography of Nash Buckingham *by Nash Buckingham*

RETRIEVER TRAINING: The Cotton Pershall Method *by Bobby N. George, Jr.*

SHOTGUNNER'S NOTEBOOK: The Advice and Reflections of a Wingshooter *by Gene Hill*

The following Countrysport Press titles are also available in DELUXE LIMITED EDITIONS:

BEST GUNS

THE BIG-BORE RIFLE: The Book of Fine Magazine & Double Rifles .375-.700 Caliber

CALL OF THE QUAIL: A Tribute to the Gentleman Game Bird

EASTERN UPLAND SHOOTING

THE GRAND PASSAGE: A Chronicle of North American Waterfowling

"MR. BUCK": The Autobiography of Nash Buckingham

SHOTGUNNER'S NOTEBOOK: The Advice and Reflections of a Wingshooter

The Countrysport limited editions feature:
*deluxe leather binding
*gilt-edged top papers
*ribbon bookmark
*specially commissioned gold foil cover art
*commemorative title page bearing the edition size and volume number with author's signature where applicable

ROBERT CHURCHILL'S
GAME SHOOTING

The definitive book on the Churchill method
of instinctive wingshooting for game
and sporting clays

A New Revised Edition
by
MACDONALD HASTINGS

New Foreword by Bryan E. Bilinski

COUNTRYSPORT PRESS
Traverse City, Michigan

To the memory of
ROBERT CHURCHILL

CONTENTS

NEW FOREWORD   *by Bryan E. Bilinski*

FOREWORD   *by Macdonald Hastings*

PREFACE
Straight Shooting
page 19

Its similarity to golf in certain aspects – shooting temperament – age is no bar – bad eyesight no serious handicap – the necessity of gun-fitting and coaching – 'Keep your eye on the Bird' – natural overthrow *v.* calculated allowances – muscle memory and gun drill *v.* conscious effort.

PART ONE
Drill

1 THE ELEMENTS OF GUN-HANDLING   **31**
Safety first – the dangerous factors – faulty guns – shooting risks – how to carry your gun.

2 THE FIRST OR 'READY' POSITION   **35**
The stock under the arm compels you to do the right thing, encourages you to stand correctly, to move your body and to point with the left or forward hand – the position of the trigger finger – how and when to operate the safety catch.

3 FEET   **38**
The correct stance combined with perfect balance and poise of body – common faults explained – indoor drill – how to practice and improve your footwork for normal crossing shots and back birds.

4 HANDS   **43**
The position of the right hand – the position of the left hand – grip only at the instant of firing – balance the gun between the two hands – common faults explained.

5 GUN-MOUNTING   **47**
Point your left hand at the bird – put your shoulder to the stock – common faults explained.

6 THE POSITION OF THE HEAD   **54**
Keep your eye on the bird – avoid head movement without equal body movement – the head should only move with the body – individual styles – young sight *v.* old sight – how to test the fit of your gun – cures for gun headache – where to look.

7 THE THEORY OF ALLOWANCE   **60**
Speed of bird *v.* a velocity of shot charge – how the eye can be deceived – the natural overthrow allied to perfect gun-mounting and body swing which automatically makes the correct allowance although you apparently shoot at the bird – ballistics in theory and practice – judging distances – judging heights.

8 PRACTICE IN THE FIELD   **69**
Shooting discomforts and cures – bruised second finger – bruised cheek – bruised mouth – bruised arm – bruised shoulder – bruised chest – how to open, load and close gun at speed yet with perfect safety – shooting rules – the danger zone – the poacher – some notes on etiquette.

9 SHOOTING FOR WOMEN   **77**
If they care to learn, women can shoot as well as men – a correct beginning half the battle – the approach to full-size gun must be carefully carried out – the small bore gun – the new 2-in. gun – gun drill – shooting clothes.

10 INSTRUCTIONS FOR THE USE AND LOADING OF A PAIR OF GUNS   **80**
Perfect team work is an aid to good shooting –the shooter's position – the loader's position – a perfect exchange of guns – some hints for quick loading – keeping the count.

PART TWO
Field Notes

1 THE RULES OF SHOOTING   **85**
The interpretation of the code varies in different company – shooting etiquette – shooting accidents – ricocheting pellets – syndicate shoots – eight very important rules for your safety and enjoyment – your legitimate field of fire – how to dispatch wounded game – shooting averages – keepers' tips.

2 CLOTHES AND ACCESSORIES   **104**
The right clothes for the shooting party are still anybody's fancy – the choice of your wardrobe will have a direct and noticeable influence on performance – the best jacket for shooting with a specification for your tailor – footgear – camouflage clothing – cartridge bags and belts.

3 HOW TO SHOOT GROUSE   112
Habits and environment – walking-up over dogs – driven birds – the grouse butt – on the
alert – where to look – always pick your bird – when to shoot – unsafe butts – unsteady shots.

4 HOW TO SHOOT PARTRIDGES   125
What not to do – analyzing the expert shot – stance and footwork – effortless
gun-mounting – where to look – how to mark your birds – some important 'don'ts' –
walking-up: everybody must help in marking birds – how to mark and gather birds.

5 HOW TO SHOOT PHEASANTS   135
The important difference between shooting grouse and pheasant and partridges and
pheasants – it is not a snap shot – indoor drill for overhead shots – high pheasants in theory
and practice – the confusion of 'conscious' allowance – the born shot analyzed –
some important 'don'ts' and a few very simple rules.

6 HOW TO SHOOT GROUND GAME   147
Even the most experienced shot is tempted to take chances – some shooting 'don'ts' –
some shooting hints – ferreting rabbits – rabbits bolting across a ride – hares –
how to make quick snap shots.

7 HOW TO SHOOT WILDFOWL   155
Dawn excursions and night attacks – the choice of gun, ammunition and clothes –
the best wildfowlers are always first-class naturalists – shooting from boat or hide –
the value of camouflage – tall birds.

8 VARIOUS   163
The odd and interesting additions to the main bag – the woodcock flight – the knack of snipe
shooting –wood pigeon decoys, jays, magpies, crows, rooks, grey squirrels and other vermin.

PART THREE
Trap Shooting

HOW TO SHOOT CLAYS   171
As an aid to improvement in shooting – the special technique necessary for 'down the line'
shooting – Skeet shooting, the varieties of stance and bodywork for the eight different
stands and sixteen different kinds of birds – the lay-out of a shooting ground.

PART FOUR
Gun Know-how

1 GAME GUNS OF TODAY   183
The all-round increase in hidden strength to meet modern conditions – single triggers –
barrel boring – length of barrels – the 'XXV' gun – second-hand guns.

2 THE COMPONENTS OF A GUN   192
The barrels – the various degrees of choke – patterns at forty yards – diameter of spread –
the body or action – sidelock v. box lock – easy-opening models – various shapes of fore-end –
leather handguards – triggers and weight of pull – the shape of the trigger guard –
the shape and size of foresight – the top rib – the shape of the butt – recoil pads.

3 THE MEASUREMENTS OF A GUN   204
Various shapes of stock – gun-fitting – weight of gun – length of stock – testing gun fit.

4 CARTRIDGES   209
Sizes of shot for various purposes – tests for pattern and penetration – powders and loads –
non-rusting primers – my ideal cartridge – bores of guns and their approximate weight
and shot charge – pellets in game charges – shot-gun patterns.

5 THE SHOOTING SCHOOL   218
Seeing the shot in the air – diagnosing results – curing the inconsistent shot – methods of
coaching explained – physical handicaps and cures – the one-arm shot.

6 THE CARE OF A GUN   232
How to assemble and dismount without effort – cleaning equipment – how to clean
gun-barrels – repairs in the field – faulty cartridges – the real value of a best gun.

Conclusion
page 241

Old and dangerous guns – teaching the young idea how to shoot – when to start a boy – shooting
is indeed a great field sport – summing up for the last time.

INDEX   249

FOREWORD

by Bryan E. Bilinski

> *'Nobody expects to play golf well without proper coaching and regular practice. Yet, although 'swing' is as important in game gun shooting as it is in golf, and although there are other notable similarities in the two sports such as, for example, the prime necessity of keeping your eye on the object you are aiming to hit, most men who get an occasional day with a gun are disappointed with themselves because they fail to put up a good performance. The secret of straight shooting, like playing scratch golf, is constant practice, a steady temperament and a knowledge of the game.'*
>
> ROBERT CHURCHILL

In the modern history of shotgunning, there is not another wingshooting technique so universally accepted and utilized by bird hunters worldwide as the "Churchill Method" properly that is explained and taught in this definitive book, *Game Shooting* by Robert Churchill and MacDonald Hastings.

Virtually every shooting school and shooting grounds in the United States and Europe currently teaches an exact or modified version of the "Churchill Method" in its program of instruction. In addition, wingshooters from the United States have been recently introduced to a whole new world of shooting opportunities through the wonderful and challenging game of "sporting clays," a game that has finally brought our hunting guns out of the gun cabinet during the long drought between bird seasons.

Sporting clays courses and grounds are unique clay target shooting facilities, laid out in natural, field-type hunting condition environments, with a primary purpose of replicating the numerous varieties of shots a wingshooter might encounter during the course of the upland bird or waterfowl hunting season. The tremendous response to and popularity of sporting clays have opened a new window of interest in the Churchill wingshooting method, and rightly so.

I'd prefer to not have to mention the other various techniques that are unfortunately based on telling the shooter to make and see varying "forward allowances" or "leads" (God forbid) on targets or birds traveling at different speeds and angles.

The only reason I am compelled to mention these other systems is to warn you that they are very complicated, "mind-consuming" and truly open-ended ways of teaching shotgun work. In reality, the shooter who tries to mentally make such calculations and field judgements of "lead," really ends up poking his gun, attempting to aim a gun meant to be pointed, focuses on his gun barrels or front sight, checks and interrupts his swing, stops the gun, and ultimately misses the bird or target.

The basis of the Churchill method is to simply swing and point directly at the bird or target and trust, in proper form, your God-given gift to unerringly hit anything you point at via the perfection of hand-eye coordination. If your gun fits you relatively well, it's shooting exactly where your eyes are looking, then relax, concentrate on your target, utilize a practiced Churchill style and technique – and you'll connect on a much higher percentage of game birds and targets. And you'll do it with more consistency and enjoyment than ever before in your life as a wingshooter. The Churchill technique is a proven method that sincerely *works*.

Therefore, it is my pleasure and honor to present *Game Shooting*, the definitive book on the Churchill wingshooting method for bird hunting and sporting clays – and a classic volume dedicated to a lifetime of one man's experience, a legend of our time, the famed Robert Churchill, fine gunmaker and authoritative wingshooting instructor.

Bryan E. Bilinski is an authority on fine shotguns, a crack field and sporting clays shot, and one of North America's most skilled shotgunning instructors and gunfitters. His capacity to put shooting technique and theory into practice through clear, concise instruction would have made Mr. Churchill proud.

Bryan's credentials are impressive – including the fact that in 1984, while the manager of Orvis Houston, he designed and supervised the construction and operation of the first nationally recognized sporting clays course in the United States.

In 1985, this course, known as Orvis Houston's Pin Oaks Shooting School, hosted the first-ever National Sporting Clays Championship. Shortly thereafter, the United States Sporting Clays Association was formed in Houston, with the use of the shooting grounds as the foundation of this group's activities. Now, the sport has grown so that thousands of shooters each year participate in sporting clays, and manufacturers are developing products especially for this new sport, which threatens to displace other clay target games in popularity. If anyone anywhere deserves the title of "The Father of Sporting Clays in the United States," it is Bryan Bilinski.

But the school – and Bryan personally – always had the teaching of wingshooting as the primary goal and focus, and as sporting clays has grown in this country from that early beginning to over 700 courses across the nation, the best ones all follow Bryan's early lead and offer instruction as well as competition and "fun" shooting. It is fitting that Bryan should write a new Foreword for Mr. Churchill's work on wingshooting and shotgunning technique.

STEVEN R. SMITH
Countrysport Press

FOREWORD

by Macdonald Hastings

In my preface to the first edition I quoted the epitaph which Colonel Peter Hawker composed in 1835 in honour of his friend the great gunmaker Joseph Manton. I added that I wasn't sure that it wouldn't do equally well, in our own time, to describe the achievement of Robert Churchill. Bob, who was no literary man, didn't appreciate that I was summoning a quotation. Until I explained the matter to him he thought that I was flattering him too much by half. But when he died on June 30, 1958, three years after the first publication of this textbook, I had no hesitation in his obituary in the *London Times* in quoting Hawker again:

'An everlasting monument to his unrivalled genius is already established in every quarter of the globe, by his celebrity as the greatest artist in firearms that ever the world produced, as the founder and father of the modern gun-trade, and as a most successful inventor in other departments, not only for the benefit of his friends and the sporting world, but for the good of his King and Country.'

Big words, in the large and sentimental language of the Victorian period. But in many ways Churchill's contribution to his trade and his times was an even greater one than Manton's. He certainly enjoyed a wider fame. In every police department of the world the name of Churchill remains a legend as a pioneer, and the unquestioned authority, on the identification of bullets in criminal cases.

He was official firearms expert to Scotland Yard for almost fifty years. He was called as an expert witness by the Directorate of Public Prosecutions in nearly every murder trial involving a shooting in this century. His evidence, based on the scientific examination of firearms and bullets, was often decisive.

His reputation in the criminal courts was unique. Whether or not he was 'the father of the modern gun trade,' as Manton undoubtedly was its grandsire, is a matter of opinion and of controversy, too. In the years when he was introducing and improving his newly designed game guns with short barrels, the arguments for and against were so embittered that people in the same shooting field, never mind what was said in other London gunshops, could scarcely discuss the subject with equanimity. Some still can't.

It remains arguable whether Churchill's 25-inch guns were an improvement on the 28-inch barrelled guns which are still generally more popular. It is probably true that his short-barrelled weapons are better suited to a short and stocky man of Churchill's own build than to a long-necked lean one like myself. Nevertheless I have shot, not badly, with Churchill's stumpy guns all my life. I doubt if anybody who has used them, even though he thought he didn't like them, has killed one head of game the less.

The average shooting man will be wise to discount a large part of what any London gunmaker tells him about his competitors. Since Manton's time it has always been a jealous trade; and Churchill himself was no exception to the rule. The fact of the matter is that there is not much to choose between the guns made by half-a-dozen of the leading makers. They even share the same hand-craftsmen. Enough that Churchill's best guns compare with any built in London in the twentieth century; and that's saying something because, to a connoisseur, there's nowhere else on earth which, by comparison, even counts.

Whether you shoot with a Churchill gun, or any other, is of no consequence in the study of this textbook, the purpose of which is simply to teach you, Churchill's way, to shoot straighter than you have ever shot before.

The only authoritative book on how to shoot, apart from a library of books on what to shoot at, is a manual originally written in the nineteenth century. In the fashion of the times, it teaches the old system of shooting at moving targets by telling the sportsman to make varying 'forward allowances' at game travelling at different speeds and angles. It is an appallingly complicated way of teaching shot-gun work and, in practice, the man who tries to make arbitrary calculations of 'forward allowances' usually pokes his weapon and shoots below and behind.

The essence of Churchill's method is that he taught his pupils to swing on to the bird; to trust the unerring ability of the eye to make the necessary forward allowance, and to leave it to the gun to do the rest. It works.

I am sometimes asked whether Churchill himself was a great shot. He was sometimes described as 'one of the best shots in

Europe'; but he wasn't that. In any company he was a very good shot, a beautiful stylist with a gun and magnificent at breaking clay-pigeons. But he could miss with the rest of us. His great quality was that, when he was off his day, he didn't get hot and bothered. Selecting his birds, reserving cartridges rather than blasting at everything that moved, he quietly shot himself into form again.

I think that it was just because he wasn't what's called 'a born shot,' because he had to experiment and practise to find out why he missed, that he became the great shooting coach he was. He was fallible enough himself to be able to diagnose the troubles of others.

He knew that, with a gun that fits, the reason why most people miss is out of sheer lack of self-confidence. And it may come as a surprise to tens of thousands of shooting men who went to school with him that, to begin with, they were children of his remarkable psychological insight. In the preparatory class, he lobbed over clays you could hit with a stone and loaded the cartridges with what amounted to dust-shot. It was only when his pupils could scarcely stand on the ground with self-esteem that he made it more difficult.

I had the rare fortune, on many days as his guest in the field, to have Churchill on his own insistence as my loader. Under his direction, I shot so unexpectedly well that the captain of the shoot protested that he hadn't enough pheasants to support the combination. What Churchill taught me is in this book.

Learning from a book is obviously a more difficult way of learning than by taking lessons at a shooting school. But it can be done. I taught myself how to use a fly-rod that way. And not everybody has the opportunity, or the money, to go to school. You won't go far wrong if you accept the direction of a man who, in the world of guns, was a master.

The reader may reasonably enquire what qualification I myself have to revise this new edition of *Churchill's Game Shooting*. Sufficient if I say that the words in the original edition were mine, too. Churchill was my friend and, in shooting, my mentor, for twenty years.

Between the wars, in collaboration with Major Hugh B. C. Pollard, he published a brief guide on how to shoot which is now out of print. Subsequently, I persuaded him to undertake this more ambitious work.

After his death, I learnt that he had named me as one of his literary executors. In due course I found myself in possession of the papers connected with his great criminal cases. After hedging a bit at the immensity of the task, I became his biographer. This revised edition of *Churchill's Game Shooting* is published to coincide with the publication of the story of his life.*

In recommending it to sportsmen, it is important to emphasize that I have recorded his teaching as faithfully as a piece of blotting paper. If my own personality impinges, it is only here and there. I have taken care to separate what I think from what he said.

In the few instances where the hard information was out-of-date, I have corrected without comment. Churchill would have wished me to do that. For the rest, whenever I have intervened to disagree or to put a viewpoint which, since the first publication of this book, has been the cause of discussion, I have set my own reflections, and others, in italic type. The device will enable the reader to distinguish between the authorized version and the apocrypha.

In preparing this new edition, I have had the benefit of the expert comments of Mr. Norman Clarke, formerly gunfitter and coach on Churchill's own shooting grounds, and now of Messrs. Holland & Holland. His advice has been peculiarly valuable because, since Churchill's *Game Shooting* was first published, Norman Clarke has probably heard every possible criticism that could be levelled at the original text; and, under field conditions, he has had a unique opportunity of discovering passages, even words, which are liable to misinterpretation. I have faithfully referred to the points of controversy, and added explanations to phrases which appeared to require further clarification.

The advice I have had from others, including Colonel J. K. Stanford and Mr. Frank Law, F.R.C.S., the distinguished ophthalmologist, gives me cause to hope that this manual may now be regarded as definitive.

I was tempted to excise the photographs of Churchill himself, in that awful check suit and the stockings which are worse, from this edition. As Bob very well knew, they are not the sort of clothes which are generally welcome on the shooting field. But they are almost the last pictures of him; and it is appropriate that he should appear in this memorial edition as he looked

* *The Other Mr. Churchill* (Harrap).

towards the end of his days. By contrast, I commend the reader to the earlier photographs of him between pages 128–129, when he was at the peak of his form. His style is impeccable.

Norman Clarke had the unenviable task of modelling for the illustrations showing the wrong ways of handling a gun. It is typical of his loyalty to the memory of 'the old guv'nor' that he hasn't wanted them changed. Anyhow, it will be self-evident to all shooting men that it requires just as much knowledge to show the wrong way as the right.

To anyone who believes that he learnt all 'the don'ts' long ago, let Norman Clarke himself, whom many of us count the best shooting coach today, have the last word. 'If there were an advanced shooting test, in the same way that there are advanced driving tests, I wouldn't pass eight out of ten.' The aim of this book is to raise the number of would-be successful candidates.

AFTERWORD

I have not altered the foreword I wrote in the revised edition in 1963. It is proper that a book of this kind should preserve continuity. It is now (1971) over fifteen years since it was first published, twelve years since Churchill's death. Produced in many countries, and many editions, it is accepted as the standard work on its subject. Since I wrote in 1963, Major Hugh B. C. Pollard and Mr. Norman Clark have both died. Norman, a modest technician, was a genius in showing how to make a man feel good with a gun. Major Pollard was a high intellectual who, in a series of books, taught the charm of field sports.

I have written my tribute to Major Pollard in a monumental work, *Pollard's History of Firearms*, which I am told may be published a few years from now. Meanwhile, I salute the memory of a man who did so much to help this contemporarily definitive work.

In this new edition, I have had no occasion to change the drill of gunmanship. I have excised parts of the text, from earlier reprints, in the chapters on cartridges and the care of guns. So much has changed in a decade. I have had to add only a few comments to keep it completely up to date.

MACDONALD HASTINGS

Straight Shooting

NOBODY expects to play golf well without proper coaching and regular practice. Yet, although 'swing' is as important in game gun shooting as it is in golf, and although there are other notable similarities in the two sports such as, for example, the prime necessity of keeping your eye on the object you are aiming to hit, most men who get an occasional day with a gun are disappointed with themselves because they fail to put up a good performance. The secret of straight shooting, like playing scratch golf, is constant practice, a steady temperament and a knowledge of the game.

Shooting knowledge can be acquired by anyone who takes the trouble to learn that there is more to shooting than being able to distinguish which end of the gun to keep clear of. Temperament, unhappily, is more difficult to control. But in shooting, as in other sports, coaching and sheer gunmanship can do a great deal to combat it.

The essential, and encouraging, difference between shooting and most other sports is that, under the guidance of an expert coach, a complete duffer can be made into a fair shot after a few hours' practice.

In the first place, unlike most sports, age is a very small factor in game shooting. As muscles become set, limbs stiffen, it becomes more than ever important to use a gun which has been tailored to fit the user. But, with good coaching and a gun that fits him, a man of seventy is capable of 'wiping the eye' of a stripling; and in fact, often does. The mistake that so many men make, who take up shooting late in life, is in thinking that any old gun will do and that they learnt all about it when they handled a rifle in the army. In fact, a knowledge of rifle shooting is a questionable introduction to handling a shot-gun. A shot-gun is a weapon of movement. A rifle is a weapon of immobility. And it is rare, in my experience, for a man to excel with both. Normally, it is advisable to concentrate on one weapon at a time.

Secondly, unlike most sports, keen eyesight in shot-gun shooting is comparatively unimportant. A man who cannot hit a golf ball, or pot a black, to save his life, can shoot driven game with fair precision, provided only that he can see well enough to distinguish a flying pheasant from a partridge, at about thirty yards.

In practice, shot-gun shooting takes place at such short ranges that faults of vision which debar a man from accurate rifle practice won't make any material difference to his performance in the coverts, on the marsh or in the stubbles. Whether you wear glasses or not, providing you can see well enough to indentify, for example, the number of a London bus in time to raise your hand to stop it, vision is going to present no difficulty to you in the shooting field.

(In the first edition, Churchill enlarged here a personal theory on 'the master eye' which is scientifically unacceptable. For that reason, I have deleted the passage. There is no doubt that he sometimes reached the right conclusion the wrong way. Vision, see editorial note on page 117, was his Achilles' heel.

For example, he persisted in his belief that, in shot-gun work, it is essential to keep both eyes open. He argued that faults of vision could be corrected by gun-fit, and modifications of style. It is a positive doctrine, typical of him, which most will do well to accept. Nevertheless, there are some who will shoot straighter with one eye closed.

Never mind 'the master eye.' It is just one of those vague phrases which shooting coaches are prone to.)

If you are not too old for the gentle exercise of shooting in coverts, you are young enough to use a shot-gun as well, if not better, than a young man who is in good enough physical condition to play for England at rugby football.

But you can't be a good shot unless you're prepared to practise as thoroughly as a good golfer practises for his game, and unless you realize that just knowing how to put a gun to your shoulder and pull the trigger isn't enough to be an average, never mind a first-class shot.

While the shooting school can never reproduce the actual conditions of the shooting field proper, it is safe to say that a man who can hit clay pigeons consistently is unlikely to make a complete 'blot' of an important day in the coverts. And, if his gun fits and the coach knows his job, he will be hitting clay pigeons—if not consistently at any rate often enough to give a wonderful lift to his morale—before he has fired a hundred rounds. The fact is, if you present a well-fitting shot-gun properly to the shoulder, and keep your eye on the quarry, you cannot possibly miss.

The reason that all of us do miss—much too often—is entirely the consequence of bad style. We drop our heads or fail to thrust the shoulder well into the gun. We shoot off balance through bad footwork. We fail to hold the barrels of the gun straight in the cup of the left hand. We 'poke' instead of swinging. We hang on to the trigger. Every miss is a fault in style. So much so that it is comparatively easy for an expert to tell whether a man has killed his bird or not simply by watching his gun handling and without looking at the target at all.

Obviously, faults can never be entirely eliminated. If that were possible, there would be no fun in shooting. But nobody can hope to improve performance without recognizing that, providing the gun fits and is throwing an even pattern of shot, a miss is always the consequence of bad style. The moral is that, if you wish to improve your shooting, the first necessity is to recognize your own weaknesses. Anybody can miss. Everybody should know, every time, why he misses. When you can say, with precision, that you shot high or low, too far in front or too far behind—which is not a very difficult thing to do—you are more than half-way to being a good shot.

When first-class shots are asked how they do it, they often have considerable difficulty in explaining their technique: what conscious allowances they make for the speed of the bird; how they judge the moment to fire; and how they deal with targets at various angles. The answer is that they don't have to think about it because they have largely solved this problem of style.

The footwork, bodywork, and gun-mounting of a first-class shot is as pretty to watch as a first-class batsman at cricket. But although stylish shooting is difficult to achieve, there need be no mystery as to how it is done.

There are two techniques of learning shooting at driven game. The older method (and, I think, the archaic method) is based on the principle of 'forward allowances.' The shooter is supposed to calculate the speed and angle of the target, and then swing the gun ahead of it, or above or below, so that the charge and the target meet. Many gun coaches still teach on this principle.

You will find in this book that my method is to tell you: 'Keep your eye on the ball,' swing your body with the target and shoot straight at it, varying the speed of the swing with the speed of the bird.

(*Words have limitations. Since this text-book was first published, it has been pointed out that the instruction 'shoot straight at the bird' could be misunderstood. It might lead some to stop in the middle of their swing. It is important to emphasize that the gun must never lose the rhythm of movement. Keep your eye on the target—if you're missing, concentrate on a particular detail of the target, it doesn't matter what—come up from behind and press the trigger as you sweep through. Never, never consciously point your gun at the quarry. The gun won't miss if your eye is on the target and your body movement, and follow-through, is smooth and balanced.*)

Admittedly, it is easier to write about it than to achieve it. But in my experience it is far simpler to shoot in the way of my school which tells you 'to stroke the birds out of the sky' than the one that suggests a different lead to every bird that comes. The truth is that a mental calculation of allowance will let you down again and again. The man who shoots straight at his bird, and automatically overthrows as he fires, is leaving his eyes to work out allowances for him. The eye is never wrong. If you miss, you can blame your failure on faulty body movement, bad gun holding, erratic trigger pulling, or a similar error.

The purpose of this book is to put down, in practical terms, the reason why we miss and to teach a technique of straight shooting.

Simply reading this book won't make you a better shot. You won't improve your average performance, whether you are an experienced shooting man or a novice, unless you build muscle memory.

Your mind may accept the new knowledge, but only practice with the lesson in mind will ram it for ever into your subconsciousness. Take my instructions, especially in the first section of the book, as drill; accept them, practise them, and, above all, master them, not only in abstract theory but in actual practice. Concentrate on the rules and practise the technique; then, like swimming, you will never forget it.

When a child masters the difficult feat of walking he forgets how to walk—he knows how—but he is unaware of his knowledge, as it is forgotten by his conscious mind. He does it, in fact, without thinking. If anyone starts thinking about walking, such as when crossing a narrow plank over a stream, he immediately does it unnaturally and without confidence and is apt to falter. Until the motions of swimming become a habit to a man, the learner is awkward, clumsy and lacks confidence. But as soon as the motions become a habit to him, when he is expert, he does it without thinking. In other words he has forgotten how to swim.

All this is to assure you that if you will practise the drill I recommend to you you will gain muscle memory and you will be able to mount your gun properly without conscious thought or effort. Accept my teaching as you accept any formal drill. Practise what I tell you as a purely physical technique—without argument —and you will find that your shooting has emerged from the mist of hazard to a very steady average basis upon which you can build your individual style.

There is no fixed standard of style in shooting as there is no fixed standard in any other sport. When all is said and done the personal equation is always paramount. A long-armed, narrow-chested tall man will inevitably have a different style as compared with a short, broad-chested, short-armed man; but, when you come to analyse comparative performance, there is very little, except the purely physical difference, to influence the mechanics of the process. The methods I advocate suit all physical variations, are easily learnt, and once learnt never forgotten.

A secondary but no less important characteristic will always intervene—temperament. This is a more disconcerting quality, for you will meet the quick, impatient type and the slow velocity, enduring, patient slogger. The first is the hardest problem for himself as well as for the gun coach because he is always in antagonism to himself. Mind outreaches his physical performance, and he is likely to swing to the other extreme, becoming casual, half-hearted and disappointed. Here discipline counts; practice and success will cure that man. His biggest enemy is his own despondency, his quick reaction to failure. But if a mercurial spirit like this once sees that he is getting better, there is no more adept pupil and the mastery once gained lasts.

Your low velocity, patient slogger, presents another condition; yet in a sense his shortcomings are his virtues. Slow to put into practice what he learns, yet once there it remains for ever. Nothing will shake it. He will always be a sound, clean shot.

In brief, there is no fixed style in shooting; every man must develop his own style, but the basis of shooting is always and invariably dependent on first learning the routine which I outline in this book. First, learn to play the game with a straight bat.

If you do that there's plenty of room for you to develop your own special technique.

Not until you make a critical survey of the wealth of books on shooting and sporting subjects which have appeared, do you realize how few of them contain any practical instruction on how to handle a shot-gun.

The English language, so rich in its output of technical and sporting literature, is strangely lacking in an authoritative treatment of the science of shooting and the sort of detailed analysis of the sport that has been accorded to style and performance in other sports and other games.

This, in essence, is due to the radical difference which exists between games which can be witnessed by a large audience and the comparative seclusion in which shooting is practised.

The average sportsman who shoots is seldom able to criticize, or rather analyse, the performance of his brother guns in the field. He is too busy, and his attention must necessarily be concentrated on his own sector of the beat or drive. His own style in nine cases out of ten, is a standard of unconscious proficiency, joint product of a well-fitting gun, a good eye and past experience. Questioned by an eager novice he can find few golden rules to explain 'how to shoot,' and in most cases admits that it is more a matter of knack than any conscious formula or system of technique.

But as I am a gun-maker who, as well as being a practical shot, is accustomed to studying the actual performance of men at the shooting school, I naturally approach the problem from a different standpoint. I am teaching you from my experience not only as a shot but as a critic and analyst of individual styles. What I am telling you in this book is not limited to casual glances at field performances during the shooting season but is based upon a routine of experience throughout the year. You can approximate me to the coach, amateur or professional, whose value and authority are admitted in every other branch of sport from lawn tennis to boxing.

At the beginning of this book, I am anxious to persuade you that the art of shooting is one that is just as capable of being taught or learnt from fundamental points of style or technique as golf and tennis. In such games the attention paid to such matters as grip, position and stance is rightly recognized as the highway to proficiency. It forms the basis of training which, with practice, develops into satisfactory achievement and a good style. My method is to deal with the use of the game gun and the attainment of shooting skill on these modernized lines. Expert rifle and pistol shots have long since insisted on correct physical technique as the basis of all teaching in their particular branches of shooting. Careful study of shot-gun shooting over many years has taught me that certain fundamental rules, which can be defined, are at the bottom of all good shot-gun work and the disregard of these rules accounts for nearly all the bad shooting attributed to bad luck or other impersonal causes.

Good shooting is an indefinite term at best, for we all have varying standards by which we gauge our own and other people's performances. But in shooting there is no system of gauging proficiency like handicaps at golf. We just form our own impressions of the people we see at the game.

We all know bad shots, poor shots, ordinary shots, fair shots, good shots, brilliant shots, and those happy beings known as born shots. But these are all purely comparative terms. Personally I would make a difference between 'good' and 'brilliant' shots. A 'brilliant' shot is a man whose standard of accuracy is as high as that of the 'good' shot; but, where the latter is cautious, and does not fire at difficult birds, the 'brilliant' man takes chances and, as a result, shows a lower percentage of kills to cartridges expended. On the other hand he probably kills more game in the day than the 'good' shot, who is content only to take birds at easy angles. And, of course, the man who takes sporting chances gets a good deal more fun out of it.

The 'born' shot is the rare man who enjoys the consistent accuracy of the 'good' shot in combination with the less calculated style of the 'brilliant' shot. The success of the 'born' shot is, however, due to the fact that consciously (or far more probably entirely unconsciously) he automatically obeys the underlying rules of the art and achieves perfect co-ordination of muscular movement and aim.

Having read as far as this, the average to bad shot may well ask: 'Am I too old or too set in my bad habits to develop into a good shot as late as this?'

Certainly he can. In fact, the man who is used to handling a gun, even inaccurately, will improve far more speedily than an absolute novice. The absolute beginner is perhaps the most difficult of all people to teach because he makes hard work of each shot. In a word he uses far too much physical energy in his movements and expends too much mental calculation on his aim. He looks at the gun rather than the bird, tries to improve his first aim. He puts enough vigour into his swing and 'follow-through' to lift a steam engine and finally he stops to pull the trigger, shooting behind his target.

(*The statement that the beginner is the most difficult pupil is arguable. Churchill was properly concerned in encouraging shooting men, who had lost faith in themselves, to try again. He had enormous success in re-educating the disappointed, proving to them that it was faults of style, and not inherent inability, which was why they missed. But, obviously, the beginners in any sport are the richest material. Otherwise, there would be no future in it.*)

Faults of style are easier to correct in men who have done at least sufficient shooting to have got over the preliminary troubles of awkward muscular action with the gun, who no longer flinch from fear of the noise or recoil, and who have overcome the feeling of strangeness inseparable from an introduction to any new sport. Experience proves that bad shooting habits can be eliminated at almost any age and that the experienced shot learns, on the whole, very swiftly.

The next question which might be asked is 'Can a man teach himself to shoot?' He can, and a careful study of this book will help him enormously. But, of course, he can never see his own faults as clearly as a bystander, and inevitably an expert coach can teach a man more in half a dozen lessons than he is likely to learn by himself in three times the time.

If a man cannot find opportunity for a little work with a skilled coach he can do a good deal for himself by persuading a friend to go over with him the technique laid down in this book and then go out with him in the field. The friend, if he is an alert critic, will be able to indicate what appears to be the shooter's faults in the light of what he has just read. One of the best ways in which a shooting man can double-check himself and compare his actual performance in the field with the instruction laid down in this book is to persuade a friend to photograph him in action with a cine-camera. Using a home movie you can make a point by point examination of the individual gun action. I have already used the cine-camera a great deal myself and found it invaluable for demonstrating to the sportsman his idiosyncrasies. For example, a gun may fit perfectly but a momentary hesitation, or an error in mounting, will negative the result of the best-fitting weapon which ever left a London workshop. Yet, if you know where your own fault lies, you are three-quarters of the way to curing it; the cine-film shows precisely where the error lies, and, once known, a correction is easy.

I want to emphasize that the teachings in this book are not directed either to the novice or the expert in particular. They are for all shooting men. A lot that I have written in the earlier chapters will seem familiar to experienced shots, but any man who ever misses a bird—and who doesn't?—will find that his own failures can be corrected by referring back to the drill. On the other hand, I like to think that the novice with little or no experience in handling a gun will find that he can start here right at the beginning.

I have already referred to a man with a well-fitting gun. Ideally no man can expect to shoot at his best unless his gun has been tailored to fit his own physical conformity as carefully as his suit. But this drill will be equally valuable even to someone who can't afford to have a gun specially made to his own measurements. The man who can't afford it will almost certainly be a younger man. All I need say to him is that gun-fit is not so important to a man when his muscles are limber and he is able, to a very large degree, to fit himself to his gun. Gun-fit becomes increasingly important as a man grows older and his muscles get set. But whatever old gun you use—providing you take care to see that it's proofed for modern cartridges—you will shoot the better for taking my advice.

Finally, blame nobody but yourself if you bruise your fingers on the trigger guards, get a sore jaw, or suffer from what is called 'gun headache.' Gun-makers will be delighted to sell you various accessories to relieve the trouble. But, if you held your gun properly, you wouldn't need them. The proper cure is to find out what you are doing wrong. If your style improves, you will not need rubber padding and the birds you shoot at will mysteriously discard 'their tin drawers.'

PART ONE

DRILL

I

The Elements
of Gun-Handling

UNLIKE the muzzle-loaders of our forefathers, loading
and letting off a modern shot-gun is a simple matter. So
simple that although the mechanism of game guns today
is as safe as human ingenuity can devise and the mere process of
charging and discharging calls for no explanation, the temptation
to use a gun carelessly is greater than ever before.

In the nineteenth century, in the days of Colonel Peter Hawker,
the father of modern game-gun shooting, the muzzle-loading
flintlock and percussion gun of the period involved so many
hazards to the user that the wonder is that there weren't more
accidents.

If you read Colonel Hawker's diaries, you will find that it was
a fairly common occurrence for shooting men to blow off their
hands loading black powder into the muzzle of a barrel in which
the spark from a previous charge was still burning. Powder flasks
blew up in the shooter's hands and pockets. Barrels burst when
somebody forgetfully put in a double charge.

Sometimes, when a man had fired with one barrel and stopped
to reload, the second one went off in his face. In moments of
excitement the shooters forgot to draw out their ramrods and
fired ramrod and all at the departing quarry. The back flash from
a flint gun occasionally blinded the user. Badly made copper caps
in percussion guns exploded like shrapnel. Not surprisingly, the
most important lesson a novice had to learn before the coming
of the breech-loader, in the latter years of the past century, was to
avoid flinching when he pulled the trigger.

With modern game guns and modern smokeless cartridges the
only dangerous factors the shooter needs to consider seriously are
himself and the other gun.

The first and most important convention of the shooting field prescribes that in no circumstances shall a gun, loaded or un-loaded, point towards anyone. The second rule is that, in theory at any rate, a gun is always loaded.

Every gun, with what is called a safety catch, carries the legend 'SAFE' when the catch is engaged. It is a dangerous word; but the gun traders, and the shooting men who patronize them, are a conservative breed and custom rules that that word 'Safe' remains: 'CHECK' would be better. The safety catch simply checks the trigger. The sears and tumblers of the actions are *never* locked.

I recommend you, as a drill, to use your safety catch. But I beg you to regard it as an extra precaution rather than a basic one.

The best of guns can become unsafe through neglect or climatic causes. Slight swelling of the wood, for example, may prevent the sear from fully entering its bent and the gun can jar off when closing. A very old 'springy' stock may cause the sears to be partly lifted during closing. I remember one of our famous gun-makers could take one of his own lock plates and, with a sharp flick on his bench, jar off the lock.

In my time as an expert witness called in many civil and criminal cases I have had to examine I-don't-know-how-many faulty guns. In one case heavy damages were awarded in a civil action to a sportsman who lost his leg as a consequence of an accident in which a gun, which another guest was carrying quite properly under his arm, went off unexpectedly. The safety catch was engaged; but the lock failed. A stranger case, fortunately without serious consequences, was one in which the owner loaded, put his gun at 'Safe,' and was astounded, a few minutes later, when it went off. He emptied his gun and put it under the back seat of his car. A few minutes later he heard a click. Once again, the action had operated of its own accord.

When the gun was brought to me I found the right lock had been fired. Closing it very carefully, I laid it down while I made my notes. To my own great surprise, it went off again after several minutes. Before stripping the gun I had a record taken of the time lapse over several days. This varied from two to eleven minutes and, on examination, I discovered that a combination of chances had been at work; the safety work, sear spring and sear nose and tumbler bent had all contributed to the main fault which was that the gun was, as we say, 'wood bound.' The consequence was that the sear nose could only hang on the bare edge of the tumbler bent whilst pressure from the mainspring caused the sear to creep slowly until the tumbler (internal hammer) was released. I think that was the most extraordinary case of gun trouble I have ever experienced; but it shows what *can* happen.

Whenever I am handling a gun myself, demonstrating as I am daily to other people, I make it a rule as soon as I pick up a gun to break it and show the empty chambers to the person who is with me. As I do so, I say 'Empty.'

You may believe that I am over careful, but a very large part of my professional career has been occupied studying the evidence, and giving my opinion, on the causes of gun accidents of one kind or another. The commonest cause is that somebody didn't know that his weapon was loaded.

You will never be criticized, just the opposite, for being punctilious in your gun-handling. When you are carrying an empty gun, as every game gun should be unless you are in readiness to shoot, make a practice of carrying it under your arm WITH THE BREECH OPEN. Let everybody see, including yourself, that an accident cannot possibly happen. Incidentally, the most comfortable way of all of carrying a gun is in this manner, broken across the crook of the arm.

There are two basic positions in which sporting guns are customarily carried when shooting is not afoot:

(1) In the crook of the elbow, in the manner I have described to you, with the muzzles pointing downwards.

(2) On the shoulder, with the muzzles pointing skywards, not horizontally inclined.

The former is the favourite method of carrying a gun and though, theoretically, it is slightly less safe than the shoulder position, it is as good in practice.

When walking-up game, the gun is held, tilted slightly upwards and forwards, in both hands in easy position. Even the most experienced sportsman, walking in line or in company, should constantly check himself to make sure that, in his concentration, the barrels of his gun have not swung across his chest, which is the more natural position, but the position in which anybody on the flank will receive the full charge if the gun goes off by accident.

Drill yourself to hold your shot-gun on the march in the field, not at the port arms position of army drill, but pointing straight out in front of you.

c

Shooting in covert, or from any sort of stand, the technique may be a little different. Sitting on a stick seat, the most comfortable way to carry the gun is to hold it in one hand with the butt on the knee and the barrels pointing straight in the air. When you are expecting birds, rise to your feet and present the gun forward and tilted upwards in the ready position. Apart from considerations of safety, the gun is thus correctly poised to come on to a bird with the minimum of delay, and in the case of birds at an angle the turn of the body carries the arms with it and so achieves the correct alignment without motion of the arms themselves.

You may be seated with muzzles erect, you may be walking with a gun under your arm, you may be holding your weapon in any of the comfortable and safe positions but when it comes to actual shooting you must learn before you mount the gun to your shoulder to assume the correct 'ready' position.

Some of my readers will be left-handed shots. It is important to point out here that in the following sections the drill applies to right-handed shots only. Left-handed men will appreciate that they must reverse my instructions, from right to left, to meet their own personal requirements.

II

The First or 'Ready' Position

IN readiness for gun-mounting, the stock must be tucked in well under the arm. You are inviting a miss if you hold the gun slackly with the butt at elbow-level. Place the stock with the small of the butt just forward of the right arm-pit, and squeeze it between biceps and ribs.

(*Watch that word 'squeeze.' Churchill meant it to mean, in the love sense, that the shooter should be one with his gun. He also meant that it is necessary to feel firm, confident and collected, before shooting. But the advice can be misleading. Don't make a job of it. Make love to your gun in the ready position, but don't make yourself so taut that, when the whistle blows, you sacrifice smoothness of action.*)

The man waiting to shoot with his gun under his right arm and his left hand free should naturally reach this position before he raises the muzzle in readiness to shoot. In any other position, there is an inclination to rush the gun to the shoulder with the result that it never comes to the same place twice running. To do that is to invite a miss. Consistency in style is the vital concomitant of consistent shooting. The method I advocate, practised until it becomes automatic, will compel you to do the right thing.

Tuck the stock well under your arm because (1) I want you to *push* your left hand forward as you mount, not merely raise it. (2) I want you to push your left hand forward because I am going to show you that the left hand is the aiming hand. (3) By pushing your left hand into the aim, you take a proportion of the recoil of the charge through your left arm and thence to your body rather than take it all on the shoulder. (4) In squeezing the gun under your arm-pit you are taking some of the weight off your hands and encouraging the muscles in your arms to relax. (5) This method will train you to put your shoulder to the stock instead of making the common error of putting the stock to your shoulder. (6) It's the quickest form of gun-mounting because the butt simply slips from the under-arm to the shoulder, without losing contact with your body (that is important) and the gun comes easily and smoothly to eye-level. (7) The gun comes up to your face instead of the head going down to meet the stock, and faulty head movement is one of the commonest causes of poor shooting. (8) The system checks hasty gun-mounting, and encourages correct timing. (9) It prevents the incidence of bruised cheek and jawbone from the recoil. (10) It encourages the right hand to adopt the correct position on the side of the stock and so prevent a bruised middle finger. (11) It not only keeps you squarely on to your target (as your body is checked from turning too much sideways) but it also encourages you to adopt a natural stance.

Finally, and this is most important of all, it encourages you to start your body swing whilst the gun is coming up.

With that I hope I have given you sufficient good reasons for asking you to begin by adopting a ready position for shooting which may at first seem odd and unfamiliar to you.

Practise the ready movement and, at the same time, don't be ashamed, however long you have used a gun, to check yourself on the rest positions, too. Are you sure that you are instinctively carrying a gun safely and correctly? Do you always break and unload it when you cross wire or a ditch or a hedgerow? Are you sure that when you are walking in line you never swing the muzzle towards the man walking beside you?

It is always dangerous to walk-up game with the gun cradled in your left arm or to proceed with the barrels pointing anywhere but in the region of your own feet. Walking potato ridges, for example, the natural body sway is enough to make a gun held horizontally between the two hands point down the line every time you put you right foot forward.

When you shoulder your gun, if you adopt that position, do you always carry it with the trigger guard uppermost? You should do. Normally, I myself never shoulder a gun except when following single file. There is a reason for it when walking in single file. In single file, there is a risk that mud flying off the heel of the man in front will plug the barrels of the man walking behind if he is carrying his own gun-muzzles pointing downwards in the crook of his arm. I've seen it happen; and it was lucky I was there to notice it. If the mud-plugged gun had been fired in that condition the barrel would certainly have burst.

As you practise the 'ready' and the 'rest' position accustom yourself to another safety habit.

Never let your finger touch the trigger until the actual moment of firing. In the 'ready' position the trigger finger should lay straight along the right lock plate. And it should stay there until the barrels are aligned on the target and your shoulder comes into the butt.

Under actual shooting conditions you will often find that you come to the 'ready' in anticipation of a shot which doesn't materialize; that you are 'on your toes' and in those circumstances it is unnecessary and often unwise to go back to a full rest position. But you have a loaded gun in your hands.

This is the time to adopt the semi-rest waiting position. Keeping the stock well up between your upper arm and hip, lay the gun sideways in the palm of your right hand keeping the trigger finger straight out as an extra cover to the guard, using the second, third and fourth fingers to hold the small of the butt with the thumb crossing to meet them. The barrels are held sideways in the left hand with the left thumb on the side of the left barrel. (*See Further Comments on Walking-up Game.*)

Some experienced shots cock their gun by slipping the safety catch forward as soon as they assume the ready or semi-ready position. I can't recommend the practice. It's so easy to acquire the habit of pushing forward the safety catch as part of the drill of actual gun-mounting. But it must be a habit. Nothing is more exasperating than to align on a bird, pull at the trigger and then to find that nothing happens.

You mustn't slip off your safety catch too soon and neither must you leave it too late; too soon is any time when the quarry is not in sight, too late is any time after the gun is raised to eye-level. If you actually shoot with your thumb pushed forward on the safety catch you will pull it back again with the recoil of the discharge.

Practise slipping the safety catch on and off with the side of the first joint of the thumb, not the ball of the thumb. If you use the ball of your thumb—and most people do—there is a risk that if you happen to pull the trigger at the same time, you will get a jolt from the lever. But, more important, if you use the ball of your thumb instead of the first joint you are altering your grip which is never to be recommended. The whole of your right hand should always remain in its correct position on the stock.

III

Feet

YOU will often notice that experienced shots, standing in a ploughed field, waiting for a drive to begin, are at some pains to select a position where there is no obstacle to impede their stance and footwork. They tread down a ridge, or select a wide furrow, to secure a position for their feet which is both firm and free from obstructions such as would prevent their pivoting.

Like the batsman who takes his stand at the wicket, looks round the field and taps out the rough spots in the wicket with his bat before he accepts the first ball, the wise shooting man gets himself set before he begins. And, like the golfer who makes a practice swing at the ball before he hits it, you will often notice that expert shots, long before the shooting starts, seize the opportunity to limber their muscles, practise their gun-mounting, footwork and swing and get themselves into a proper condition to give their best.

I mention that because I can imagine an impatient reader thinking that by this time we ought to be getting on with the actual shooting. I can only assure you that, if you master the proper way to use your hands and feet, and practise it until the drill becomes automatic, you will find that the problems of hitting what you are aiming at become relatively easy.

In shooting, as in most other sports, stance, footwork and poise of the body are all married together to blend into one smooth action. Above all, the balance and poise of the body must be firm and comfortable with the weight supported evenly on *both legs*. The only exception occurs when using wildfowl guns or unusually heavy charges in which case the greater proportion of the weight may be thrown on the left leg.

The toes of the feet should be about nine inches apart and the heels about three inches apart, although this distance will of course vary slightly with the general build of the individual. But, generally speaking, it is better to take too narrow a stance than too wide a one.

I have introduced a series of figures here because that is the simplest way of demonstrating the commonest faults in stance as compared with the correct position.

Figure 1 shows the common fault of standing with heels too close together. The result is that the bulk of the recoil is taken by the shoulder without assistance from the legs. This is not only unnecessarily wearying for the shooter, but also prevents him firing a successful second barrel until he has recovered his poise. In addition it is a frequent cause of bruised cheek or a bruised second finger. Shots who may suffer from these troubles should always suspect their stance and be at pains to correct it.

Fig. 1   Wrong

Figure 2. Another fault. Right foot immediately behind left. This twists the body in such a manner that the gun-stock is not

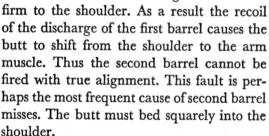

firm to the shoulder. As a result the recoil of the discharge of the first barrel causes the butt to shift from the shoulder to the arm muscle. Thus the second barrel cannot be fired with true alignment. This fault is perhaps the most frequent cause of second barrel misses. The butt must bed squarely into the shoulder.

This is also an 'infirm' stance which will cause the shooter to drop the right shoulder and shoot underneath the bird crossing on the right but with the reverse effect on his left where the left shoulder will be uplifted and shoot well over the top of the bird crossing on the left.

Fig. 2   Wrong

Figure 3. Another common fault. The stance is too wide. The shooter is unable to transfer body weight from one foot to the other without a sway of the body with the consequence that he will drop a shoulder on side shots and shoot underneath them. On uneven ground the

Fig. 3   Wrong

recoil can even knock him over or drive him back a pace or two; which of course means a risk to the neighbouring guns.

Figure 4. The correct position. The balance and poise of the body is even, weight can be transferred left or right without body disturbance; it allows the shooter to put his right shoulder to the stock and to absorb recoil bodily instead of all on the shoulder. Any turn is easily and quickly accomplished and the heels are about three or four inches apart.

Fig. 4   Right

Having placed your feet in the correct stance, assume the ready position. Now take your own gun and practise moving your trunk to the right and to the left. The turn of your body to the right should compel you to transfer body weight on to the right leg. The turn of the body to the left should transfer the weight on to the left leg. Practise this body swing at angles of 45 degrees right and left where only a transference of weight is required.

Having mastered this movement, increase the body swing to a full 90 degrees right and left and it will be found that the opposite foot, instead of being firm and flat on the ground, will quite naturally begin raising its heel around the 45 degree mark and will turn outwards to allow you to get to 90 degrees and beyond.

Do not mount your gun yet. Remember that part of this body and foot movement must take place before gun-mounting. A short heavily-built man may notice that heel-raising begins before reaching 45 degrees whereas a tall thin man may almost reach 90 degrees before it happens. Regardless of this you will find that it is a natural swing which will allow you to pivot on your toes and to cover much more than one-half of the circle without alteration of stance. With a forward inclination of the body, practise a low shot at a rabbit on the right or left. Then, with a backward inclination of the body, practise shooting at an imaginary pheasant crossing in front of you. Finally, although I have a personal distaste for the 'eye-level' bird which, in the interests of safety, must be shot at with caution in front or behind and never down the line, it makes very good dry practice to try the swing for the whole 180 degrees all around you.

A middle-aged man especially may find it difficult to swing more than three-quarters of the complete circle. In that event, it is proper in certain circumstances to move one foot more to the rear of the other one. For example, when birds are immediately behind, you may be able on firm ground to move one foot more to the rear with the toe turned as much as is conveniently possible in the direction of the bird; and then raise the other heel and pivot.

To get round to the right, shift the right foot a few inches to the rear of the left and the reverse for the opposite side. Do not take a step with the foot, since to lift it off the ground disturbs the balance, rather 'scrape' it round to the back of the other one.

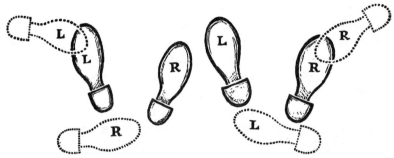

SWINGING TO RIGHT BEHIND   SWINGING TO LEFT BEHIND
(1) Scrape right foot behind left.   (1) Scrape left foot behind right.
(2) Pivot on left toe.   (2) Pivot on right toe.

In partridge driving, fast birds often get out of range before a gun can get round, and this movement should be practised in your room against your usual method to enable you to decide whether you can adopt it for such shots. It is difficult at first, but after practice you will become more confident and will be able to do this movement very smartly whilst retaining your balance. With a little indoor drill the motions become automatic.

When walking-up game, as apart from waiting at a stand for game to be driven over the guns, the essential footwork is unchanged, but on sighting a target, the walking gun must accustom himself to a routine movement which will place his feet in the correct position.

As the gun is mounting, the shooter should simply scrape back the right foot to bring himself into the position shown in *Figure* 4.

Again, with gun in hand, held in the ready position with the barrels pointed straight ahead, walk up and down a room, or a lawn, and practise the movement of stopping in your tracks, scraping back the right foot so that you assume the correct position as the gun mounts to your shoulder.

If you shoot, as you put your left foot forward, you will shoot under the mark. If you shoot with both feet together, you will take recoil without assistance from your legs and you will be off-balance and miss with the second barrel.

Don't fool yourself that you can remember your foot drill—like all the other drill in this book—without dry practice.

This business of indoor drill is important. Just as a boxer uses a punch-ball for practice and exercise, so a shooter can improve his style and get into better muscular trim for field work by indoor gun-handling.

The preliminary manual of rifle exercise of the army is not solely to teach the recruit how to open and load his rifle. It is very largely designed to accustom him to the muscular exercise involved. If you give a man unaccustomed to guns a weapon to handle his movements are relatively slow and uncouth. He has to exert far more energy than the trained man.

Normally, we put our guns away at the end of January, and when August or September arrives, even if we have been accustomed to shooting all our lives, we are to a certain extent slack and out of this particular form of training. That is why very many of the very best shots, men with established reputations as leading performers, go down to the clay-pigeon schools and fire on one, two or three successive days in order to get into training. The practice braces them and accustoms them to recoil, and it must be remembered that the physical effort of lifting a $6\frac{1}{2}$-lb. gun or more and firing a hundred or so rounds is considerable. It puts them into physical training as well as 'getting their eye in.' Not everyone can spare the time for these visits, but indoor drill, although it lacks the element of actual practice and the reality of recoil, is by no means a waste of time. It is sound physical training.

Those who live in the country or pay frequent visits there can find many more opportunities for carrying a gun and firing a sufficient number of rounds than a townsman. They attain what I might term contact with their weapon. If you want to shine as a shooting man you must make an effort to keep in reasonable practice all the year round.

You are bound to be disappointed with yourself if you only take up a gun on the occasion when somebody sends you a shooting invitation or somebody lends you a gun for a day's sport in the country. There is no game on earth in which you can achieve a mastery without constantly playing it and giving your attention to it. But, oddly enough, shooting is one of the sports in which I notice that singularly few men are prepared to take the same trouble as they take over their golf, their cricket or their football pools.

IV

Hands

NOW that you have found your feet, or I hope you have, take your gun and go over this section carefully with the weapon in your hand. Grip is a very important matter and it is necessary that the detail should be understood.

Right Hand.—Most people think that they grip a gun naturally and correctly. All too often they do not. The tendency is to carry the right hand far too much round the top of the stock. This checks it coming up and forces the knuckle of the second finger hard against the rear of the trigger guard (another cause of bruised finger).

Make this test: lift your gun to your shoulder with your thumb purposely too far round the top of the stock. You will find that you cannot lift the gun without raising the elbow as well. That in itself causes muscular constraint and awkwardness.

And, again, starting with your usual grip, readjust so that the finger-tips of the right hand are rather more round the stock than usual. You will find that the gun fits comfortably into the hollow of the hand and that it can be lifted without any elbow work far more quickly and comfortably than usual. You will also be able to bring the gun up to the cheek instead of having to put your cheek down to meet the gun.

A frequent cause of bad grip is the tendency for shooters with a short thumb to keep it in contact with the top lever. This is not necessary, as the fraction of time lost in shifting the grip of the hand is immaterial, whereas a bad grip means bad shooting.

The strength, or pressure, with which the stock is held should not be exaggerated. The gun should be brought up with a fairly light grip which should be tightened *only* at the instant of trigger pressure. If you grip too tightly while mounting the gun to the shoulder you may relax on the instant of firing. Bruised cheek or finger is sometimes an indication of too light a right-hand grip at the instant of firing, though more usually it is due to the error in stance indicated in the previous section.

Sometimes a man may use a gun which he has inherited or

bought second-hand. It *may* fit, but, more likely, it does not. Stock length, bend and cast-off represent only approximations to fit unless we also take into account the circumference of the narrow portion of the stock where the right hand grips it. Men's hands vary considerably. One man may have a long-fingered, trim and flexible hand; another a broad-palmed, capable hand, that of a surgeon rather than an artist, while a third may have a short-fingered, podgy hand. Even if all these three are relatively the same in the circumference which they can grip, the width of the hand varies. When fitting a gun I pay considerable attention to this factor. One man may need the comb of his stock cutting back half or three-quarters of an inch more toward the heel than another, simply in order to make a comfortable bedding for his hand. There is no particular novelty about this attention to manual anatomy, for, in the old days, when duelling was in vogue, a gentleman would be measured for his pistols, the selection of an appropriately shaped stock having been part and parcel of the gunsmith's craft. They had to fit perfectly in the individual hand. Similarly, in these days, we must ensure that our game guns are stocked to fit not only the bodily dimensions of shooters, but also fit their hands.

In my opinion the grip of every normal gun should be tapered from the direction of the breech; that is to say, it should be thicker in front of the hand than at the rear, and thus offer a cone to prevent the hand slipping forward on recoil.

Very often ones sees a grip tapered the reverse way. Such guns tend to slip through the fingers on recoil with bruised second finger for result.

Left Hand Grip.—The right and left hands should each do an equal share of the work of mounting the gun to the shoulder. The correct point of reach is found by balancing the gun between the two hands until the point of equal distribution of weight is found.

If the left hand is too far back the stock will mount earlier than the barrels, which will 'sag'; also the recoil will be more heavily felt on the shoulder.

If the left hand is too far forward the barrels will come up before the stock. This is almost as bad.

The gun should be balanced to encourage horizontal mounting, so that, by the time the butt touches the shoulder, the barrels should be pretty well parallel to the line set by the eyes.

A badly balanced gun has no right place for the front grip, but one properly balanced will allow firm grasp to be taken near the front of the fore-end.

The left thumb should not be curled round the barrel but, rather, be held lengthwise and made to project, or, at least, be noticeable. This serves a double purpose for it cuts out disturbance of aim due to left eye vision and also prevents the fingers covering too much of the barrel and encroaching on the sighting rib; it also prevents the barrels jumping out of hand on recoil, another cause of bruised cheek.

While lifting the gun the barrels should only be held lightly; but they should be gripped at the instant of firing.

You may adopt a correct stance and you may also take a perfect grip of the gun, yet you can still miss certain birds if your body or legs are wrongly braced. The rifle shot holds or expels his breath as he shoots: but the man with the shot-gun does, or should do, something more.

Perhaps I can explain it most effectively by pointing out a few of the differences that I notice between the expert shot and the novice.

You can always recognize the expert, as he takes his stand to shoot, because his feet are never too wide or in an unnatural position; his toes are pointed at their usual walking angle, the forward foot is not much in advance of the other, and the shooter's balance enables him to transfer his body weight from one leg to the other without disturbing his bodily control. In conjunction with legs and body, he can take recoil properly.

The novice, you will notice, may never stand twice alike. He puts one foot behind the other, with the effect that it turns his body sideways. His toes are turned unnaturally which means an insecure foothold, and, if his stance is too wide, it causes a drop of the shoulders in the side shot.

The expert shoots with a stiff knee, either left or right, or to be more precise (if he is taking a going-away shot on the left) the left leg is very firm or stiff and the right is the reverse. All the weight is on the left leg and the right leg, with heel slightly raised, is helping to push the weight forward. Of course, everything is reversed for the overhead shot and for the crossing shot on the right.

The novice often bends both knees, or simply stands free, with-the really using his legs as part of the machinery to ensure rock steadiness, regardless of wind. He hasn't learnt how to take up recoil without disturbance and so allow a quick recovery for the second shot.

The expert braces up his body by means of both arms and legs. The stiffening of the knee tightens the leg muscles and thus serves to stiffen the hip joint; consequently stiffening the whole side. The action of gun-mounting, with elbows and both arms kept down as much as possible, helps to stiffen the back muscles and, altogether, the body is very rigid.

The novice, with his bent knee, is also loose at the hip. If his elbows are outwards, he can wobble about so much during his gun-mounting that the odds are very much against his ever making a consistent performance as a shot.

The expert clenches his teeth, slightly inclines his head and slightly shrugs his shoulders to stiffen his neck muscles. The novice may keep his mouth open, hold his head loose, or be out-breathing at the instant of firing, all of which aggravate looseness in general, causing irregular gun-mounting.

In its proper place, I am emphasizing in this drill the necessity of keeping the eye on the bird, pushing out the left hand, relaxing the right-hand grip and putting the shoulder to the gun. For that reason, the shot must plant himself firmly, not only to withstand recoil, but also to allow of perfect gun-mounting.

All the good shots I have ever known have been men who, perhaps without thought, have naturally braced themselves at the instant of firing. Some of them, whom I have seen emerge from the ranks of the mediocre and middling to fair-class shots, have altered with practise from a nervous and jumpy style to one of firm rigidity which, without a shot being fired and simply by gun-mounting alone, shows the onlooker that here is a man who has perfect control of his gun; who is keen and who, if given the right tools, will shoot well.

Again, and you must not overdo it, this whole muscular bracing progress occurs during gun-mounting. Confidence, plus keenness, causes the majority to do it, more or less properly, and the perfect action is a smooth gradual mounting culminating in rigidity at the instant of recoil. Nothing here, of course, refers to the grip of the hands. We brace up the body yet relax our grip, as explained in the next chapter.

V

Gun-Mounting

THIS is perhaps the most critical process of shooting, for it co-ordinates all the mechanical functions of stance, footwork and grip with the conscious function of aim.

When you point your finger at an object you aim at it and there is unconscious adjustment of the line of vision with the axial line of the pointing finger. Point at an object, glance along your extended finger and note how, without conscious sighting, you have taken a true aim.

The left or forward hand must not be considered simply as a lifting lever for the gun. You must, so to speak, mentally aim or point at the object with the left hand which holds the gun. You point just as straight with your left forefinger as you do with your right. Drive the left hand forward with a rather vigorous pointing movement, pointing at the bird the whole time.

The left hand does the real aiming. But the right must keep pace with the left, doing its share of directing the muzzle on the object the whole time that the gun is coming up.

Here is where gun-fitting and, to a lesser extent, the clothes worn need consideration. The gun must not be too long in the stock or the clothes bulkier or tighter than those normally worn while shooting. On the other hand, though the stock should not get in the way of the coat, neither may it be too short. In practice, the butt should scrape your clothing as it travels up your arm to bed in your shoulder. The slightest clearance between butt plate and shoulder is all that is necessary or desirable; and the *thrust* of the left arm automatically provides it.

At the completion of the mounting movement or, rather, this first portion of it, the gun is up to the eye-level and the butt of the stock in touch with but not home on the shoulder. The left arm (hand) is pointing at the object in subconscious co-ordination with the sight or line of vision from the eye.

Now, put your shoulder forward to the stock and at the same time contract the trigger finger so that as the gun is firm against the shoulder the trigger is pulled exactly at the limit of the movement. Swing is combined with this movement.

It is in appearance almost a 'snap' and the jar of the shoulder against the stock aids the trigger finger in precise timing of its pull. Analysing this apparently simple yet complex movement we find that the left arm pushes forward while the right finally neutralizes the push and adds the bit extra that brings the gun back. Thus the left arm absorbs a large proportion of the recoil which would otherwise be received on the shoulder.

The pressure of the stock against the shoulder by the right hand involves the necessity of gripping with the right hand and so avoids the occasional trouble of too slack a grip. You should actually be *pulling* the gun between your two hands as you fire. With practice the opposing movement of the two arms becomes so automatic that the trigger finger can remain in a semi-rigid position and trigger pressure to fire can be made (indeed should be made) part and parcel of the butting of the gun to the shoulder. Trigger pulling is thus timed to occur at the instant that the butt of the gun is met by the thrust of the shoulder coming forward to meet it.

If you perform this mounting movement correctly—thrusting the shoulder forward to meet the butt, butting the gun into the shoulder with the hands, and applying trigger pressure at the moment the two meet—you won't feel the kick of recoil from the gun.

(*In cold practice, you will always notice recoil more than you will in the heat of shooting in the field. I recollect an occasion in the African bush when, shooting for the pot, I picked up my .404 magnum rifle to shoot a small buck. It was only afterwards that I realized my mistake. I thought at the time that I was shooting with a 7-millimetre. The answer is that, if you are with your gun, recoil goes through your boots.*)

The analogy is the old one of grasping the nettle. If you handle your gun indecisively, it will 'sting' you. Handle it firmly and determinedly, and you'll know you're handling it right because you won't feel recoil.

The precise position where your shoulder should meet the butt of the gun in the instantaneous action of completing mounting and applying trigger pressure, can be established by folding your arms. When you fold your arms, you will notice that your shoulders come forward, in just the way that your right shoulder should come forward to meet the butt, and that you create a muscular bed between your collar bone and the ball in the shoulder socket. That natural bed in your shoulder is the point where the butt should meet it as you fire.

The proper movement in gun-mounting is, in fact, the precise reverse of what many novices, and nearly all women, tend to do when they lift a gun warily to their shoulder for the first time. They draw the shoulder away from the butt. They're unable to take recoil and can easily be bowled off their feet, or lose a tooth, on discharge.

As an experiment—but choose a safe place to make it—try firing a gun, held firmly in the hands, without lifting it to your shoulder. It will remind you what an ugly kick a 12-bore has when it is held improperly. But, held properly, the arms and shoulder absorb the full shock and do so without the shooter being aware of it.

What the novice does is to hang on to his gun with grim determination at all times when he isn't actually firing it. But, when he fires, he loosens his grip, draws away his shoulder, and catches the recoil on his jaw.

The expert carries his gun, except at the instant of firing, with a relaxed grip. But, as he fires, his muscles tense in perfect time with the action of gun discharge.

From the foregoing you will see that the eyes have been left nothing to do but look at the bird. The hands and arms automatically obey the eyes, and if the gun is mounted correctly, discharge occurs automatically and in perfect time as the butt comes to the shoulder.

Provided the gun fits and that the quarry is within range you will shoot exactly where you are looking and should kill every time.

Obviously every bird killed is proof that the muzzle must have been pointed in the right place. Next, that, as the barrels lie in the left hand, the left hand also was pointing in the right place. Combining the two propositions one shoots wherever the left hand points. If weakness or injury prevents or makes this ordinary procedure at all difficult, there are remedies which are dealt with in another chapter.

When this formula is properly carried out, misses occur from one cause (and one cause only): not looking at the proper place. Curiously enough, when you have mastered the knack of correct gun-mounting, misses which you could not analyse or diagnose before, but attributed vaguely to some fanciful cause, are easily

D

resolved. You know instinctively what you have done wrong and are able to correct the error. The only explanation I can offer is that the shooter knows where he is putting his charge because the slightly upward movement of recoil lifts the muzzle of the gun into view and the eye takes cognizance.

A common complaint of shooters is that they 'do no good with their second barrel.' This is often caused by a disturbance of the grip or shoulder-bedding of the gun brought about by the recoil of the first discharge. The method of gun-mounting I am teaching you eliminates this. If the left arm is correctly pushed forward, it not only serves to keep the butt from catching against the clothes (so that an extra heavy coat in hard weather does not so seriously disturb or upset the fit of your gun) but, acting as a girder under compression against the backward pull of the right hand, it takes the main stress of recoil and absorbs it without transmitted shock to the body. A bad mounter, on the other hand, takes the full recoil shock on his shoulder instead of on his left arm and in consequence is swung slightly round, so that for his second shot he has perforce to correct his aim again.

Needless to say, bad footwork is another reason for second barrel misses. The shooter fires when, as a consequence of bad style, he is off balance.

But, although shooters themselves have a common tendency to complain that they miss with the second barrel, I fancy that the complaint is more often that they are looking for an alibi for poor shooting all round.

A man who can consistently kill with his first barrel can usually put up a good show with his second. Under the test conditions of the shooting school, what we usually find is that a pupil who is 'trying too hard' misses with his first barrel because he pokes at the bird, and makes a clean kill with his second (once we've taught him not to be afraid to use his second barrel quickly) because he hasn't got time to stop and think, and makes a natural swing on to the target, and fires at 'first aim.'

It's a paradox of game-gun shooting that, if you see the barrels as you fire, or indeed hear your gun go off, you have missed. There is no mystery about that. If you see the barrels, it means that you can't be looking at the bird. If you hear the gun go off, it means that you are not giving the target, which is all that matters, your undivided attention.

To cure that trouble, we use various coaching devices. We

tell the shooter to try and miss the bird; just behind, or just in front. It doesn't matter where. By making him concentrate on hitting a particular part of the target, we make sure that he looks at the target and not at his gun.

If you are missing in the field, it is always an effective corrective to make up your mind to place the charge not at the target in general but at a specific part of it. Promise yourself to shoot that next pheasant in the eye, or in the left leg, or in the beak. Look at that, and nothing else, as you fire.

A man with his eye on the bird can often kill clean, if his footwork and gun-handling are correct, by pulling the trigger before the butt of the gun is into his shoulder. Some snipe-shots shoot that way for choice; although I wouldn't recommend it, except as an experiment, to anybody but a very experienced gun-handler.

Most of the foregoing remarks deal with the 'going-away' bird, perhaps the simplest shot of all; but the subsequent instruction detailing the adaptation of the technique to more difficult shots are all dependent on this first mastery of the knack of correct gun-mounting.

A novice is inclined to snatch the gun to his shoulder. This is wrong. The whole sequence of movement for ordinary shots should be easy and steady, becoming in time so purely mechanical that once learnt it is never forgotten.

Contrast this technique with the practice, so often seen, of raising the gun at an angle rather than parallel to the line of vision, then bringing the muzzle down on the bird. In this practice it is obvious that, not only is the line of vision temporarily intercepted by the barrels, but that the gun is spinning windmill fashion, and it has to be got out of its spin before firing takes place. With proper technique the muzzles are finding the bird during the whole process of mounting, and even a slightly premature, or belated, trigger pressure does not necessarily involve the miss that is unavoidable in the case of the man 'tip-catting' his gun or otherwise not keeping his muzzles in the general direction of the bird.

In the field it is not possible to ensure a succession of simple 'straight away' shots for practice purposes, but a good deal can be done with simple manual exercise in one's room at home. Practice simple gun-mounting with a pair of 'snap caps'* in the

* Snap caps are dummy cartridges used for 'dry' practice. They are necessary because, unlike a rifle, the action of a shot-gun is jarred, and can be severely damaged, by releasing the pins on empty chambers.

barrels, and you will, in a day or so, get the necessary muscular control or 'knack' which is half the battle.

Timing the discharge is rather more difficult at the start and can really only be learnt by practice, preferably at clay birds. In essence there should be a ratio between the speed of the bird and the speed of mounting the gun to the shoulder. The swifter birds need a quicker movement.

After a little practice this soon ceases to be a matter of conscious calculation. It becomes an automatic or reflex effect accomplished instinctively and without thought.

Those who are dogged by persistent failure are sure to ask the question: 'Does my gun fit me?' It is not one which can be answered in general terms but, if you do not shoot well and your gun-fitter has not seen you shoot, it is highly probable that some alteration is needed. Never have the stock of a gun bent or cast-off to compensate for faults in gun-mounting. These should be corrected not by deforming the gun but by improving your style. Unless a man has been properly trained or has unconsciously and naturally evolved a good consistent technique of his own, his very errors are inconstant and it is useless to try to attempt a fit until a standard or basis has been established.

A perfect fit with a gun is dependent on the establishment of a preliminary normal method or standard of shooting, with subsequent small alterations and adaptations to suit the maturing style. No gun-maker or fitter, however expert, can hope to make a gun a perfect fit by forecasting what a pupil will become when he has mastered the groundwork of gun-handling.

I realize, too, that many good sportsmen who read this book will be using guns that haven't been specially built, or fitted for them. The majority, perhaps, will perforce have to use a weapon which they have inherited from somebody else or purchased in circumstances when skilled alterations for fit were out of the question.

Ideally, I must insist that no man can shoot at his peak performance without a gun that suits him. But I admit it is possible to fit a gun to yourself, especially if your muscles are supple and you study how to get the best out of the marriage between you and your gun. As a professional, I'm shooting for test purposes with guns of all shapes and sizes. I am able to use them effectively because I make allowance of grip and presentation to correct the misfit factor.

Much more important than gun-fitting are the basic requirements of good shooting: proper stance, grip and a stylish technique of gun-mounting. A man who looks after that will always
outshoot the bungler with the best-tailored pair of game guns
that London can produce.

Further, any shooter with a gun that he himself finds is comfortable to use will be at no significant disadvantage, whatever
his weapon, walking-up in a rough shoot or pot-hunting along
the hedgerows or in the marshes. Where a man's gun-fit will find
him out is in a really hot corner at driven partridges or in the
coverts, when pheasants come taller than the trees. But a man
who can afford that sort of shooting can afford to have his guns
made-to-measure. He will never get the best out of himself until
he does.

VI

Position of the Head

IT is said that Head Movement is the cause of one-half of the misses in shooting. This saying is true of the 'going-away' bird, when, with your eyes on the quarry, you move your head by burying it down on to your gun-stock.

Begin this lesson by making a simple experiment. Point your finger at some distant object. You will find that, on first aim, you come straight on to it every time. Now, lower your head as you raise your finger and you'll notice that you are all over the place; never on the mark.

The cause of head movement is, commonly, that the shooter is using a gun which is too heavy for him. He puts down his head to meet the stock instead of allowing the stock to come up to meet his head. In that event, the cure is to practise gun-mounting until this bad habit has been eliminated. Another fault, which may be yours, is to put the head down and subsequently re-sight the bird; few shots made in that fashion make a successful kill.

THE HEAD SHOULD ONLY MOVE WITH THE BODY. Never shoot 'out of the corner of your eye.' And, if you find that you are shooting underneath going-away birds, don't mistrust your gun until you have made absolutely sure that head movement isn't the reason why you are missing. How often it happens that a sportsman reports that he is missing underneath the target and, as a consequence, the gun-maker sets up the stock with the object of making the gun shoot higher. Yet, in practice, it has absolutely the reverse effect if head movement is the real cause, because, when the head goes down, it arrests the stock from coming up. In such cases, the higher you build up the comb of the stock, the lower the shooter will be on the mark.

Head position varies very much with the individual. The short-necked man doesn't move his head about nearly as much as the long-necked individual. The tall man has a natural tendency to use his neck like a swan. The desideratum to aim at, when you are shooting, is to be stiff-necked rather than otherwise. If you can keep your head from moving about and retain this during gun-mounting, you should come up on the mark every time.

Oddly enough, the position of the shooter's head is closely associated with eyesight. A boy will usually lower his head to meet the stock, but a middle-aged man will hold his head erect and raise the gun to his face.

These two classifications cover the difference between 'young sight' and 'old sight.' Nothing is commoner than a marked falling off in shooting due to an unsuspected change in eyesight in middle age. A man may have been shooting all his life with a straight-stocked gun. A change of vision occurs and he finds that he is right off his shooting. The cure is not glasses, but a bending down of the gun-stock about a quarter of an inch at the heel or bump. This will compensate for an alteration of alignment due to the new head position.

While on the subject, it is as well to mention that a relaxation of the muscles, from age or sedentary habits, also alters gun-fit, and, generally speaking, a shorter stock will be found more comfortable with increasing age. Similarly a novice, who has yet to learn how to extend his arms fully and naturally in the normal shooting position, should begin with a gun which is rather short for him. When properly practised, he can be fitted for exact length, a simple matter of different depths of heel plate.

To test your own gun: first, follow out the section on correct gun-mounting, and note if, at the moment you press the trigger, the rib and muzzle of the gun are correctly levelled 'on' the object.

The best position for the head is fairly erect and turned very slightly to the right.

If you have to put down your head too much to the stock, you are not properly fitted. Above all, your head must be naturally, normally and comfortably poised. It is hopeless to try to adapt the poise of the head and the neck to a badly fitted gun, for it induces rapid fatigue and a consequent falling off in shooting performance. A proper grip of the right hand will allow the stock to come up to the face. The head is inclined slightly, to avoid the cheekbone or jawbone pressing hard on the stock, and the cheek should touch midway between the two.

Head position is an arbitrary matter which varies with the individual. It should be first and, above all things, 'natural'; very erect and definitely firm. Gun headache is due, in nine cases out of ten, to neglect of one thing only: the neck muscles are not braced and the head is held 'loose.' The shock of recoil jerks the head and the effect is that of a minor 'knockout' blow. The old remedy of holding a rubber band between the teeth is a good one, for the act of clenching the teeth steadies the head and stiffens the neck muscles, so that the automatic throw-back of the head is lessened. Most shooters automatically retract their neck muscles and bring their head down to the shoulders when firing. A minority—and particularly the swan-necked minority—do not do this, and complain of headache in consequence. Alter the attitude and alter the gun to fit is the real remedy for headache. It is a curable trouble.

Sometimes, indeed very often, one finds people who believe that, by adopting one particular load, or one particular brand of powder, they escape from headache. Once, when a great variety of powders were available, some would claim that they were headache-free from using one brand, and others swore by another; but there was no common agreement on the universal panacea for gun-headache. There couldn't be because the powder in the cartridge is not the cause of it. Recoil, the note of vibration of the explosion, are all called in to account for the trouble; but, actually, gun headache is simply the consequence of a fault of style. It means that the shooter is taking the recoil shock with a loosely-held head. Set the head down into the shoulders, though without raising the shoulders; stiffen the neck muscle, and gun headache will vanish.

The position of the head and, above all, the rigid maintenance of that position are vital matters in shooting. In golf, it is recognized that head movement, while a shot is being taken, will seriously affect its direction; a lift of the head may cause you to miss your ball, a slight inclination may lead you to hit below it. Golfers know that if they look at the ball as a whole, they are prone to 'top' it, whereas, if they concentrate on the back, on a point on the ball, greater precision is achieved.

The underlying principles apply in a similar sense to head movements during gun-mounting. A great many of those unaccountable misses of seemingly easy 'away birds' are due to too much head movement during gun-mounting. One's vision is centred on the bird, and, as the gun is raised, there is a risk of a final unconscious squeeze of the face down to meet the stock. In consequence, there is a loss of the instinctive accuracy of *first aim*.

Remember that, if you lift your head, you tend to shoot over the top of your bird. If you lower your head you tend to shoot low.

To summarize, you must remember that, once the eye has found the object, the head should be carried rigidly and not moved independently of the body. This requires practice and, at first, concentration; but, once learnt, it becomes instinctive, and will often show both improvement in speed and in accuracy.

Keep your eye on the bird; but don't make the very common error of looking at birds which aren't there. There is no more certain way of tiring your eyes* and assuring that, when the target comes into range, you will miss. If you are shooting in open country, in a grouse butt for example, where you may see a mile or so ahead of you and you are continuously focusing and refocusing your eyes, searching the heather for birds that possibly won't be put up until the beaters get rather nearer in another ten or twenty minutes time, the odds are that, when a covey passes over you, it will be absolutely unseen and gone before you can throw a shot.

If you are continually looking up and down the line in partridge driving, you can count on it that when the birds come they will seem to be travelling twice as fast as they really are and disappear over the next hedge before you can bring your gun to them.

You will never be any good as a snap shot at rabbits in a narrow ride if you persist in trying to anticipate where you're likely to see them.

REMEMBER THAT IF YOU FOCUS ONE OBJECT IT TAKES TIME TO RE-FOCUS ON ANOTHER OBJECT.

There is nothing which is so fatal to good shooting as lack of confidence. If, for one reason or another, through allowing your eye to roam or getting into a panic because birds came over you, or a rabbit ran across your path, for which you were unprepared, all the faults of style which I have talked about will show themselves. You will be caught out making the hasty snatch, the elaborate swing and the steam-roller effort. You will miss again and again and again. Your faults will multiply the more you try to get back into form.

The secret is to master yourself. All you have to do is to concentrate; keep your eye on the bird, count it dead before you

* See page 117.

pull the trigger, trust your first aim, and remember you only have to kill one bird at a time. I know it is very much easier to write about it than to do it in practice. But, in practice, you can master yourself to an enormous degree by realizing what is going wrong.

Of all the faults which are the consequence of over-anxiety, the commonest is checking the swing of the gun. It is what you do when you see the first bird of the day or the last, or the one you have promised the kitchen for dinner. You make too sure of it, and, nine times out of ten, you miss behind. Good shooting is never hasty, never over-cautious.

I have often helped temperamental shooters by telling them that every cock pheasant flying towards you gives you time to say slowly to yourself 'What a beautiful fellow you are' before you shoot at him.

The reason why some men are born shots, and others perpetually erratic, is almost entirely a state of mind. The great shots are usually phlegmatic shots. Most of us have occasional serene days when we could hit anything. Most of us, too, know the other days when we are shooting with increasing exasperation all over the shop.

I have a friend who, on his day, is a first-class shot, but he is such a chronic victim of nerves that he hardly ever shoots well if he is out with people who are strangers to him. The trouble is that he is much too conscious of his company. If you find that you are off form, almost the first thing to convince yourself is that it doesn't matter (as, of course, it doesn't). Pretend that you are quite alone. Next, make up your mind not to be in a hurry. Finally, concentrate on shooting not at a given bird but at a part of the bird. Shoot off his tail or prick his beak. This has the effect of forcing the shooter to concentrate on the target instead of fluffing about trying to look after the other guns' business. If you remember some of these tips, and if you are a reasonable shot, you ought to get back into form before the day's shooting is over.

In addition, never try to pull off a showy shot at the beginning of the day. A fine partridge shot once told me that he always shot the first bird of the day behind him. The idea was to get his eye in. After the first kill he went on to shoot birds on the flanks. Only when he was mounting his gun sweetly did he shoot his birds well out in front and calculate on killing a brace. And he was a man who could put two birds down out of a covey before most of us could get out guns to our shoulders.

If you are missing driven pheasant, it is quite a good policy to wait until the birds are almost over your head so that you have to bend backwards to reach them. You will often kill them directly overhead because, in that position, you have no time to hang on the trigger and no choice but to keep your eye on the bird.

I have discussed all these matters again, in greater detail, in subsequent chapters; but I have no hesitation in repeating myself because repetition is the secret of instruction. I like to think that, when you are out shooting, you will remember an occasional phrase from this book; and that an occasional phrase from this book may be enough to bring you back into form in one of those black moods when you feel you couldn't hit a haystack.

The best illustration of the right attitude of mind on a shooting day is the story of a friend of mine who was invited shooting after a lapse of many seasons when he hadn't handled a gun at all. It happened that the company he was in was composed almost entirely of first-class shots. He went through the morning without hitting a bird. Subsequently, when the party was moving from one stand to another, his car was in front in a narrow lane where only one car could pass at a time. Half-way up the lane my friend came to a haystack. He stopped the car, got out, slowly produced his gun, loaded it and, while all the cars at the back were hooting to encourage him to get on, he raised his gun to his shoulder and fired two barrels into the haystack. Then he solemnly turned round and made a rude gesture to all the men behind him. He was quite right. He had cultivated that happy frame of mind which banishes all fear of missing. In that mood, anybody will very quickly become a very good shot.

VII

The Theory of Allowance

THE man who has mastered the technique of dealing with the straight-away shot will find that it applies equally well to crossing and overhead shots so soon as the need for extra allowance in these cases has been appreciated.

The action of keeping the left hand pointing at the moving bird automatically compels a correct swing of the whole body. And the gun comes to the shoulder without a check for aiming, or trigger pressure, but all in one harmonious movement.

Contrast this with the style of a man who shoulders his gun and chases the bird with the muzzle, making either a calculated or an empirical 'allowance' forward of his target. His endeavour to compensate for speed may be justified in theory, but bad trigger pulling results in practice.

The 'allowance' principle, when permitted to enter into shooting as an abstraction, is quite unsuited to the average sportsman, and if imperfectly understood, is a prolific source of irritation and error. Take a simple demonstration of its difficulty.

A charge of shot takes one-twentieth of a second to travel twenty yards; one-tenth, thirty yards; one-seventh, forty yards. A bird travelling at forty miles an hour covers one, two or three yards respectively in the same time intervals (one-twentieth, one-tenth and one-seventh of a second), and we know that the gun must be pointed these distances ahead to score or kill. But measure out the ranges in straight line, in an open field or paddock, and erect three poles twenty, thirty and forty yards apart. Now attach a piece of whitewashed board one yard in length as a crosspiece to the pole at twenty yards, a two-yard one to the thirty-yard pole and a three-yard one to the forty-yard pole. Then return to the firing point and look at them.

They will present a very neat example of how easily the eye can be deceived, for in perspective they all look about the same size and they all look far shorter than they really are. The inference to be drawn is that a constant angular allowance suffices; to be modified and made more precise as experience increases.

A short study of the example will convince you how hopeless it is to attempt to calculate precise allowances for varying ranges in the heat of shooting.

Once you appreciate that allowance is needed, let eye and swing collaborate to produce the correct measure.

The whole secret is to regularize your movements and mount the gun properly to the shoulder so that the hand and eye co-ordinate. Your barrel must always be aligned precisely where your eye is looking. The eye learns its job quickly enough. Apparently you are shooting straight at the bird, but, unconsciously, you will be making all necessary allowances.

PRACTICE THE POINTING OF THE LEFT HAND AND BODY AT THE BIRD FROM THE 'READY' POSITION UNTIL YOU ARE DOING IT IN-STINCTIVELY WITHOUT BEING CONSCIOUS OF DOING IT.

The difference between shooting at birds overhead and crossing, as compared with going-away, is that, besides being in more rapid flight, their line of travel is more or less at right angles with the line of fire. Therefore, theoretically, the gun must be directed further ahead than with the going-away bird.

What I propose to teach you is that the more rapid gun move-ment, caused by the body swing, automatically carries the aim more forward. If you mount your gun at a speed that is equal to the speed of the bird; or, in other words, if you keep your left hand pointing at the bird during the whole of the gun-mounting, then, if it is a slow incomer, the unconscious overthrow is very slight; but all that is needed for correct forward allowance. On the other hand, if it is a very fast crossing shot, your own speed is increased; the overthrow is proportionately greater and is, again, the correct forward allowance.

TRAIN THE EYE AND HAND TO TAKE CHARGE OF THESE MATTERS AND LEARN THEIR JOB WITHOUT BRAIN INTERFERENCE.

Once again, remember the remark on hands and feet.

If your technique is sound, you will find that the right angle target, whether overhead or wide out, presents no difficulties. Once again, dismiss all ideas of calculated allowances. Look at the bird, pivot easily and smoothly, and complete the movement as for a straight-away shot, but without in any way checking your swing.

If it seems difficult to begin with, then adopt a slow, smooth body swing before mounting the gun. Above all, do not mount the gun and then swing. This procedure is hopeless.

You will note that, in the foregoing sections, I have never told you to look along your barrels or to keep the sight in view. *Don't.*

In practice, the shooter should not be conscious of his gun-muzzle, the rib or sight. His eye, or rather his attention, should be fully occupied with the bird, and, if he holds his gun properly, he will hit whatever he is looking at.

When the gun has been fired, recoil jars the barrels up and the shooter may then see them, but, with proper action and a well-fitting gun, he should not be conscious of them until he has fired.

The scientific basis of this is the fact that the eye cannot pay attention to objects at different ranges at one and the same time. In rifle shooting it is necessary to focus the target, and yet at the same time see the front sight. The back sight intrudes up to the foresight first of all, and then deals with foresight and bull, usually by means of an intermediate focus. Shot-gun practice is different. There is no time for focus to pass from one object to another. Gun-fitting gets breech and sight into line with the eye. For the rest, the close range and then widespread circle of pellets will compensate for any small inaccuracy of alignment or centring.

At the moment of striking, a billiard player looks at the object ball, not at the cue or his own ball. The golfer, after he has adjusted his stance and rehearsed his swing, has to keep his eye on the ball and not on his club. In lawn tennis, cricket and, in fact, all such games, the eye must be kept on the object. So the shooting man must keep his eye on the bird, and ignore his gun.

If your eye is focused on your gun you will mount behind an incoming bird, and will have great difficulty in catching up with him.

If I haven't already persuaded you, let me explain to you in greater detail the difference between aim in theory and aim in practice.

Figures are all right on paper. They can be immensely valuable in theoretical calculations. But I want to prove to you how ridiculous it is, in practice, to suppose that everybody can calculate the intricacies of muzzle and shot velocity in relation to a variably moving target in the actual field.

A ballistician, knowing the recorded decrease in shot velocity for a cartridge from initial muzzle velocity to ranges of twenty, thirty and forty yards, can calculate the *time* occupied by the shot charge in covering different ranges, and he can also calculate the distance covered by a wind moving at the rate of twenty, thirty or forty miles an hour in equivalent time. Normally, these would be

computed for a bird crossing at an absolute right angle to the line
of fire but can, of course, be calculated for any angle.

Let us take a simple example. Consider a shot from a standard
12-bore cartridge at ranges of twenty, thirty and forty yards used
against a crossing bird flying at thirty miles an hour. Twenty
miles an hour is about the rising velocity of a pheasant bustled out
of a hedge by a spaniel. Forty miles an hour is the average speed
of a driven pheasant in full flight.

Now let me confuse the mathematicians by recording that the
lateral movement of the gun-muzzles by one inch makes a difference of thirty inches at thirty yards. From that it can be calculated
that the gun-muzzle movement necessary for forward allowance
is:

     $1\frac{1}{2}$ inches at 20 yards
     $1\frac{5}{8}$ inches at 30 yards
     $1\frac{3}{4}$ inches at 40 yards

From this we may calculate that, in general terms, the slow bird
needs only half the allowance of the fast one and the birds of the
short twenty-yard range only require 40 per cent of the allowance theoretically necessary to the forty-yard bird. Even these
figures only relate to the birds crossing at right angles. For a bird
quartering at 45 degrees all figures have to be halved. The
bird seen straight in front, unless it is climbing steeply, needs even
less allowance, and, if a bird twists as you lift your gun, no calculation is any good at all to you.

But, for the record, all theoretical forward allowances may be
calculated from the following tables:—

A shot charge in flight, travelling at a thousand feet a second,
takes approximately:

     0·06 of a second to reach 20 yards
     0·09 of a second to reach 30 yards
     0·12 of a second to reach 40 yards

A bird travelling at thirty miles an hour travels:

     44 feet per second
     11 feet in 0·25 second
     8 feet in 0·18 second
     6 feet in 0·13 second
     4 feet in 0·09 second
     $2\frac{1}{2}$ feet in 0·05 second

Therefore a calculated forward allowance for a bird crossing at thirty miles an hour is approximately:

> 2½ feet at 20 yards
> 4 feet at 30 yards
> 6 feet at 40 yards

These figures, of course, are calculated from the gun-muzzle. The shooter should add the length of time he takes to pull the trigger, in addition to the time taken by the lock mechanism and primer to explode the charge. If all the birds flew across at this level speed of thirty miles an hour, if we had a range-finder, and provided we did not hesitate in pulling the trigger after having made our mathematical calculation, then all might be well. But I hope I have said enough to establish that it is beyond the capacity of even the most expert shot to work out forward allowances on a mathematical basis.

Forget all about them. Leave them where they belong, in the pages of this book. Your job is to keep your eye on the bird; forget all you ever knew and heard about the thousands of different allowances and the thousands of varieties of shots and let your eye and the natural overthrow of the gun take care of everything else.

My considered opinion is that these tables of allowances, which I give here simply to prove to you how confusing they are, are not only misleading, because very few people can interpret them properly, but they are one of the basic causes of bad and sometimes dangerous shooting. It is high time that the whole allowance system was deposited in the wastepaper basket. It is not practical, and it establishes an entirely false foundation of thought at the back of the shooter's mind.

It can never be practical for, among a thousand men, it would be impossible to find half a dozen who were alike in their judgment of distance, their sight and reaction to speed, or their timing. The time taken to press the trigger is another factor which varies enormously with the individual and, indeed, varies from shot to shot according to empirical factors such as how soon the target was sighted.

All systems founded on 'allowances' are inherently unstable and unscientific. Indeed, it is only in the sport of shooting that the matter even arises. I have never heard the question raised in any other form of game where the hitting of a moving object, such as a ball, is involved.

Ballistics, so far as rifles are concerned, is a fairly exact science; but shot-gun ballistics are far more a matter of compromise based on a theoretical 'mean of average.' Even in matters which do not concern ballistics, matters of sight displacement in minutes of angle, we should find some tables stating that the lateral move-ment of gun-muzzles should be 2·5 inches to give a forward lead of forty inches for twenty yards and three inches to give a forward lead of seven foot six inches at forty yards. Now this lateral move-ment obviously varies with the length of the gun, and it also fails to take into account that this lateral movement is carried out in a different way by different people. The pivotal point of time may be with the stock home or it may be a far looser movement with the left hand as the pivot, and it is very often accompanied by head movement as well. It is indeed difficult to resolve this $2\frac{1}{2}$-inch movement into anything really practical unless a great many other factors are taken into account.

Now consider the question of timing, the precise adjustment of forward allowance, in terms of the ordinary shooting man. Take the man who, with the best will in the world, is trying to improve his shooting or to correct his faults, and is studying the thousands of figures involved in any moderately full table of allowances with his potential variations in range, angles, speed of birds, loads of varying velocity and all the other technicalities. Assuming that he gauges the distance right (of which more later), one man will jump the required distance but stop to press his trigger; the next will fire before he has really completed the movement; while a third and dangerous type takes a long time to get to the desired point of lead and, by the time he reaches it, has swung round and is pointing down the line of guns before he is aware what has happened.

Now let us come to the question of judging distances. It is an enormously variable factor and is undoubtedly affected by a purely physical consideration in the individual. A short-sighted man, or one whose eyes are relatively wide apart, is, as a rule, slow at focusing distant objects (and, oddly enough, a one-eyed man can, as a rule, hardly judge distances at all). To people with this disability a bird, thirty yards away, but near the ground, looks far nearer than the one thirty yards almost overhead, although the distances are equal.

This is a very common fault, and it is concerned with back-ground. A low bird is seen against some form of a subconsciously

E

imaged 'measuring stick.' In a way its size is related to the hedge, a tree or some object, and it is seen in proportion, and the range is based on that. Against the sky, of course, there is no standard of proportion.

In addition to the physical limitations of the individual, we have to take into consideration normal 'optical illusions.' We traditionally see things in our own perspective, although the Japanese, for instance, have an entirely different value of perspective as can be seen in their prints. In one of his experiments, Payne-Gallway fitted a measuring device to his gun-barrel, and a dead pheasant, at forty yards horizontally, appeared to measure more than twice the length of the overhead bird hoisted to forty yards in the air. It was clearly a matter of optical illusion; for the same bird at the same range is clearly the same size.

A man may be a fair judge of distance but not good at judging heights. The reason is, perhaps, that most men have some mental standard of distance; a cricket pitch, a miniature range, or some familiar unit of longitudinal measurement. Height, though, is less familiar and the average man is usually sadly out in his guess at the height of a tree or a T.V. mast. Very few men realize that the average oak or elm tree in England, which looks quite tall, is seldom taller than some thirty-six to forty *feet*; that is, twelve yards or so. And may I remind you that the effective range of a shot-gun is somewhere between forty and sixty yards. So much for those out-of-range pheasants that shooting men talk about. You will constantly notice stories in the papers of falls from third-storey windows, in which the report says that 'The victim crashed sixty feet to the street below.' The fact of the matter is that the average third-floor window-sill is twenty-four to thirty feet above ground level.

With a 20 per cent factor of error in horizontal range judgment, and a 50 to 60 per cent factor of exaggeration for height, we are unlikely to judge very accurately the matter of widths at a distance. Here again, an optical illusion operates. An interesting experiment, which will afford you an opportunity of testing your friends' judgment as well as your own, is to paint a board forty inches long and four inches wide with white paint, and erect it crosswise on an upright thirty-five yards away. Then set up a similar board forty-eight inches long but *eight* inches wide. Paint it black on a lower post, some twenty or so yards to the side of the white one, but forty-five yards away from the observation point. You will very seldom find anybody who can make a correct guess as to the distances, and, in most cases, people insist on pacing them out as they literally can't believe their own eyes.

Practical experiments of this nature, and some practice in checking and estimating ranges and the size of objects at a distance, will soon give you sufficient experience to decide whether calculations are the least help at all in the field, or whether a more practical method isn't to subscribe to the system of shooting that I personally advocate.

In my method there is no question of trying to compute muzzle movement, allowance, or any other complicated matter. All I ask you to do is to look at the bird, and, by correct mounting and body work, shoot naturally without constraint or effort *apparently* straight at the bird; but subconsciously, overthrowing a little and so giving the necessary lead or compensation for time flight; and, in that way, arriving at what, in any other terms, is a complicated mathematical problem.

When I say 'look at the bird,' I mean it. You must glue your eyes to it, focus it and see nothing else. At first, it is not easy to forget the gun, but, once proper concentration on the bird is achieved, you are two-thirds of the way to becoming an expert shot. It is more difficult to do it at long ranges than short ones, for, thinking it over, you will realize that we all look things 'straight in the eye' at short distances.

In the law courts, I have noticed how the jury shift their gaze from Counsel to Witness as questions are put and answered. All twelve heads move like automatons. Yet the crowd in the stands at a race meeting are all stiff-necked. I know the field of view renders movement unnecessary; but, to get down to the refinements of shooting, if you want to hit a pheasant in the neck, you must look at his neck and not at the bird as a whole. There is a lot to be said for a steady eye as well as a steady hand.

(*The neck, for preference. But if you concentrate on a wing tip, legs or breast, the result will be much the same, because the spread of shot will cover the whole bird. The vital thing is not to see your gun barrels.*)

Finally, I must tell you, once again, never to be afraid of missing. I am reminded of Wild Bill Hickok, the great gunman of the frontier days of the West, who had a remarkable reputation as a marksman. Yet, in his biography, it is stated unequivocally that Wild Bill was never a good shot. He couldn't cut ace pips out of playing cards. The secret of his success was that he could shoot whilst he was being shot at. If you can cultivate that attitude of mind, if you can resist the temptation to get excited, and use your gun at game when you are in no danger yourself of being shot at, with the same coolness that Wild Bill could handle a gun in a fight in a saloon, you'll be well on the way to become the calm and collected shot that I want to make you.

VIII

Practice in the Field

ASSUMING that you have carefully studied what I have so far said, and endeavoured to build up your *muscle memory* by practising at home, you will be anxious to test out your technique in the field. Unless you are a natural stylist, or you have been particularly economical in your use of ammunition, the chances are that you will be bothered by a number of trifling discomforts which are common to everybody who uses a game gun, except those expert shots whom all of us envy and so few can emulate.

If your shooting style is perfect, you shouldn't be bothered with minor bruises caused by the recoil of the gun. Gun-makers can provide various material sedatives to mitigate various conditions, but you would do much better to know the cause and, by style, try to correct it. Here are the commonest troubles with their cause and the proper way to overcome them:

Bruised second finger: This is caused through loose grip, relaxing grip in firing, too short a stock, or the bad habit of using the pressure of the second finger against the back of the guard to squeeze the trigger pull-off. If the stock is gripped too lightly, it will occasionally slip through the hands after firing and knock the finger that way.

You may wear a finger guard, or unscrew the guard and roll on to it a rubber umbrella ring (doubled) which will hold it in the spur of the guard and take off most of the blow. But if you will study what I have said about right-hand grip, you will notice that the pulling back of the right hand and the pulling-off of the trigger with a semi-rigid finger, helped by the shoulder meeting the butt of the gun, will completely clear the finger. If it doesn't, the stock needs lengthening. If the stock is the right length your second finger should be well clear of the back of the guard and the pad of your index-finger comfortably placed to touch off the trigger. Beware of hooking the first joint of your index-finger over the trigger. If you follow these rules you will never be bothered with bruised finger again.

Bruised cheek.—If the face is, for example, half an inch off the stock, the recoil is likely to jar the head into forcible contact. If the head is too erect and too square, the jawbone comes on to the top of the stock and the jar of recoil will bruise the flesh. Further, if the head is too much 'down', the cheekbone comes on to the top of the stock.

Avoid sandwiching your flesh between either jawbone and stock, or cheekbone and stock; and note that the head should be pivoted slightly to the right to avoid jawbone or cheekbone coming into contact, and that the gun-stock should firmly touch the cheek midway between the two.

Bruised mouth is more often than not caused by the fingers of the right hand coming back with the recoil. What this means is that you have taken an incorrect stance or that the stock is too short by at least half an inch.

Bruised arm is due to incorrect stance or too long a stock.

Bruised shoulder is due to incorrect stance or too wide a butt. A recoil pad should cure this ill. Get one that is rounded at the corners, smooth and well-varnished and always soft and pneumatic (not hard, as the wood itself is).

Bruised chest is due to incorrect stance or, more often, too long a stock. If the stock is too long, the gun won't come properly to the shoulder. Other causes are insufficient cast-off at toe or too much toe on the stock of the gun. Sometimes an unsupported brace buckle is the cause.

Shooters should pay particular heed to the position of the buckles of their braces. Myself, I recommend all who can to dispense with this article while engaged in shooting. A little attention to the fit of the trousers round the hips and the avoidance of a long waist cut, such as necessitates a high lift of the buttons, will usually render any support, other than perhaps a belt, unnecessary. The shoulders are more supple without the confining effect of braces and the body less liable to perspiration. But, if braces must be worn, the buckle should on no account be situated where the butt beds into the shoulder. If the elastic has stretched so as to necessitate this position, the remedy is to remove some inches of the webbing and have the fitting resewn. I have discussed this matter in rather greater detail in the latter part of the book, but I want to emphasize here that shooting clothes can be very important. Rifle shots are so particular about it that, at Bisley, most of them won't go to the ranges unless they are wearing the same clothes which they always wear when they are shooting at the targets. I know one Queen's Prize winner who, even in the hottest weather, always wears the same old mackintosh to make sure that the feel of the gun in his shoulder never varies, whatever conditions of weather he may have to shoot under.

This may seem late in the day to talk about the proper method of opening and loading a gun; but, generally speaking, I don't bother my pupils with matters of that kind until they have mastered the more elementary elements of gun-handling. When you know that you can hit what you are shooting at, when your confidence has been built up, that is the time to think about the finer points of gunmanship.

Of course, anybody can open a gun; but few people effect the operation in the smooth and effortless manner in which it should be conducted. More often than not, one sees a man who ought to know better hurriedly fumbling, dragging on the barrels and attempting to break the gun before the lever has been completely opened.

To open the top lever, knurl the first finger against the right lock plate. With thumb on lever, squeeze both the lock plate and the lever together. The leverage will be sufficient to open the stiffest lever you are likely to come across.

To open the breech, hold the stock under the arm with barrels turned slightly sideways to give body leverage to assist easy opening. Draw down the barrels with the left hand whilst the stock is gripped between the right side and right forearm. Don't try to do it with your right hand, as this should be just leaving the lever to reach bag or pocket or belt for fresh cartridge or cartridges. Handled in this way, a self-ejecting gun will throw the cartridges away to the right and not immediately over your right shoulder.

When I am loading for my pupils at the shooting school, many remark 'I wish I had you as a loader when I am in the field.' Yet, although speed comes with practice, the method of quick loading is easy to learn.

Whether you have got your cartridges in a pigskin bag, or in your pocket, begin by giving the pocket or the bag *a good shake* before shooting. The heavy weight of the lead shot in the head of the cartridge, compared with its much lighter base, will cause it to turn 'head uppermost.' It is consequently long odds that, when you put your hand in your pocket or cartridge bag, you will find that the heads are waiting in the position in which it is easiest to handle them.

If you have only expended one cartridge, picking a second one out of your bag and popping it into the chamber of your gun is a quick process. Where time and effort is so often wasted is in fumbling with a second cartridge when both chambers of the gun have been expended. It may be that you are in no hurry to reload but, in game shooting, it is always wise to assume that the best chance of the day will come at the moment when you are the least prepared for it. Get into the habit of reloading your gun in the field as quickly as possible.

This is the method which you should practise until, like everything else in shooting, you can carry it out without thinking:

When you break your gun, to eject the fired cases, your right hand should be on its way to your pocket or bag at the same time. Two cartridges are taken and, if you have shaken your bag or pocket as I recommend, you will find that they come to your fingers easily. Take two cartridges and as you collect them in your hand make a movement of your fingers to provide that the lower one is more prominent than the top one by about three-quarters of an inch; in other words, pick them up out of your pocket or your bag between your fingers in an over-and-under position. Insert the nose of the under cartridge into the right barrel but don't let go of it. Using it as an axis, twist your wrist so that the other cartridge turns over the left barrel. Let both go and the gun will be loaded at express speed without barked knuckles.

I don't expect you to master this trick just by reading what I have said about it. Practise it carefully, following the instructions and referring to the photographs. Once you have mastered it, you will get a reputation for quick loading which will be the envy of your fellow shooting men.

Closing a gun is an important matter because the factor of safety is involved. Never close your gun by lifting the barrels to the stock because the process involves raising the muzzle of the gun to what can so easily be a dangerous angle, if, by accident, you release the charge. The proper method of closing the gun is to lift the stock to the barrels. This is the way it is done: having dropped the cartridges into the chambers, grasp the stock of the gun with the right hand, making sure that the fingers are well clear of the trigger. Pressure of the right hand against the grip of the stock, with a slight forward inclination of the body, will close the gun. Alternatively you can close the gun by holding the barrels pointing towards the ground and raise the stock to meet them with a lift of your forearm.

Having learnt the drill, and adopted all the safety precautions that I have emphasized so strongly, you will still be an unwelcome guest at a shoot unless you also master the etiquette of the shooting party. The etiquette isn't merely a matter of ceremony; it is based upon sound principles of safety and good sportsmanship, too.

For driven birds in the British shooting field the shooters are usually numbered for the first drive: number one being on the left; and, thereafter, they move up two places every drive. Thus, number one in the first drive will be at number three stand at the second drive, and so on. The reason for moving up two places at each stand is to save a gun being on the outside twice in succession; so better distributing the chances of sport.

(*Although the system of moving-up two places for each drive is that most widely practised, the positioning of the guns is always at the discretion of the host. Sometimes, it may be the host's wish to give special guests favoured treatment, to have more walking guns on one stand than others; or, in unexpected weather conditions, to put guns where there are no numbered sticks at all. It's a movable feast in which it is always incumbent on the guest to ask the form. Churchill has also omitted to mention that the numbered cards in general use are coloured red against the oncoming traffic of birds. The shooter should place himself facing the white side with the number on it.*)

When you are shooting birds in an organized party there are certain rules which must be carefully adhered to.

The first is that, in the normal course of events, a line of men will be driving the ground in front of you putting birds forward so that they will fly over the guns. At a certain point in every drive it is extremely dangerous to shoot at an angle below forty-five degrees in front of you. When the beaters are close-in it is the duty of every shooting man to be very careful indeed about any shot he takes in front. Normally, especially if a low-flying pheasant, flushed out of covert, or a rabbit makes a last-minute rush as the beaters come up with the guns you should take the shot, if you take it at all, behind you.

At any time, when you are in an organized drive, examine the ground and the landscape carefully before you start shooting. For example, if you are standing in a ploughed field which is heavily littered with flints, it can be extremely dangerous to shoot at any ground game which isn't well behind anybody else in the vicinity. Pellets can ricochet off flints in the most dangerous and devastating manner. If you are shooting in hard weather remember that the ground itself can ricochet pellets like a steel plate. And never fire your gun unless you are perfectly certain where the charge will finish. To shoot into foliage at ground level, however far away you think the beaters may be, is inviting an accident.

(*MANY OF THE MOST EXPERIENCED SHOTS REFRAIN, ON PRINCIPLE, FROM SHOOTING ANY DRIVEN FUR IN FRONT.*)

One of the most rigorous rules of organized shooting is that you mustn't steal another man's bird. It is only your bird when it is coming to you more than to anyone else, or otherwise in your own proper angle of fire. Shoot only at an angle of 45 degrees right or left; do not shoot immediately in front of, or just behind, adjoining gun.

Most of the great shots pride themselves on their courtesy. I remember one senior member of the Royal Household who, when he was shooting, almost invariably took time off when he saw a doubtful bird to say to the next gun 'Yours, sir.' If the adjoining gun replied 'No, yours,' the old courtier took pride in still having time to spare to shoot the bird clean. That doesn't mean that, among friends, it isn't permitted to have a bang at a bird which your neighbouring gun may have missed with both barrels altogether. It is a part of the etiquette that, if that happens, you are fully entitled to have a go to 'wipe his eye.' And, if he is a good sportsman, he will be the first to congratulate you on doing it.

Remember that, in the sport of shooting, you are not only there to enjoy yourself: you also have a responsibility to your host to help him harvest an important food crop. You also have a humane duty to see to it that you kill your birds clean, and if, by chance, you wound them that you take every precaution to see that the game is ultimately picked up by the beaters or the dogs.

As you shoot it is your responsibility to mark your fur or feather as it falls, making a note how many head of game falls in front of you, on your left or on your right. Some men are exceptionally good at this, others cannot remember whether 'it was

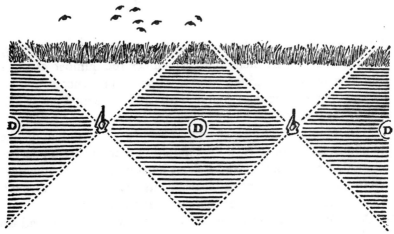

DRIVEN GAME SHOOTING: DANGER ZONES AND LEGITIMATE FIELDS OF FIRE

In this diagram it is assumed that guns are standing thirty yards apart and well back from a high hedge during a partridge drive. Except when standing close to cover, when an inevitable 'gap' will occur in front, all birds are covered while still well in range (forty yards). The legitimate fields of fire (the white areas) for each gun are 90 degrees in .front and 90 degrees behind. The shaded portions are the Danger Zone.

It is permissible to shoot at a high-flying partridge covey in a Danger Zone or to pick the nearest of a bouquet of pheasants to the gun. But it is a matter of etiquette to be certain that you are not poaching a fair bird from your neighbour. *Ground game should never be shot in the danger zone.* Above all, the shooter must train himself *never to follow through* into the shaded areas. Whilst turning to shoot behind, the gun should be down from the shoulder and the barrels pointing skywards during the 90 degrees traverse of the Danger Zone.

five or seven' that they got down. Never hang up the field to hunt for a mythical bird. Alternatively, if you are certain that you have got a bird down, tell the keeper or the head beater where you think it is. It won't hold up the shooting and the keeper will be grateful to you for telling him where to look when he is going round on the pick-up afterwards.

Even in the best organized shoots, with the most proper guests, it often happens that two men fire at the same bird. Always let the other man claim it; it goes into the bag just the same. And, anyhow, the lookers-on see most of the game.

The most important rule when you are walking-up game—as opposed to occupying a stand and waiting for it to be driven towards you—is always to keep in line. Remember to walk in line 'as steady as a farm labourer.' Remember that birds usually prefer to run than fly. Partridges, if gently pushed forward, will run until they are tired to get into cover, and will then squat.

But, if you walk fast, they will run fast and, in all probability, rise out of range. If men could remember the number of times they have chased partridges all day without much success and on walking home tired had found birds sit for them, they would realize the importance of slow walking.

To sum up, it is far better to miss a chance of a bird than to take the slightest risk, or to earn the reputation that you are a poacher of another man's sport. Never shoot horizontally into hedgerows or cover; some very remarkable accidents have happened through the shooter not seeing where his shot was going to end.

Don't fool about with your safety catch, working it to and fro until you don't know whether it is on or off. Accustom yourself to push it up with the first joint of the thumb as the gun reaches the 'ready' position.

Whether you shoot well or badly during a day in the field, make sure that at the end of it you can congratulate yourself that never for a single second were you caught off guard in your safety precautions or did you do anything which might have caused a fellow gun to think to himself that you are a jealous shot or that you don't know the rules of the game.

Over-keenness, which is such a virtue in most sports, is one of the things in shooting which mysteriously results in your host refraining from inviting you to share his sport again.

IX

Shooting for Women

I HAVE deliberately refrained, up till now, from making any reference to women as shots, although quite a lot of women shoot really well, and with enthusiasm. The trouble is that very few women are properly taught how to shoot. This is the more regrettable as a correct beginning is half the battle.

If they care to learn, women can shoot just as well as men; but, in most cases, their approach to the sport is from a different angle to a man's. Boys, as a rule, like guns and noise but girls, as a rule, have a distinctive dislike of firearms and fireworks; and, whereas a boy comes to a gun with a natural desire to be able to use one, girls usually have a doubt at the back of their minds.

I think many more women would shoot but for the unfortunate factor that, in many cases, they have tried the experience of a few shots from a borrowed gun, and found it a painful affair; as a result of this, they abandon all desire to use a gun again. This is exactly as if, in an endeavour to learn swimming, they tried to dive off the highest springboard for a start. On a modern properly-equipped shooting ground, special provision is normally made for women. They begin with practice in proper gun-mounting and snapping with an empty gun at various marks. For this purpose a very light ·410-bore try-gun is the best weapon. This is a measuring gun, which is adjustable until the individual need is fitted. As the gun is a very small bore it can be fired without any perceptible recoil and is indispensable for the first steps in shooting.

These early exercises have to be taken steadily at first, for they are bringing into play muscles not usually exercised and can be a little tiring. As soon as muscular familiarity is realized (this means perhaps a lessening of rigidity, for one always exerts too much energy in an unfamiliar effort) a beginning is made with recoil discharges at stationary birds set up in front of big steel targets. This is where the instructor teaches the importance of proper grip and stance, and co-ordination of hand and eye, during the rests in practice.

Women are inclined to flinch from an anticipation of the noise;

but this is very easily cured, and they usually regain complete-self-confidence in half a dozen rounds.

Within six lessons, at the most, a novice has probably graduated to the next size gun, again an adjustable try-gun, but of a larger bore.

This approach to the full-size sporting gun has to be very carefully carried out, as no risk can be run of bruising of the shoulder. Women have a much more easily marked skin than most men, and though recoil may not in any sense be felt as uncomfortable, slight bruising may occur from any error in gun-mounting or firing before the gun was properly set to the shoulder.

The tendency of most women is to square their shoulders much more than men. This also throws out the breast which is exactly the attitude we want to avoid for shooting. We do not want a woman to stiffen her back, square her shoulders and bring the gun up. She must not stand square, but very slightly sideways, and she must practise putting her shoulder to the gun rather than the gun to the shoulder. The reason for this is that, in the rigid position, there is no natural shoulder abutment for the gun-stock. She will probably fire the gun with the stock against the arm muscles, which is wrong and painful.

Take anything—a walking-stick will do—and keeping the shoulders and the arms-folded-on-breast, simply move the arms from the elbows to allow gun-mounting. You will note the following:

(1) The breast is perfectly clear of the toe of the gun-stock and safe from the risk of injury.

(2) A proper 'bed' or abutment for the stock is made within the right shoulder.

(3) This is not a rigid braced affair of bone and muscle but cushioned and elastic and free to move back with recoil, and absorb it.

In fact, the body is, so to speak, poised to catch the recoil, whereas if the woman stood square and rigid, backing away from the gun rather than leaning towards it, she would experience the recoil. But as she would not 'give to it' it would punch harder than was comfortable. If the stock of the gun rests on the bone of the shoulder-joint a thin layer of skin is pinched between un-yielding bone and hard wood by the recoil, and extensive and painful bruising may result. If, however, the correct position and method of gun-mounting is properly drilled home, any woman can fire normal-sized game guns with absolute confidence. The main thing to remember is that nothing must be rigid; the shooter relaxes rather than stiffens and she must not grip her gun tightly but hold it as lightly as a riding switch. There is no bracing to withstand recoil, but an easy yielding to it. All muscles have to be relaxed, not tensed, the only bracing or contracting movement is that tightening of the right-hand grip which occurs as you press your trigger.

The new 12-bore two-inch chambered gun* is excellent for women. It is a modified version of the standard 12-bore game gun with two-inch cartridges. But in every case women should begin with a small bore gun and work up gradually. The 20-bore try-gun —a very nice gun to handle—can never equal the performance of the larger bores and its slender barrels are not adapted to some rather long and graceful hands; they tend to slip through the left and the recoil of the 20-bore is often more perceptible than with the more massive 12-bore.

For shooting clothes for women, nothing is better than rough tweed with pivot sleeves loose cut at the elbow, as most practicable golf jackets are now cut. As women tend to wear thinner materials than men it is also always a good idea to have a quarter-inch thick pad of fine rubber sponge sewn into the shoulder of a light-weight shooting coat, inside the lining. This will take the sting out of any careless shot fired in a moment of excitement.

It is not easy to lay down any hard-and-fast rules for women, as their physical capacity to handle the weight of a gun is variable to the individual; but, in general, anyone who can drive a moderately powered car without fatigue will not find the slightest difficulty in a day's shooting, providing that they begin the right way and learn the essentials first.

So far as footwork and grip and all other matters are concerned, the rules are the same as for men, but it cannot be too strictly stressed that this matter of a correct shoulder resilience is vitally important in the interests of a woman shooter. The proper fit of a gun is even more important to a woman than to a man. Silhouettes may change with the march of fashion but the exact setting of a stock to fit perfectly, yet allow for changes in figure and fashion is rather a skilled art. It may take a little longer to get a woman fitted to perfection; but it is really vital to her success in the field.

* See page 189.

X

Instructions for the Use and Loading of a Pair of Guns

SHOOTING with a pair of guns and a loader is not as common as it used to be, because these days the opportunities for that sort of shooting are more limited. But a pair of guns and a good loader are the equipment of every good shot. Undoubtedly, the combination is highly effective, and it is doubtful if a good shot could show such a high percentage of kills to cartridges were he only to use a single gun and load it himself.

I am assuming that the shooter is using the normal double-barrelled game gun. In the English shooting field, anyhow, the pump gun is not welcomed except in the roughest of rough shoots. Apart from that, even an automatic gun is not so effective a weapon for quick shooting as a pair of guns in the hands of a first-class shot and with a loader who knows how to pass them.

There are various reasons why you make a much better performance when you are able to use a pair of guns. You are able to keep head and body in 'set' position and your eyes on the look-out, whereas with a single gun the disturbance of loading the gun does not help towards such composure.

Many shooters find their loaders more bother than they are worth, but this is not a fault of the system. Ill-trained loaders make you wait for a gun, they knock barrels, drop guns or hand you an unloaded or partly-loaded one. On the other hand, many good loaders are handicapped through their master not knowing the right thing to do.

I have seen shooters change guns over their left shoulder and over their head, and I have heard of a novice with a brand-new pair of guns throwing the first gun to the ground to grasp the second gun. I think these are the first instructions that have ever been printed and I hope that they will be of service to all. Further, I hope that there will be a marked increase in the number of 'two-gun' days in the future.

Both shooter and loader must work together to allow smooth and quick exchange of guns.

The shooter must keep his stand and not run about (such fidgety shots disturb adjoining guns).

Even if he has fired on his left, and needs the second gun to shoot again on the left, he should come back himself for the gun and not expect the loader to follow him round unless he has a succession of such shots and alters his stand. He will get his gun quicker, it will be put in the right place in his left hand and there is no chance of falling on his loader provided the latter keeps to one position and the shooter always returns to it for exchange of guns.

The shooter, after firing either one or both barrels, pulls back the safety catch with the first joint of the right thumb and brings the gun back with the right hand until the muzzle is upright and the breech is near the right of the shoulder. The left hand has meanwhile left the gun as soon as the catch is on 'safe' and is thrust over to the right to receive the loaded gun, which must be grasped immediately it touches the hand.

The loader takes the empty gun with his left hand, and with his right hand simultaneously puts the loaded gun into the shooter's left hand, which is extended to receive it.

The photographs show a perfect exchange of guns, and the diagram shows position of both the shooter's (A) and the loader's (B) feet.

It will be seen that the loader is standing sideways to the shooter and is thus able to turn his body towards the shooter when exchanging guns and to turn away from the shooter to load and close the gun, and to bring it to the upright.

The loader should have his cartridge bag slung over his left shoulder with the lid of the bag folded back and the bag hanging well in front of the body.

He should take hold of the gun with the left hand about five or six inches above the breech and, swinging away from the shooter, bring the stock under the right arm on to the right hip, the right hand meanwhile opening the lever (first finger pressing on the side of the right lock and thumb on left side of lever—on no account allowing the fingers to touch the triggers or even the

F

guard). With a jerk of the body and a pull of the left hand he opens the gun and ejects the fired cases; whilst doing this his right hand has left the lever and has gone to the cartridge bag to get the one or two cartridges required. (He should never grasp more than the one or two cartridges required at the time.) His hand is back ready to insert the cartridges by the time that the other has completed the opening of the gun.

He should drop the cartridges into the breech—not ram them in. (See Chapter VIII.) Then, with an upward jerk of the right hip, he closes the gun by bringing the stock up to the barrels (never close a gun by bringing the barrels up to the stock). The golden rule is that the muzzle must always be pointing to the ground during the loading and closing. It should never point at a spot more than a yard away from the loader's feet.

Now his right hand grasps the stock, the gun is lifted upright and the body swung round ready to push the gun into the shooter's left hand, at the same instant taking the fired gun.

In this method of loading both hands are working at the same time and a remarkable speed can be attained. I do not recommend the method of holding any cartridges in reserve between the fingers of the right hand. The best of loaders can be seen to fumble with them at times. Your man should be practised or drilled at his work and should start slowly as speed will come with practice.

The shooter should call as he kills his birds—either counting One—Two—Three; or, Dead—Dead—Miss—Dead. In the latter case the loader counts them up and gives the total at the end of the drive, as the shooter must always know how many birds he has got down. The loader will only mark a fallen bird when told to do so, or when his preoccupations allow.

Remove cartridges after every drive.

When carrying a pair of guns place one of them with the breech open in the crook of the right arm. The second gun should be gripped by the right hand with the barrels (trigger guard uppermost) resting on the right shoulder. In this position they will be quite safe, and there will be no likelihood of the two guns knocking against each other.

Whenever a gun is carried under the arm it should always be open at the breech. As few loaders do this the point should be noted. Shooters always look kindly on such evidence of safety. Excess of care is never a fault.

PART TWO

FIELD NOTES

I

The Rules of Shooting

THE rules of shooting, which is a sport not a game, are unwritten. The interpretation of the code varies in different company, in different countries, and at different times.

In some company, and the individual is the only judge of that, it may be counted part of the game to kill a bird before the next man can raise his gun to it. In rough shoots, where the chief anxiety of the host is the hope that enough game will be killed to give everybody something to take home, it is permissible to take every chance that offers. On occasion it may be regarded as reprehensible to pass by the opportunity of adding to the bag. On rough shoots the simple rule is to ask your host what the form is.

'Are we standing on ceremony today or not?' 'Do you want us to shoot hen pheasants?' If your host says, as he probably will, that we are shooting everything today we can catch up with and it is up to you fellows to make a bag, then of course you are entitled to do your best to drop everything that comes into view. But if it is a big day in the coverts or on the stubbles with numbered stands carefully organized, you can very easily blot your copybook by being over-zealous, as surely as you can, in your own estimation, by missing your birds.

The rules of shooting are unwritten because they vary from shoot to shoot. In one shoot the rule may be 'cock pheasants only' and only to the man they fly to; but everything else free for all. On another shoot the etiquette may be strict on game but it may be the custom to have a sweepstake on the head of vermin shot. In that event you are fully entitled to try and kill jays, crows and squirrels before your near neighbour can get his gun to them. But, if in doubt, don't take a chance.

In many ways it was easier in the old days when the host of the shoot exerted a discipline as strict as a Master of Foxhounds. Before the First World War, in the heyday of driven game shooting,* a gun could expect to be publicly rebuked, if not ordered home, if he made the slightest mistake in etiquette. On the great shoots the people who were invited were not even supposed to have their 'off-days.'

The tradition was so severe that Lord Leicester, the son of Coke of Norfolk and great grandfather of the present earl, would stop the shooting at Holkham if he considered that his guests were not performing up to standard. On one occasion he halted the beaters in the middle of a partridge drive on the grounds that the guests weren't proving themselves worthy of the birds he was showing them. It was with the greatest difficulty that the head keeper persuaded his lordship to carry on, pointing out that the guns were shooting in a full gale and that, on later drives, they would have a better chance of making a good bag.

In our own time Lord Leconfield, 'Lordy' to everybody who knew him, would walk down the line of guns on a big day in his coverts at Petworth, when he wanted the game for his tenants' annual supper, and announce: 'Two hundred pheasants before lunch, gentlemen, or no grace birds for you.'

The standard of etiquette in shooting in the nineteenth century is exemplified in the story of Lord Walsingham and the Marquis of Ripon. On one occasion these two great sportsmen, who were counted among the finest shots of their day, were surprised by a covey of eight partridges which swept overhead of them in the middle of a pheasant drive. Immediately the two men fired two barrels, changed guns, and fired another two barrels into the covey. Between them they shot the lot. The story was quoted in their own time, not for the brilliance of their feat in bringing down four birds each out of the covey, but for the fact that they were so experienced, and they knew the etiquette of shooting so perfectly that neither of them shot at what might have been counted the other man's bird.

I have instanced these stories, not in the hope that any average gun can achieve that combined perfection of manners and marksmanship, but to indicate the ideal that every shooting man should endeavour to attain to. If it was true in the old days that a man was likely to be ordered off the field if he offended the code, it is no less true today that, although shooting hosts are more

---

* *Driven game-shooting is just as good now, perhaps better. But Churchill couldn't be persuaded that anything was ever as good as it was 'in the good old days' of his youth. Neither can most of us.*

reluctant to speak their minds out loud, they think much the same way as their forebears.

For the man who offends, the situation is rather worse today because, very often, when he finds he is not invited out shooting again, he doesn't know what he has done wrong.

Further, it is useless to pretend that, however safe a shot a man may be, he will ever be as welcome as a shooting guest as one who shoots really well. Nothing is more exasperating to a host, who has gone to considerable trouble and expense to present game as effectively as he can over the guns, than somebody who is unable to make his fair contribution to the making of the bag. But, while a poor shot will obviously never get the invitations to shoot that a really brilliant shot invariably does, it is well to remember that the most brilliant shooting will never make up in the eyes of your host and your fellow guns for a breach of the rules of safe shooting.

You may feel that I have already said enough about the importance of safe shooting in the earlier parts of this book. But, as a gun expert, I am consulted continually by the police and by the insurance assessors about shooting accidents, and for that reason alone I am more conscious of the dangers than an ordinary shooting man who has probably never had personal experience of a serious gun accident in his days and who, I hope, never will. But I can assure you that shooting accidents are far commoner and far more surprising than any member of the ordinary public would think possible.

There is always an element of danger in shooting which, from long experience, I am inclined to believe is inevitable; but it can be reduced with care and experience to a negligible factor. On the whole, there is a far greater risk of an accident driving in your car to join a shooting party than in using a gun in the field, but just as we seek road safety we should seek gun safety too.

I can think of no better way of emphasizing the dangers than to relate to you details of some of the accidents that have come my way. It is surprising how many of them reveal a quite singular succession of circumstances.

There was the case of a keeper, an exceptionally careful man, who, while standing by a five-barred gate, cautiously lowered the hammers of his gun and rested the butt on one of the top bars of the gate while he lifted his knee to tighten a button or strap on his leggings. The way he stood the barrels were on his shoulder and the butt on the gate; but, by some accidental movement, the butt slid off the rail and the gun slipped down between the bars of the gate until it was arrested by the heads of the hammers. The impact was sufficient to fire one of the cartridges. As the barrels had now slid off his shoulder the keeper was shot just beneath his shoulder blade. Fortunately, it was not a fatal wound; but it was an accident which most people would say was not only improbable but impossible.

This accident, of course, would not have occurred if the keeper has been using a hammerless gun. In very many hammer guns, with rebounding locks, the hammer can be pushed forward into contact with the striker without using a great deal of pressure. A doubtful advantage with the majority of hammer guns is that the gun cannot be opened until the right hammer is lowered from full cock position. In winter, I should prefer to open the gun and then lower the hammers as it is so perilously easy to let one of them slip under the thumb. By my method, it does allow one to follow the strict rule: always take cartridges out before you do anything.

In another case I remember, a man who was ferreting for rabbits lay down his gun fully loaded whilst he knelt down to listen at the bury for the sound of his ferrets working. His companion accidentally kicked the gun and the man who had his ear to the hole was shot.

The all too common accident is that caused by a man crawling through a low gap in the hedge and dragging his gun after him by the barrels. A bramble, wire or unseen stump catches the triggers and there is another inquest to which I am called in as an expert witness.

Today fencing is not kept up as it ought to be. One cannot blame the farmers who use wire because it is the cheapest form of fencing; but wire is almost as dangerous to the shooting man as it is to the hunting man. And the danger isn't only wire. On an average day's shoot we all encounter gates so rickety on their hinges that they won't open; stiles in advanced decay, rotten rails and untrimmed barely practicable gaps, not to mention very slippery mud and awkward ditches. Never, never, never leave a cartridge in your gun, especially when you are alone, if you have to negotiate any sort of obstacle at all. Never mind how agile or confident you are. I know.

But what you do by yourself is your own business. What I am principally concerned with is to advise you how to behave in company, because, if you are shooting regularly, you will find that you are usually shooting in the company of other people.

There is no question that the greatest responsibility which falls to anybody in the shooting field is the host. If the host doesn't belong to the old-fashioned school which said what it thought in a loud voice and with decorative expletives, he none the less has a very large responsibility. If the host has the misfortune to have a guest who is, for example, shooting dangerously, one formula is for him to approach the offender and other likely offenders and say: 'Sorry, old man, but one of the guns—I won't tell you which—recently had a nervous breakdown and, as a consequence, he is very jumpy. Would you mind making a point of it today to open your gun immediately we finish each drive and keep it open until you are in position for the next drive? Show it to the other guns if you will, not ostentatiously of course, but show it to them just to prove it is empty. And if you notice anything let me know as soon as you conveniently can.'

If a delicate hint of that kind produces no improvement the host must decide whether to order the guest home or, if he prefers to avoid that unpleasant responsibility, at least wangle the numbers so that the offender is kept on the flank and can then hazard only one neighbour.

Incidentally, drawing for place and maintaining a routine movement is a device which might well be done away with in the shooting field. On many of the best shoots today it is no longer practised. The host selects the guns for each beat. It is not, of course, a working principle for syndicate shoots; but, even on a syndicate shoot, the captain can seed the draw by putting all the odd numbers to one side of his case and the even numbers on the other side, giving the best shots all even numbers and moderate shots the odd ones. This device at least ensures that the good shots don't get bunched together but are placed in positions in which they are able to assist their less accurate neighbours.

If you shoot with a party of country gentlemen, you will notice that they never take low pheasants down a ride. They never shoot a rabbit in front unless it is against a bank and dead safe, and they seldom shoot hares in flat country until they are through and behind the lines. The sport is a commonplace to them and they have a true sense of proportion. They never take a shot which might pepper a beater, or a dog, which they can't see, but who might be there.

The novice, perhaps a townsman, who shoots irregularly, is usually keener than the countryman and must always watch out lest in the excitement he falls into an error of judgment. A very good rule for the novice in his first season as a game shot is never to shoot at anything on the ground. Afterwards he will learn never to shoot at ground game at all until past the line or in a place where experience tells him that to shoot is safe. Remember that beaters are usually near when rabbits are flushed. Every gun should know exactly where the other guns and the beaters are placed before he raises his own. Rather let a hundred rabbits go by than risk a ground shot in which you don't know where the charge will finish.

It is good manners on all shoots to kill vermin; jays, magpies and, if possible, crows. Jays are a pest; but they have a low lilting flight which takes full advantage of cover. Better not shoot at them at all, even if there is a sweepstake on the vermin bag, unless you are absolutely confident that the bird can be shot at with safety. I mention this because even the most responsible shots tend to lose their heads when a jay plays hide-and-seek in the trees in front of them.

The sort of thing that happens is that one gun in the line will fire at a jay at a perfectly safe height. If he misses it the bird, more often than not, will make a downward dive. If the dive is in the direction of the next gun, who is ready and waiting, the latter may have a hard job to restrain from firing. Apart from scoring a direct hit on a beater there is then a risk of a ricochet as well. Pellets can hit a glancing surface, such as a tree branch, and after that they can go anywhere. If they hit another suitable surface they may double ricochet and the possibilities of accidents would then become enough to defeat an Einstein.

It is on record that on one occasion a sportsman shot a rabbit at forty yards in a grass field. The rabbit was central between two beaters over thirty yards apart. The rabbit was killed but *both* beaters were peppered. An accident of this kind is not so abnormal as one might imagine; but what appears quite credible to people like me, who know a great deal about guns, is often received sceptically by those who only think they know about guns.

Take the possible reasons for the foregoing accident. It is possible, though it is more possible than probable, that the wads blew through the charge and so dispersed it over a wide area.

This is the phenomenon which accounts for so-called 'cartwheel' patterns we occasionally get when plating guns, when only half the pellets can be accounted for on the steel plate. No one knows how wide the other pellets have flown.

In practice there is a risk in shooting ground game, or birds below the ten-foot level from the ground, not only to those in line with the gun but to those parallel to the target and within twenty yards of it on either side.

The ordinary sportsman may well say that for years he has shot rabbits ferreting and never known a ricochet. This is probably true; but most rabbiting is close-range work and it must be remembered that at ranges of ten or twelve yards pellet energy is so high that the pellets are either smashed to fragments or penetrate and lodge in the earth. At ranges of forty yards pellet energy is much reduced and contact may turn them rather than destroy them. They can glance off a stone or other hard surface and proceed with their mass unreduced yet with sufficient velocity to penetrate. At low velocity and longer ranges the danger is rather more from the wide dispersal of pellets than from ricocheted ones, the pellets having lost energy being almost killed on contact.

I have fired many thousands of experimental rounds and have brought pellets back to within a couple of yards of my feet at twenty yards' range. By an arrangement of plates I have succeeded in getting double and treble ricochet pellets zigzag to almost any direction of the original target. The basic safety of shot-gun shooting is that nature has provided targets which fly in the air, but though the patter of shots falling about one from somebody else's gun is normally harmless there are conditions when it can be very dangerous indeed.

The effective range of 6½-size shot has been calculated by one 'pen shooter' as fifty-four yards. Even if he clothed his back in two copies of *The Times* and three copies of the *New Statesman* I feel sure he would be uncomfortably reminded of his schooldays if he put his theory to the proof. The real range of a shot-gun on a windless day is at least two hundred yards. The maximum for number 6-shot is three hundred yards. Of course, at two hundred yards the shots have little potentiality of penetration, but it must never be forgotten that a pellet which would not penetrate tough and resilient skin can yet blind at one hundred and fifty yards.

These figures only relate to a normal charge. In some cases cheap cartridges mean cheap methods of production and cheap materials. In that event, high pressures and badly fitting wads can permit a condition to occur known as 'balling' or the fusion of a few pellets. This condition may be produced by tilting wads or through the gases from the powder touching the sides of the shot column which fuses a few pellets together, and it can also be caused by undue pressure pressing very soft lead pellets into close adhesion.

However, 'balling' is possible and three or four pellets may join together and fly in a compact projectile mass. I have cut holes in a mild steel plate at thirty yards, and although extreme range is unknown yet it is at least five hundred yards. According to its mass it would of course be capable of causing a serious wound at very long range.

The law takes a very odd view of these strange cases and there are far too many people going about with no notion of how deadly a shot-gun can be beyond fifty-four yards. As the majority of accidents arising out of 'balling,' and other circumstances, are settled out of court without report the emphasis of danger isn't rubbed home as much as it ought to be.

But the main consideration is not how to settle or account for accidents, but how to prevent them. You may not be a very good shot, but never let anybody say that you are not a careful one. Never fire at anything you cannot clearly see and, more important, see beyond. Know that a hedge may have anything on the other side of it from a couple of rustic lovers to blackberrying or mushroom gathering villagers or their children.

Remember, too, that the fact that you didn't know they were there, or that they had no business to be there, doesn't free you from your liability in civil law.

Because it *can* happen to any man using a gun that he may be indirectly, even excusably, responsible for an accident to somebody else, I'd say that it was a prerequisite of going into the shooting field that every man who carries a gun should take out an insurance against accidents. Sportsmen's premiums are very low indeed and they can cover you for third-party risks as well as risks to yourself and your guns for a few pounds up to a liability of £10,000.

Never make light of those far too common incidents when people get 'peppered' or 'tickled up' in the course of a shooting season. For the person who is hit, even at long ranges, it isn't funny. To be hit with a few shot-gun pellets with only enough energy left in them to penetrate the skin is like being hit hard with the flat of a cricket bat. The shock is considerable. That it should happen at all always means that somebody has taken a risky shot which shouldn't have been fired and which he is very lucky has ended without more serious accident.

Rabbits and vermin are the chief sources of offence, and also the woodcock which flies at head level. The old axiom that when shooting in untested company you should lie flat on the ground on the cry of 'Cock over' until the fusilade is over has a lot to commend it. Some quite steady pheasant and partridge shots lose all their steadiness where rabbits, woodcock and vermin are concerned. In the tail end of the season, when the host wants to get the rabbits down, the best rule is that, as soon as the beaters are within fifty yards, the guns on the ride should face about and only shoot away from the drive as the beaters advance.

At the annual farmers' shoot, which is so often held on Boxing Day, it is quite the best method to split up the party into smaller parties to localize the danger, giving them a drink and a sandwich at one o'clock and finishing around 2.30 p.m. to sit down to a hot meal. The beagles and mixed bag of dogs that collect on these occasions tend to lose some of their enthusiasm in the afternoon at the time when the farmers after an excellent lunch are ready for anything.

Indeed, in winter, when the days are short and an early start is impossible it is probably a mistake to have a lunch break at all, which usually wastes rather more than an hour and a half or so. Far better to have a sandwich and a drink at midday and carry on till 2.30 or 3.0. Then you can take your time over luncheon, have much more to talk about and have your necessary rest after a good meal or get on the road to go home as early as you wish.

In the old days, at the beginning of the present century, and in the latter years of a past, a great deal of attention was given to seeing to it that the guns stood in a true line. That was a wise precaution. Today, there is a tendency to place guns, not in relation to their neighbours, but to the best advantage to the bag. As an axiom of safety the line should always be as straight as possible. The guns who are walking-up with the beaters are usually in unknown territory and the keeper who posts them has duties elsewhere, but it is best that they stop at a safe distance before reaching the 'all out' end of the beat. The keeper should delegate this duty to an experienced beater who knows the ground. The beater can tell the 'back' gun when and where to stop.

As I said in the beginning of this chapter, there are no general rules of safe shooting; but it is possible to lay down a code of proper conduct:

(1) Always unload after a drive. Always unload before passing a hedge, gate, stile or other obstacle.

(2) Never shoot ground game in front of the line unless you know exactly where everybody else is and unless you can see beyond the quarry. Be very careful of shooting into the ground if it is in a stony place which might cause ricochets.

(3) Keep the safety catch always back at 'SAFE' and practice until it is a habit to push it on as the gun-stock leaves the 'ready' position under the arm and the forward hand is raising the gun to eye-level and pointing at the bird. Many shots can acquire this routine easily, using the side of the first joint of the thumb instead of the ball of the thumb and thus retaining correct right-hand grip. But, regardless of how distracting this effort may be at first, it is a very necessary precaution.

(4) When using a pair of guns, be sure that your loader is really well trained. He must be drilled parade-ground style. Don't use a second gun at all if the only loader you can find is a borrowed gardener or a chauffeur who may blow your toes off or cause an even worse calamity in his anxious effort to please. If ever you are given a bad loader put one gun down and shoot with the other, letting your man hand you the cartridges. It is not worth risking an accident. If, on the contrary, you are shooting with a man regularly you will be advised to have him properly trained which won't take longer than three or four hours' tuition on a shooting ground. If you are determined to take risks, with an untrained man, quadruple your accident insurance policy.

(5) If you shoot with a handguard on the barrels, make sure that it fits tightly. Handguards can usually be squeezed tight by hand if the fit is loose. Remember that, when using a pair of guns, you take the second gun in the left hand while passing the fired gun back with the right hand. If the handguard is loose the gun may slip through it to the ground with most serious consequences. As a matter of technical detail a stud catch can be fitted by a gun-maker which will save this particular annoyance and danger.

(6) Always carry your gun safely. When there is any doubt about the going, open it. The loss of time, closing your gun again and bringing it to your shoulder to shoot, is infinitesimal. The man who makes a habit of always opening his gun and unloading at any stop or obstacle, allowing it to remain open until a fresh start is made, then loading and closing his gun in readiness, will never shoot as the careless ones often do with an empty gun.

(7) Train yourself so that your forefinger never touches the trigger until the gun is up to eye-level, otherwise a slight insensitiveness in cold weather or a stumble may apply pressure before you realize it. If you wear gloves in cold weather always have the trigger finger cut off. In practice, a woollen mitten gives greater warmth and far better grip.

(8) One shoots many days and no game is really very important. Don't try to kill everything and never shoot when there is the slightest doubt of human safety. No one will ever blame you for not shooting. You are much more likely to get the blame for killing a bird which isn't properly coming to your gun.

Many shooting accidents happen at the end of the day when guns get tired and rather casual. The novice is usually more of a danger with his left barrel swinging down the line after he has missed with his right barrel. It is in order to avoid this that, on the shooting grounds, we often take out the left mainspring of a double gun until a novice learns his job. Actually he learns quicker and, further, it encourages him to use his first barrel effectively instead of letting it off as an explosive gesture.

The mechanical side of really good guns is seldom likely to be the cause of accidents. Design is very stabilized and always provided guns are kept in good order mechanical danger is a very rare hazard.

If by any chance the cartridge misfires, don't bring the gun down from the shoulder until you have pulled again. Then pull back the safety catch and lower it carefully, taking care that the muzzles are kept pointing to the ground. In some cases of mechanical fault, the gun may go off with the movement of the safety catch whilst it is being opened.

The modern British game gun is chambered for $2\frac{1}{4}$-inch cases, and the duck gun for 3-inch cases. When these cases are loaded the usual quarter-inch turnover or crimp makes each cartridge a quarter of an inch shorter. Therefore the 3-inch cartridge can be loaded into the $2\frac{3}{4}$-inch chamber; but, on firing, the turnover is unfurled into the narrow coning into the barrel, there setting up an abnormal high pressure and so straining the action of the gun. In Britain, perhaps the most serious danger lies in the fact that the 20-bore cartridge, if accidentally loaded into a 12-bore gun, will lodge in the bore, and the user, unaware of the obstruction, may load and fire a 12-bore cartridge behind it. A DANGEROUS BURST WILL ALMOST CERTAINLY RESULT.

The same danger, perhaps even a greater danger as the two cartridges are so alike and are principally used by beginners, occurs when 28-bores and 20-bores are used together. For the 28-bore lodges in the 20-bore in the same way as the 20 itself lodges in the 12; and, incidentally, as the 28-bore also lodges into a 16. Luckily the 20-bore is becoming an obsolescent size and small bores generally may be replaced by the new 12-bore which is chambered to 2-inch cases* and weighs a little over five pounds. As long as 20-bores are made the danger will remain unless the case is standardized with a far wider rim. In the same way, 28-bores could well be made with a deep wide rim as well.

There will always be fatal accidents which are difficult to understand. It is often reported how people get shot cleaning their weapons in circumstances which leave no real explanation as to why the victims, who alone could have told, got into the positions they did. Some accidents happen with most unusual weapons. I knew a keeper who was seriously wounded by an alarm gun which was loaded with a short cartridge inserted in a barrel block at the base of a rod. At the top of the rod was a heavy weight secured by a pin. When the pin was drawn, the weight was released and fell on the striker of the barrelblock, thus firing the cartridge. The keeper was careful to secure the falling weight, but he picked up the gun and turned it upside down allowing the barrel block which held the cartridge to slide down the rod and back on to the fixed weight which fired the shot. The result was that the keeper was wounded. The moral is that with this type of alarm gun, a very common model in wide use today, all bottom blocks should be fixed.

Once in a while, cases are reported of weapons, which have not been used for a generation, being found still loaded. It is not uncommon for firearms collectors to find old muzzle-loaders in which the charge has been left in the gun and which they at once boil out and draw. The action of all magazine and

* See page 189.

automatic self-loading weapons causes a fresh cartridge to be carried from the magazine to the barrel every time a fired or 'unfired' cartridge is extracted from the barrel. Many accidents have happened owing to forgetfulness or the belief that the ejection of the live round from the barrel has unloaded the gun.

If, having read as far as this, you feel that the risks and the dangers of game-gun shooting are so great that it seems almost impossible to believe that you won't get into trouble, let me comfort you by saying that, although I have probably fired as many, if not more cartridges, than anybody else living today, I have only been badly shot once and tickled up not more than a few times, although I have had many bad scares. Neither have I ever been present when a serious accident has happened, although I have been called in so often after the event. But there have been many occasions when I have had to take a deep breath.

Once, when I was loading for a very important personage, I said 'No' and stopped him just in time from shooting at a rabbit which ran in front along the hedgerow. As we later left the stand to pick up the game which had been shot, two children crawled out from under the very bush where the gun was pointed to shoot the rabbit and raced to our stand to gather up the cartridge cases as mementoes of the world-famous personage who had left them behind.

The discipline of a shoot is probably the most important factor to its safety. The better the manners, the safer the shoot. Guns must keep to their stands and never move to pick-up until the drive is over. Beaters must beat slowly and make a noise, light tapping with a stick or a couple of pebbles. The absolutely silent beater, who uses his stick to walk with, and moves like a ghost, is a danger. It is best for all concerned that a beater within range should be visible and audible. The really important shoots have a regulation beater's uniform of a light-coloured mackintosh, rather like a hunt servant's, and bowler hats with a scarlet hat-band. The bowler hat may be rather a nuisance in thick cover and perhaps white boiler suits and white waterproof caps could be preferred by beaters who wish to save their clothes. But, wherever possible, the beater should be dressed so that he is visible, and obviously the men would do better work wearing clothes which resist water and which they needn't be so careful of as their own everyday suit.

The correct handling of a gun in company is largely a matter

G

of good habit, and the drill should be inculcated into every young man using a gun for the first time. It is proper for a gun walking with the beaters to fire in the air to signal the start of a beat. (Incidentally it also helps to get birds on the move.) And normally speaking, especially at the end of the drive, he should not shoot at birds going forward. During one pheasant drive, where there were a lot of birds, I remember seeing a flanking gun shooting low and medium pheasants. He seemed to have no idea that he was dropping his shot not only on the beaters but on his fellow guns standing in the front line. If you are on the flank, or indeed, wherever you are standing in a drive, your first responsibility is to identify precisely the direction from which the beaters are advancing and the position of all the other guns. Experienced guns, when they take their stand at the beginning of a drive, make a practice of carefully identifying their position to the man on either side of them by waving a handkerchief or their hat.

Whatever you do, never change your position in the course of a drive. For better or worse, stay where you are. If, in quite exceptional circumstances, you do decide to change your position, make sure that both the adjoining guns know exactly where you are going. But on the whole, that's a matter which should always be decided before the drive begins. In practice, if you do try to improve your position, you'll generally find that you are not much better off. The bird that draws you forward, or to the left or the right, won't be typical of the way the birds will fly in the greater part of the drive. Generally speaking, you can depend on it that the keeper knows what are likely to be the best stands. It is very much in his interests to see that you get as much good shooting as possible.

The only circumstances in which, in an organized shoot, it may be advisable to move from the numbered stands is in exceptional weather conditions. If the wind had suddenly changed to an unexpected direction, if the weather is bad, it may well be that the guns can take up better positions than those already laid down. But normally speaking that is the responsibility of the host. Every gun should be very reticent indeed about changing his place from the numbered stand allotted to him. In rough shooting, in which the guns are probably their own beaters and the day alternates between drives and walking-up, it may well be that it is left to the guns themselves to take up what seems to them the most advantageous position. Even then, you are not freed of the responsibility of making sure where your neighbours are standing and establishing exactly your own proper and legitimate field of fire.

Your legitimate field of fire is an angle of 90 degrees immediately in front and immediately behind you. The 90 degrees to your left and right are a danger.

If a covey of partridges or a bouquet of pheasants comes over, it is reasonable for the guns on each flank of them to shoot at the same time; but always remember, in those circumstances, that your natural birds should be the ones which are nearest to you. Remember the story of Lord Walsingham and the Marquis of Ripon who, between them, without poaching each other's birds, killed every partridge in a covey of eight.

On any day when game is abundant, there will be many occasions on which you will not be immediately certain whether the bird is rightly yours or not. But, every pheasant, from the moment you see him, gives you time to look to your manners before you shoot. In case of doubt, your gun, which should be at the 'ready' position, should be poised ready for mounting. A typical case of doubt is when a pheasant, or very often a woodcock, flies down the line. Hold your hand until the gun next to you has had a fair chance. Don't shoot if he misses until the bird is well in your area. As a matter of good marksmanship, that is the right moment to shoot.

Harking back to the drill, you'll find, if you watch, that the man who swings his body properly whilst his gun is mounting is usually a safe shot. The man who first mounts his gun and then swings on to the bird, looks unsafe and usually is. If you have the misfortune to be posted next to a poker, particularly in grouse and partridge driving, it can be disconcerting enough to put you off your own shooting. It can be even worse if he also has the habit which such people often have, of sitting on his shooting-stick while he is waiting for the drive to begin, with his gun loaded (and his safety catch up) laid across his knees pointing in your direction.

On one occasion, when this happened to me, I elaborately pretended to imitate the offender's example. I made a show of loading my own gun and pushing up my safety catch, and then laid my weapon across my knees with the muzzle pointing in *his* direction. He at once lifted his gun and pointed it to the front, and I reversed arms and reloaded. Not a word was spoken.

One old sportsman who used to give me some delightful days' shooting, used to have a habit of saying, 'Unload your guns and follow me' when he led us on to the next drive. I remember another who would withdraw a cartridge from an open breech, with the enquiry, 'What cartridges are you using?' When the man who hadn't unloaded his gun withdrew his own cartridges for comparison, the host looked at them and then handed them back with a quiet 'Put them in your pocket, my dear chap.'

I hope I have now repeated the safety precautions and illustrated them with anecdote and example with sufficient emphasis to make an impression even on the most negligent of gun-handlers. No shooting man can ever afford to stop thinking about safety. And the moment of greatest danger is when a man forgets for one unforgiving second that he has got a lethal weapon in his hands.

But these basic rules of conduct in the field wouldn't be complete if I confined myself to the responsibility of the man with the gun to his fellow human beings. The second responsibility is to the game which he is shooting. It is a familiar paradox that most sporting men love the thing they kill. Nobody has any right to use a gun against game who isn't trying all he knows to kill clean and who hasn't studied what to do in the unavoidable circumstance when an animal is wounded.

When you are shooting it is your duty to mark down everything you hit as carefully as possible, with the most particular attention for the head of game which looks like running. The etiquette of the shooting field requires that you must not leave your stand to retrieve wounded game while the drive is on but, immediately it is over, you should send your dog or call in somebody who has got a dog to go after wounded game first and foremost. Even if it is personally unpleasant to you to despatch a 'runner' cleanly and humanely, it is your duty to do it whenever necessary. Too many shooting men have only the vaguest idea how to put a wounded animal out of its misery. It is not good form to break a partridge's neck, by taking it by the head and spinning its body in the air. Neither is it particularly stylish to pull off a pheasant's head in the effort to break its neck.

The quickest and cleanest way to kill a partridge or a pheasant, if you don't mind doing it, is to crack its skull sharply between your front teeth. Alternatively, you can break its neck cleanly by twisting the head to one side or the other and carrying it back with a sharp pull. The proper way to kill a rabbit is to give it a rabbit punch with the side of the palm of your hand in the back of the neck. You can kill a hare the same way, but I don't recommend it because hares bleed profusely and, if you pick them up by the back legs and strike them behind the ears, you'll probably spatter your clothes with blood. The way to kill a hare is to place your boot or shoe across the back of its neck as it lies on the ground. Pressing down the head, quickly pick it up by its back legs and draw its body sharply across the leg which is holding the hare down. This will kill the animal quickly and humanely and will ensure that you haven't got to send your shooting clothes at the end of the day to the cleaners.

However well you think you are shooting, always resist the temptation of boasting about it. The lookers-on see most of the game and nothing irritates a man who may feel that he has had the worst of the luck, or is off his day, than the bumptious gun next door who boasts about the head of game he has killed. Count the game you bring down by all means. In fact, the policy is to be recommended because it's a guide for the pickers-up, but don't talk about it, except in passing, and as modestly as you can to the people who are picking up the birds. And remember never to give yourself credit for any bird about which you are doubtful. Nothing makes a gun more unpopular with the keepers than if he gets the reputation of claiming game which is as difficult to find as the rabbit in the conjurer's hat. If you believe that you yourself are not an offender in this matter of claiming birds which you only think you have killed, I can only tell you that, privately, most shooting men are the victims of this harmless self-deceit. I remember an occasion at a tea at the end of the day's shooting. When the keeper brought in the figures for the total bag, the host for fun asked each of the guns to write down on a piece of paper the total head of game that he guessed that he himself had shot. All the guns, except me, put down what they believed to be their score on a piece of paper. I excused myself saying that I would take what was left over. The result of adding up the scores turned out exactly as I expected. Taking the guns' own reckoning of what they had killed and substracting it from the total bag, it left me owing many birds on the day's shooting.

Curiously enough, even some of the best and most experienced shots tend to delude themselves about their marksmanship. I have even heard a man claim that over the season for pheasant he had put up an average of 80 per cent of pheasants to cartridges expended. If he had achieved that, he would be one of the greatest game shots that the world has ever seen. In truth, I should be surprised to learn that he put up a better performance than 30 or 40 per cent of the cartridges expended.

If you can kill one bird out of three cartridges expended, you can call yourself a good shot. Lord Walsingham, who in his day was counted one of that mysterious band, the ten best gameshots in England, went farther in reducing the average to 30 per cent. Of course, there is a great difference between the average of birds fired at and killed as compared with the average of cartridges fired for each bird killed. You would probably put up a better average if you based it on birds killed out of those fired at, but, personally, I prefer to establish it on the basis of the number of cartridges fired to produce the average of birds killed. If, at the end of a day which you know your friends thought you were shooting well, you honestly add up the number of the head of game you are *quite certain* you brought to bag and compare it with the number of cartridges that you fired, you may be surprised to discover—although I wouldn't be—that your average was as low as 25 per cent.

It is not my purpose in this book to discuss matters which are outside the actual business of safe, straight shooting. There are many admirable books on game preservation and estate management and the natural history and ecology of the game animals of this country. You can read about correct relations between riparian owner and keeper, and game-rearing and game management in relation to agriculture, elsewhere. All I need remind you here, at the end of the first chapter on Field Notes, is that at the end of the shooting day it is customary, and pleasantly so, to tip the keeper as a reward for the sport he has provided. Sometimes shooting men become unnecessarily anxious as to the size of the tip they ought to give. I have often read the suggested scale on the basis of £1 for 100 to 200 pheasants, £2 for 300 to 400 pheasants, 10s. for a small rabbit day, £1 for 200 rabbits and so on, but I personally think that tips should not be based wholly on the bag. Much better to tip the keeper on the basis of the quality of the sport he has provided and, in a reasonable proportion, to the capacity of one's own pocket. If in doubt, consult an older shooting man or a regular guest at the particular shoot you are attending. Normally speaking, £1 is reasonable for a smallish day, and £2 for a big day in the coverts. But far more important than the tip is to remember to thank the keeper, and to add, if you can, a personal word of comment on the way he showed his birds. He will appreciate that quite as much as the crinkly note you put in his hand.

Finally, however tired you are, and however late you get home, DON'T FORGET TO CLEAN YOUR GUN. So many do. Nowadays, the coming of non-corrosive caps has eliminated the risk of fouling. The temptation to put guns away without cleaning them is therefore the greater. But it is important to point out that, although the manufacturers are now confident that they have overcome the dangers to the metal of cartridge-fouling, that is no guarantee that the gun is free from atmospheric-fouling. If you put your gun away without making sure that it's clean and dry, the barrels will pit as surely as they did in the bad old days. Further, it is still necessary to scour the barrels to keep them moon-bright, and free from leading.

(*The precaution is the more necessary because there is plenty of the old sort of ammunition still lying about in gunrooms and cartridge magazines. If you are still using up cartridges with corrosive caps, it's a good plan to end the day by putting a right-and-left of the new stuff through the barrels. You'll find that they will do half the job of cleaning for you.*)

II

Clothes and Accessories

THE eminent Victorian sportsman, who devised a shooting hat out of a dead hedgehog, made, I suppose, the most memorable attempt to resolve a problem which has baffled countrymen since the invention of gunpowder. It was a gesture, magnificent though forlorn, to determine, once and for all, the most suitable attire for a day's shooting.*

Although the inventor of the hedgehog hat is now in the happy hunting-grounds, it must be evident, even to the most casual observer of the country scene, that people who go shooting are still doing their outrageous best to keep his memory green. Every other recreation, even golf, seems to have sartorial limits beyond which no self-respecting sportsman is supposed to go. Not so shooting. The right clothes for the shooting party are still anybody's fancy. So much so that I shall never be surprised if, instead of a sweepstake on the bag, the ladies are invited to award prizes for the best fancy dress.

In theory, there is a convention that people go shooting wearing tweed knickerbocker suits (not baggy) in dark shades, with a cap to match and a mackintosh. But I never seem to meet those types outside the advertisements. My own impression of a typical shooting party, drawn Stands 1 to 8, is more like this:

No. 1: 'The Week-ender'	Newmarket boots, check riding breeches, deerstalker hat, and a full-skirted dun-coloured coat which looks as if it were made by sewing a lot of pockets together.
No. 2: 'The Crackshot'	Gumboots and plus fours worn under oilskin over-trousers. A sort of battle-dress coat and a fisherman's hat.
No. 3: 'The Dandy'	Skin-tight tweed knickers, white spats and porpoise-hide boots. Norfolk

* It is proper to explain that the earlier parts of this chapter are among the places where Macdonald Hastings has the bit in his teeth.

	jacket with flaps on all pockets. Green snap-brimmed slouch hat.
No. 4: 'The Farmer'	Pigskin leggings and breeches, hacking jacket and cap, old army bag across shoulder.
No. 5: 'The Eccentric'	White stockings and Scottish brogues with black ankle laces. Khaki shorts, high-necked sweater, and naval duffle-coat with hood.
No. 6: 'The Fellow-who borrows-one-of-your-guns'	Corduroy slacks, open-necked shirt, twill coat and town shoes.
No. 7: 'The Weather Prophet'	Fishing waders, unspeakably aged tweed suit, oilskin hat, and a roll of waterproof on back.
No. 8: 'The Youngster'	Jodhpurs and gumboots, silk scarf, tweed jacket and no mackintosh when it rains.

To these outfits, every shooting man I know favours an unpredictable collection of accessories in the form of whistles, lengths of rope, dog harness, shooting-sticks, devices for carrying cartridges and weird containers for food (which seems to consist mainly of windfall apples).

While I can advise you with every confidence on how to carry a gun, I realize that in the matter of the clothes that a man carries on his back for shooting, individual taste is likely to prevail.

But, if you dress for the occasion, rather than in the clothes which suit you best for shooting, you will find that the choice of your wardrobe will have a direct and noticeable influence on performance. If you turn out for a big day in a carefully tailored suit and knickerbockers, you may look elegant but you won't shoot as well as you will in the loose-fitting battered jacket you customarily wear. Shooting is a sport in which you must feel comfortable, free in your movements and familiar with the feel of your clothes. Whatever clothes you ultimately insist on wearing, make a policy of settling on the style and sticking to it.

The great Colonel Hawker used to shoot brilliantly in a heavy broadcloth coat and a top hat (which was a considerable achievement), only made possible by shooting with rather short-stocked guns. At the turn of the century, the fashion was to wear a thick

Norfolk jacket, breeches and gaiters, and a deerstalker cap. The Norfolk jacket was of thick material, heavily lined, and it was also fitted with a leather gun-pad on the shoulder, poacher's pockets inside the skirt of the coat and a multitude of other inside and outside pockets which were a survival from the time when men used to shoot with muzzle-loaders and had to carry about with them a tool chest of implements and appliances. As the season went on, more and more clothes were added until, in hard wild-fowling weather in winter, it was really quite a physical feat to mount the gun to the shoulder and reach for the first trigger.

Another tradition demanded that shooters should camouflage themselves by breaking up the colour scheme of their clothes. Men would wear a green hat, dark brown jacket and light-coloured breeches; and if only they could have procured noiseless cartridges, I presume that they would neither have been heard nor seen.

In fact, apart from wildfowling and pigeon shooting, camouflaged clothes are not nearly so important as people imagine. You are much more likely to turn birds in a pheasant or partridge drive by omitting to wear a cap and showing them the white of your forehead than you will be wearing a loud check or, as the American sportsmen do, a red hat.

The only unequivocal piece of advice I am going to give you on shooting clothes is to tell you that you *must* wear a jacket which is baggy at the elbows and has, for preference, a Raglan-type shoulder with a large armhole.* Tailors have a notion that they can make the necessary allowance for freedom of movement by putting a couple of pleats at the back of the shooting coat. The pleats help a little but they don't compare with the freedom which a wide pivot sleeve can give. Most golfers, to whom freedom of arm movement is as essential as it is in shooting, wear what amounts to a blouse. Normally speaking, the blouse or wind-cheater isn't the ideal wear for shooting as the butt of the stock rucks up the material.

The best jacket for shooting I myself have evolved, after many failures and half-successes, is one I keep at my shooting grounds to lend to people who arrive, as they often do, in town suits. Although I am a square and stocky man, my old coat fits quite well on six-footers, and I am amused how often my pupils remark that my old jacket seems to fit them better than their own.

Here is the specification: You want an ordinary well-fitting

* Here, Churchill takes over again.

jacket without inside or outside breast pockets on the right side if you are a right-handed man, or on the left side if you are a left-handed man. There should be no visible shoulder pad but a piece of thick buckram inserted between the lining and the shoulder, stitched criss-cross in the way that buckskin is stitched into the knee of riding breeches, to keep the padding flat and to prevent any ridges or puckering. The pockets should be of extra strong linen. The buttons, strongly threaded, should be of bone or other soft material with rounded edges. Sharp edges scratch the gun-stock and metal buttons make bad rucks in the woodwork of the stock.

My jacket has four buttons, instead of the usual three, and a neat lapel so that the gun can come to its place in the shoulder without the heel of the stock tripping up on it. I have also got a storm button under the lapel so that the collar can be turned up and buttoned close round the neck when it rains. The collar is made of the coat material on both sides and not lined in a way which shows up a different colour when the collar is turned up.

While you may not care to adopt this device for yourself, my own coat has, within the lining and starting at the front of each pocket, a belt on the same principle as the belt at the back of your waistcoat. This belt (inside of course) has the ordinary buckle for adjustment. This allows the weight of the pocket content to be carried on the waist instead of dragging on the shoulder. The thought is that you'll use your pockets on many occasions to carry cartridges. With a belt, such as I recommend, you will be spared the effort of lifting the weight of a pocketful of cartridges every time you lift your gun or raise your arm. As an experiment, put ten cartridges or a pound weight, which is the same thing, in each pocket of an ordinary jacket and you'll find that every time you raise your gun you have to lift the lot. With the inside strap to take the weight and loose pivot sleeves, you can fill your pockets, yet the jacket will not drag down from the shoulders; neither will you have to raise the weight of your cartridges with your arms. The theory of the extra wide sleeve with the wide elbow room is based upon the drill that, in gun-mounting, you stretch the forward arm and bend the other. There is no reason at all, of course, why you shouldn't have storm cuffs fitted for hard weather as well.

The sort of breeches you wear is unlikely to affect your shooting, but it's a sound rule to avoid long and baggy creations such as golfers favour. In wet weather, and in wet roots—and in the shooting season roots are usually sopping wet—baggy trousers quickly get saturated and, if you are doing a lot of walking, they will chafe the inside of your leg as well.

But although you can suit yourself what breeches you wear, footgear is important. If you wear the wrong sort, it will definitely have an effect on your shooting performance. Don't cripple yourself with heavy shooting boots at the beginning of the season if you have not been wearing them regularly; much better have a thick sole put on a lighter shoe. I personally prefer boots and anklets to shoes and gaiters. A boot feels lighter than the heavy shoe because of the better support round the ankles and, when walking heavy ground, is much less tiring to lift. The anklet prevents the water from the cabbages and the grass from entering, and the only disadvantage I know about them is that they take longer to put on and take off. Perhaps some enterprising boot-maker will turn out a combination of boot and anklet with a zip fastener.

Nails in the heel and round the edge of the sole of either a shooting boot or shoe are a help on slippery ground, but, if too close together, they collect chunks of dirt. The very sensitive shot will find that he can keep his balance better with low heels because high ones do have a tendency to pitch the shooter forward.

Personally I wear a cloth cap when I am shooting. In fine weather you can pull down the peak of the cap if the sun is shining in your eyes or give it a rakish tilt if the sun is hitting you at an angle. You can use it as a waterproof seat if the ground is damp and park it out of the way in your pocket if you don't want to wear a hat at all. The objection to a cap is that in pouring rain, unless you turn it back to front, you get a soaking down the back of the neck. For that reason a tweed cap with an all-round brim, such as fishermen wear, might be even more suitable.

But I repeat that this is simply the clothing that I wear myself when I am out shooting. The only firm advice I give you, whatever you wear, is to have your shooting jacket made with wide deep sleeves, because that will definitely have an effect for the better on your performance.

Rather than carry a waterproof about with them, a lot of shooting men these days seem to prefer to wear a waterproof gaberdine shooting jacket. These jackets have a good deal to commend them. The principal snags are, first, that they tear on the slightest contact with barbed wire and, alas, barbed wire is now a uniquitous enemy; and, further, they are particularly susceptible to stains, such as blood and oil marks. At the end of a very short season, they can look quite filthy, whereas tweed can still look reasonably respectable, if smelly, after years of hard work. And wool tears much less readily than most materials.

Wildfowlers and pigeon shooters, who have to take very much more care over their camouflage than the shooter in the coverts or on the stubbles, hardly need any special advice from me. Most of them are masters at concealing themselves in the mud or in the hedgerows. Most of them, too, have learnt that you can't do better than to dress yourself as nearly as possible as the modern soldier in the field. When I am laying-up for wildfowling, I personally wear a set of army surplus laverack clothing: a blouse and waterproof slip-on trousers and a hood at the back which can be pulled over the head. The whole of the nasty mixture of green, khaki and yellow looks pretty awful, but in a hide it undoubtedly works.

All I need remark about clothes, in addition, is that wild-fowlers who put on a series of sweaters and waistcoats and jackets to keep out the cold of a January day should, if possible, try to use a shorter stocked gun than the one they use in ordinary circumstances. Otherwise they will be at a definite disadvantage in their gun-mounting. But more about this later.

The Field Accessories of the fully equipped game shot can be extended as indefinitely as a fisherman's tackle. Cartridges can be carried in the pocket (which is the best place if you don't require too many); in a pigskin bag (the best is what is known as the Payne-Gallway pattern with a fixed frame opening); in a belt, bandolier, or a haversack.

The pigskin cartridge bag (cowhide is not so tough or weather resistant) is used almost universally for covert shooting. You can get a bag to hold 50, 75, 100 or 150 12-bore cartridges. The 50 size is rather small to get your hand into quickly for loading; the 150 size is too cumbersome and heavy; the 100 size, with 50 to 75 cartridges in it, is probably ideal.

If you are using a cartridge bag, it is a good idea to wrap a piece of chamois leather round the brass buckles which attach the shoulder strap to the two sides of the bag. This will effectively prevent the buckle from rubbing against the stock of the gun and rutting the wood. Gun-makers can remove these ruts from the stock of the gun but it is far better to prevent it happening in

the first place; especially if you have got a best gun with a lovely walnut stock that you don't want to spoil.

It is another wise precaution to soak the leather of a cartridge bag in one of the waterproofing oils. It not only makes the bag last much longer, but the leather becomes increasingly supple and, as a consequence, you can draw out your cartridges more comfortably and more quickly. Remember what I told you in the drill. Before you begin shooting, give your cartridge bag a good shake. This will cause the brass end of the cartridge to point upwards and the heavy lead to sink downwards.

Many shooters I know like to carry their cartridges in a belt round their middles or in a patent bandolier across their shoulders. I can't recommend it. It's the slowest possible way of drawing cartridges for the gun. The weight is essentially in the place where it will impede, however slightly, your freedom of movement in gun-mounting, and people who wear cartridge belts either find that the cartridges fit too tight and are a niusance to pull out or, alternatively, they fit so loosely that, when the wearer crawls through a hedge or bends down, the rounds of ammunition drop into the grass.

If you are shooting in the coverts, a stick seat, unless you are a particularly agile character, is an essential accessory. The only advice I have to give you about stick seats, because you will obviously choose one which suits your personal backside, is to try and have one in which the metal stop at the base is protected by a ring of rubber. Just as the buckles on cartridge bags are the most common cause of ruts in gun-stocks, so shooting-sticks have the chief responsibility for causing dents in barrels. The slightest tap with a metal stick on a gun-barrel is sufficient to make a dent which may be invisible at a casual glance but which, on close examination, will be revealed in the barrel.

If you *must* take a dog shooting with you which isn't rock steady, don't attach him to yourself with a lead. That's the most certain way of making sure you'll be off balance when the game flushes. The proper thing to do, if you are shooting at a stand, is to have one of those patent leads with a peg at the end by which you can plug your irresponsible animal to the ground at your feet.

Cartridge magazines, those great leather boxes with oak linings which used to be dragged about the place by Victorian sportsmen, are now completely out of date, except as a convenient box to store cartridges in the gun-room. The most suitable container to use, by way of a refill magazine which you can draw on between stands, is probably one of the very large pigskin bags. Better still, have two bags of the ordinary 100 size.

Game counters too—those things which used to be called 'Norfolk liars'—are now out of fashion, although it can be amusing to use them privately to keep your score on a big day. A cartridge extractor is always worth having and, if you are carrying your own game, the best bags are those with the string front which allow the air to get at the game. But never allow game to remain in a bag longer than you possibly can. Ideally, game should be hung up and allowed to cool immediately it is shot. In the early part of the season, hares, for example, will go rotten in a few hours unless very great care is taken to lay them out in a cool place and keep them free from blow flies. Even later on, pheasants, partridges and grouse will not hang nearly so well if they have been knocked about. The use of the traditional poacher's pocket is the most certain way of making your own clothes smell and making the game you carry in it inedible.

III

How to Shoot Grouse

THERE are two accepted methods of shooting red grouse: walking them up over dogs, or driving them in front of a line of beaters to the guns standing in butts. Grouse shooting has unique features because the red grouse is only indigenous to certain parts of the British Isles where the soil is predominantly acid with a bountiful growth of the proper sort of heather and adequate quartz grit.

Heather is a hard indigestible food and quartz is the only grit which suits the grouse's gizzard. Attempts to introduce the red grouse in other parts of the world have not been successful and the better authorities now conclude that it is a bird which can only adapt itself to life on soils where the requisite degree of acidity of water and a supply of heather and quartz are common. Exact ecological parallels have not yet been found anywhere where acclimatization has been attempted. So for practical purposes the limits of grouse shooting are confined to northern Britain, with a slight overflow for rough shooting in Ireland. A few grouse occur in Devon, but they are a rarity there, and, therefore, no sportsman would wish to shoot them.

Grouse shooting is unlike any other form of shooting in most of Britain and America. The majority of sportsmen, outside these islands, and even within them, can only shoot grouse occasionally and usually do so in strange surroundings. For that reason, I am going to deal with grouse first, not only because the opening of the season on August the Twelfth is the opening of the shooting season in Britain; but because it is a form of shooting in which even experienced pheasant, duck and partridge shots can be confused by the novel surroundings and conditions.

To begin with, there is a tremendous element of luck in the quality of the sport that the grouse shooter is likely to enjoy. You can rent the most expensive moor and be disappointed. You can be a guest on a moor where normally the bags are small and run into a bumper season. It is nobody's fault that nobody really

knows how the grouse have fared until the guns get among them
on the Twelfth.

It is only too true that he would be an unwise shooter who
ordered his cartridges for the season on the strength of the preliminary reports from the moors. There is no mystery why that
should be so. For two very good reasons, the prospects for the
grouse season are almost entirely assessed on guesswork.

The first and most formidable reason is the temperament of
the average moorland keeper who, even at the point of a gun,
can be relied upon to withhold everything that he knows. Characteristic of what any moorland keeper is likely to tell you is what a
friend of mine, with a small moor in Lancashire, heard when he
asked his man for an opinion of prospects during the coming
season. There was a weighty pause while pipes were primed and
dogs called to heel and then the keeper replied: 'It might be
better than it was last year, and it might be worse. Depends how
the grouse move.'

Keepers being what they are, the second good reason why
grouse-shooting forecasts are so uncertain is because the moors
are what they are. There are few prospects more calculated to
encourage short cuts, and snap decisions, than a wilderness of
knee-deep bog and knee-high heather, muscle-aching hillsides and
ankle-spraining descents. It is my experience that high-hearted
forays into the hills to see how the grouse are doing usually
degenerate into a sit-down and a cigarette in the car while the
dogs are turned out to range round the verges of the moorland
roads. If a few barren pairs get up, everybody agrees that the
moor has gone to pot. If a covey or two is seen dusting in the
road, the landlord returns thankfully to tea and decides to
double the shooting rent.

But, apart from human considerations, it is, alas, a fact that
grouse can never be relied upon to stay put. A few years ago, I
remember reading a witty story called *The Twelfth*, by J. K.
Stanford in which the soul of a calloused old shooting colonel was
transmigrated into a grouse. As a grouse, he organized his fellow
birds so that they were always on a different beat to the guns.
That state of affairs is so common in actual shooting that one can
almost believe that Pythagoras was right.

It is never safe to assume that the birds crowding a moor in
July will oblige over the butts in middle August. For that reason
alone, the non-committal attitude of the upland keeper is justi-

H

fied. Grouse are essentially vagrant in habit; and, if you drive a small moor frequently, the birds will leave it until peace and quiet have returned.

In addition, 'grouse disease,' which is an epidemic either of coccidiosis affecting the young birds, or strongylosis affecting the young and old birds, breaks out in a rough cycle of seven years. All indications suggest that in a favourable year for heather growth and when the moors are not too wet, disease falls to its lowest level. But too many birds on a moor, followed by a trying season, invariably mean an outbreak of 'grouse disease.' The law of nature allows a certain head of game to a hundred acres, but if we succeed in developing more stock than the ground will hold the epidemic of parasitic diseases of game spread, more swiftly because the feed and the ground will only maintain a fixed head of birds.

Before the first world war, 'partridge disease' was virtually unknown in Great Britain. A few birds with strongylosis had been picked up and the possibility of strongyle disease of partridges was known to a few biologists. After the first world war, many landowners tried to recover their losses on shooting rents by making ten partridges grow where only five grew before. In addition, agriculture has gone back and, as there was less standing corn and more grass, an epidemic of strongylosis (little parasitic worms in the bird gut) broke out and spread everywhere. In plain language, partridge disease is a disease of overcrowding, too; and every Scots moor manager knows that if he has a heavy head of unshot game left, and conditions of feed are bad in the hills, it will probably take five to seven years before he has a season again when bags are over-average or even normal.

The consequence, curiously enough, is that nothing exasperates the Scottish keeper more, when the landlord has made a 'let,' and when there are a lot of birds on the moor, than visiting guns who shoot badly. The lessee may be entitled to bag, say, 5,000 head of grouse in his 'let,' but if he and his guests are only capable of shooting 2,000 head by the time they go, it is then too late to get the stock down to the limit which is healthiest for the moor. If the moor is let and half the bag is made, the moor is overstocked and with the additional hazard of bad weather goes down with disease. It isn't worth shooting again until careful conservation has restored the balance several years later.

So, in general, although many of the Scottish moors are excellently managed, no system has yet been developed which allows for the vagaries of climate. In some years an adequate area of heather can be burnt in order to provide new food in the following seasons. In others, bad weather prevails in the legal time for heather burning, and little can be done. What this all adds up to is that, if you have the good luck to be in a grouse-shooting party on a moor and in a season when there are a lot of birds, there is a responsibility on you not to 'fluff' them. The landlord and the keepers require you, in the interests of the shoot, to shoot straight. To accept a grouse-shooting invitation which obviously comes at a time when you are most likely to be out of practice, and not to have taken precautions at the shooting school before you go north, is bad manners, both to your host and to the landlord whose land you are shooting. Nevertheless, it's no use pretending that to go straight to the moors and shoot grouse well is easy.

The environment is strange. It is August and it is quite likely that a stiff climb up to hill butts may find you out of condition. There is usually a very long wait before the drive begins (assuming, that is, that the game is to be driven) because the beaters will probably have to bring in an enormous expanse of ground by comparison with the shorter beats in partridge or covert shooting.

A gun having been posted with his loader in the butt is usually 'in tension.' He scours the undulation of the moors and, in ten or fifteen minutes, although he may be unaware of it, he has 'fatigued' his eye. I am not sure that it is strictly accurate to say that the eye *can* be fatigued. An oculist could probably demonstrate that all that happens is that there is a slower reaction time for the pupillary accommodation. Actually, from a shooting point of view, the man who looks for the birds for twenty minutes before there is any chance of seeing them has 'tired' his eyes and probably fatigued some of his body muscles to the point of bracing them.

I am going to concentrate on showing you how to shoot driven grouse because, if you can shoot driven grouse, you can almost certainly shoot them when they are walked-up over dogs. Apart from the unfamiliar surroundings, and the effort of walking through heather and boggy ground, it is no more difficult to shoot walked-up grouse than walked-up partridges or pheasants. It is, normally speaking, the straight going-away shot that I described so fully in the drill.

In fact, driven grouse at the beginning of the season are not—
repeat not—difficult shooting. It is towards the end of the season,
when they are very strong and the winds blow high, that they
can be such very difficult birds indeed to bring down. But it is
not the difficulty of the shooting that usually defeats the novice,
who may indeed be a very fair shot at other sorts of game, but
the curious problems associated with dealing with driven grouse.
Before discussing the actual shooting of the birds, I must once
again begin by pointing out the very special dangers attaching to
shooting from grouse butts.

A great many grouse butts are sited by a keeper with only an
eye for the bag and not much regard for safety; or, perhaps, no
conception of how dangerous some of the people from the South
may be. Butts are very often damnably dangerous because of
their site or because of the way that they are constructed. In
general, grouse fly along a line which follows closely the contour
lines on the maps, but a shift of five yards back or three yards
down the slope could make the butts much safer and without the
loss of any birds at all. So, when you step into a grouse butt for
the first time, your initial responsibility is to analyse its position
in relation to the other butts and the other shooting men inside
them.

The custom of sticking 'stop sticks' in the butts to warn guns
not to swing their barrels beyond a certain point to the right or
to the left is to be commended; but all too often you find, when
you arrive on the hill in August, that some thrifty shepherd has
used these sticks for a fire and possibly the wooden flooring of
the butt and anything else that will burn as well. At the beginning of the season, you will often discover that the butts are in
most discreditable order. The cure is to send for the keeper at
once when you arrive and, if necessary, have him send up two
stout lads and a pony load of pioneering material to make good
all the butts that are in disrepair. The foraging party can also
cut a turf drain and provide some sort of standing-place. Keepers
dislike doing this as it encourages the shepherds to revel round
illegitimate camp fires in the following year. But, if you lease a
moor, it is a job that almost certainly needs doing.

No general rule can be laid down about butts as they depend
on local conditions. Some could only be made safe with corru-
gated iron screens of double thickness.

The most fatal kind of butt is where the shooter looks up a

hillside and finds that, exactly in line with the normal height of advancing grouse, he is looking into the next butt. The butt usually has a side entrance too, facing the lower butt, thus allowing the gun or loader to get his legs peppered if an emotional shot 'follows on' unduly.

The number of people that do get peppered depends to some extent on the season; but, in a bumper year in the Highlands, slight shooting accidents rate almost second to the figures of local motoring accidents. It is not the experienced shots who get peppered. They are usually wise enough to sit down in the butt until the battue is all over, once they have become aware of the first high velocity swarm of visiting pellets coming in their direction. If you find that you are in a difficult butt, mark your safe limits on either side with either sticks or gun bags and perhaps pile up a few extra turves on left and right flank.

If you are renting a grouse moor, or going as a guest for the first time, don't count your birds before you see them coming over the guns. Nobody in advance of August the Twelfth really knows the head of game that these high and lonely moors hold, because, in the normal course of events, very few people have visited them, except the keeper on his round; and one man can only cover a small part of the ground. However many times you have been to a grouse moor before never forget the first time you walk into a new butt to assess the safety measures which are necessary to protect your neighbours from yourself and yourself from your neighbours.

After that, when you have made a careful note of where adjoining butts are situated, don't 'tire your eyes' searching the heather. Take it easy and look into the 'blue'; or better still, don't look at anything at all; but relax and think about anything else under the sun, except shooting.

(Churchill himself had faulty vision as a consequence of an accident when he was shooting experimental tracer charges for the R.A.F. in the 1914–18 war. At the time he feared that he would lose the sight of an eye. It may well have been his own slight disability which made him put the emphasis he always did on the importance of avoiding 'tiring the eyes.' But, although the phrase may be misleading and in ophthalmological terms even nonsense, the advice is sound. It was his own remedy for over-eagerness, a bug to which sportsmen in the exhilarating environment of the hills are peculiarly vulnerable. Grouse-fever is as catching as stag-fever. Churchill's cure may not suit others; but every sportsman should resort to some such

device, while he is waiting for driven game to come over, to keep his temperature at normal. Those who doubt it need only remind themselves how often the most spectacular shots of their lives were the unexpected ones.)

Don't anticipate your birds. They'll show themselves to you in their own good time, and, if you are not keyed-up waiting for them, when the first covey appears over the skyline (and butts are nearly always sighted below a convenient skyline) you will focus it immediately. If a covey flies low, a few feet over the heather as they so often do, you will see it for the first time as a sweeping shadow across the face of the moor; but you will realize it in time, and you will have plenty of time to get into focus before the birds come into shot.

You will always be told that the best practice is to kill your first birds well in front. It is excellent advice; but it takes some experience to know when unfamiliar birds like grouse are actually in range. Another school holds to the view that you can kill a bird behind at a far longer range as his feathers will not deflect the shot so much as they will if you shoot at him head-on. These are two rival and opposite schools of thought. The only point on which both agree is that a crossing shot is more vulnerable. It is more vulnerable because you are shooting at the moment when the long axis of the bird is exposed to the shot pattern. When he is coming head on or going away he exposes his shorter axis.

On the whole, if you are having your first experience on a grouse moor, I think the best advice I can give you is to tell you to treat your first few birds as ranging shots. If you feel you want a little more time when the first covey comes over, take time by all means and try to pick off, say, a single one of the laggards. Whatever you do, don't shoot all over the place because you feel you must let off a couple of barrels. I know brilliant partridge shots who invariably only fire off one barrel in front when the first birds of the day come over. They want to make sure of their swing and settle their eye on the target before they start killing two in front.

You are sure to be excited when you see your first covey. There is sure to be the temptation to shoot into the 'brown.' Resist it and endeavour to put into practice one of the pieces of advice that we often give in the shooting school. Try and hit your first bird in the tail. That will make sure that you are keeping your eye on the bird and not 'poking' or shooting into the spaces between the covey. People often wonder why it is that when they 'brown' at a covey it so seldom happens that any of them fall. In theory, the spread of the shot pattern should be large enough to fill up the gaps and hit a bird as well. In practice, what happens is that the man who shoots into the 'brown' deliberately aims into the space between the birds. And because, if the gun-mounting is good and the gun fits, the charge will always go to the place where the shooter is looking, he contrives according to the best rules of shooting to miss his birds altogether.

So don't be ashamed to take one in front and one behind at the beginning of the drive or the day. It is far better style to shoot both barrels in front but it is better to shoot steadily for a little while than to miss your birds altogether.

In theory a grouse, or any other game bird, coming with his own velocity takes a harder smash from the pellets than a bird going away at the same velocity. If an indignant cowherd threw a turnip with the velocity of 30 m.p.h. at a car moving at 50 m.p.h. towards him he would possibly make a demonstration; if he chucked a 30 m.p.h. turnip after a 50 m.p.h. car the show would be no more than a futile display of rural spleen. That's the principle.

Actually a bird shot thirty yards in front is killable. One well-known shot used to pace out the distance and pull up some heather to mark the point. I am not certain that this is the best way for most people, but it is a good idea to have a sort of aiming point notion of what forty yards is. It is a shade less than two cricket pitches and, if you can visualize two pitches stuck end to end, it seems an incredible distance.

My own advice to the grouse shooter is not to worry so much about measuring distance with his eye as to wait till the bird looks big enough to eat. That may sound rather like telling some-one to take an object 'about the size of a bit of wood,' but, dis-counting snipe, all edible birds have bulk. On the basis of waiting until the grouse looks big enough to eat you will take oncoming birds at between twenty-five and thirty yards, which is just where the crack shots take them. They probably hustle-on and fall behind the butts, but they were killed well over twenty yards away.

(*That comment, advising the grouse shooter 'to wait until the bird looks big enough to eat,' has probably stirred up more heated discussion in gunrooms and shooting lodges than any in this book. Surprisingly, in a sport in which every exponent rationalises the correct method of finding the target in a variety of ways, the larger part of Churchill's council, especially*

*on pheasant and partridge shooting, has been accepted without question.
But not that.*

*The answer requires the qualification of the debates in the original
Brains Trust:—'It depends what you mean. . . .' The phrase, indeed
he was fond of it, suited Churchill. For others, it is reasonable to argue
that if the shooter waits until 'the bird is big enough to eat', the grouse will
be gone before he gets his gun up.*

*I know what Churchill was concerned about. In the grandeur of the
moors, it is fatally easy to relate distance to the scale of the scenery. What
looks like a short climb can be a morning's work. So he searched for a
simple rule. I agree with his critics that it is not adequate.*

*In shooting partridges, which by comparison with grouse are as slow as
a suburban stopping train, most men drop their first bird twenty yards
later than they should. There can be no harm in shooting too soon at
grouse. But, since the object of the exercise is to make a clean kill in
front, it is important for the shooter to have a rule-of-thumb which suits
him. It would be useful if it could be said that a recognition mark, like
the white collar round a wood pigeon's neck, is an indication that the
grouse is in range; but the varying light conditions on the moorlands, in
addition to the difficulty of guessing ranges in surroundings of vast ranges,
precludes it. My own policy is to shoot when, irrespective of wing-beat and
expectation, I can identify the bird ornithlogically as a red grouse. But
that, too, might be the wrong advice for others.)*

Once you have killed your first oncoming birds from a grouse
butt you will probably change guns because, in driven grouse
shooting, it is customary to shoot with a pair and a loader. It is
at this moment that accidents so often happen because, believe
it or not, there is no room for the 'follow-through' shooter at
grouse. The butts are in a line, or what is worse, a curve, and
accidents are almost as easy as they are when driving a car.

Why aren't the butts set out straight? The reason is that the
flight of grouse is very closely along natural contour lines. If the
side of the brae was a tilted plain, the butts could be in a straight
line but the topography of the land does not run to plains and
experience has probably shown that butts must be placed in a
curve. Not necessarily a curve of sharp radius but one that
allows the centre butt to tickle up his left and right wing butts
with a charge of shot at, say, eighty yards if he doesn't limit his
firing angle to a restricted front. At eighty yards you will not kill
anyone but you could very easily put somebody's eye out.

(It is not as widely known among shooting men as it ought to be that

it is possible to buy splinter-proof spectacles from Messrs. Theodore Hamblin, the dispensing opticians of Wigmore Street, London. In unfamiliar company they provide a useful, and unobtrusive, protection. In the field the eye is peculiarly vulnerable. A random pellet, which wouldn't penetrate skin, can easily damage an eye. Eyes have the consistency of soft-boiled eggs.)

The story of the American sportsman shooting on the moors, who saw an eminent general, on his right flank, pepper a celebrity on the left and himself finally fired both barrels of both guns at the two of them 'to stop them fiddling as they were making the birds rise wild' is probably mythical. On the other hand, all myths have some substance in them, and a lesson. Too little care in the butts is criminal, but I am bound to add that too great care may result in the sportsman missing a lot of shots he would otherwise have secured without danger to anyone or risk of the social observances.

I have mentioned the sticks which are usually erected on the turfs or the crevices of the stone wall in well-organized butts to limit the zone of fire and the swing of the too-anxious follow-through. If the sticks are not there, put out some mark of your own to replace them. Further, remember that a slip on uneven or boggy ground where sheep used the butts may explain an accident but won't excuse it. Butts ought to be properly tidied up; but they often aren't. All too often one is expected to shoot in the middle of a quagmire. Nobody can shoot at his best, or even safely, off a couple of rocking stones in a bog, and bad butts are responsible for a lot of bad shooting. If you find yourself in a bad butt you must do all you can to make it more comfortable before the birds begin to come over, and you need have no feelings about telling the keeper subsequently what you think of his winter work and remind him, in future, to see that his butts are prepared properly.

In any case the occupant of a butt must take careful note of his neighbours and work out, *before shooting*, the safe angle of his field of fire. Assuming that you are in a properly designed butt, you'll notice that you usually enter at the side and the site of this entrance is no help at all in remembering your front. If you are not careful, in the heat of the drive, you will find that you forget your precise position in relation to the other butts. Even if stopping stakes are in position they are very often too wide apart for some shooters. Don't depend on them. The surest way to shoot safe is to shoot according to the drill in the first part of this book. Any man who completes the whole of his body swing whilst gun-mounting and fires at the precise moment that he throws his shoulder into the butt of the gun, not dwelling on the trigger and not following birds when the gun is already in position, won't make mistakes. It is the man who follows the birds round who can put a charge of shot so easily into the next butt.

In the interests of safety, and in the interest of concealing your presence from the oncoming birds, don't fall into the habit of hiding low in the butt, squinting through the turves, and popping up like a jack-in-the-box when you think they are in range. Any sudden movement like that of the shooter or the gun, or even a fluttering scarf, will frighten the covey off its course. You may get a shot but it will be a much more difficult task to kill a bird out of a scattering covey. Don't be afraid to stand in the butt as upright as Nelson on his column, but keep still and don't move your gun until the birds are within range and you are ready to kill them. You will shoot better, because you will be nicely balanced, and ready, and you won't turn the birds because they fear movement much more than your black outline in the centre of the butt.

The cause of accidents on the grouse moors is hurry. The cause that so many birds are missed is hurry. If the gun takes it easy, spots his birds well in front, he'll never be hurried and he will never make a dangerous shot. That rule applies equally to the loader as to the gun himself.

If your loader is trained to carry out the system of loading and changing guns and keeping well down he won't lose you any birds. Loaders as a rule remember to keep low on grouse moors but they are often much too vigorous. And however still you are, a jack-in-the-box loader can negative your own discipline. Never take an untrained loader into the butt; it is dangerous. If necessary, drill your loader with snap caps and rub it in to him to keep his head down.

Many grouse shots find difficulty in killing a bird which is driven against a strong wind and appears to be drifting in front of the butt. This is certainly a trick shot but, once learned, it is the easiest shot of the lot. Fire very steadily at the legs of the bird and a little right or left according to the direction of the wind. If you are meeting fast birds travelling with the wind all you have to remember is to shoot straight at them with a rather quicker gun-mounting. You can always trust your eye, as I told you in the initial drill, to make the necessary allowances. And only the case of a bird moving much slower than its normal speed requires conscious calculation.

In case of a shot behind the butt, a gun who completes the whole of his body swing relatively leisurely, with a complete 180 degree turn, will kill his birds behind with his second gun without effort or risk to his neighbours. Gun-muzzles must be raised, and kept high, during the turning movement. The turn-about in fact has to be completed with the gun erect. Only when it is completed should the gun be mounted to the shoulder. If you swing through, as many people do with the gun half or fully mounted, and try to follow-through in a complete motion from 'birds coming' to 'birds going away' you are taking a chance on an accident.

The golden rule is to KEEP YOUR MUZZLES UP ALMOST VERTICALLY WHILST PASSING THE LINE. A complete turn of the feet is essential. You can't shoot with a twisted body over your shoulder at 'going away' birds. You are wasting cartridges if you do.

Grouse have a habit of jinking in the air and slipping sideways the moment a barrel is thrown. If you stand still, as the birds come towards you, there is a good chance they won't jink. If you make a movement they will. But if you find grouse are jinking for one reason or another, don't be tempted to adopt the jack-in-the-box tactics which I have already warned you about. Whatever happens stand still and MAKE SURE THAT YOUR LOADER IS NOT DODGING ABOUT BEHIND YOUR BACK.

In theory, grouse are driven straight over the butts. In practice, a single bird or a pair from the covey may traverse the line of butts, and be missed by all the guns. This is particularly true if they are flying into a crossing wind. To handle this sort of bird calls for a trick shot. But, once the trick is mastered, it serves. Fire steadily just *underneath* the bird and very little towards the line of progress, right or left as it may be. Don't over-estimate pace.

To deal with very fast birds, borne on a thirty-mile-an-hour wind, the sort of birds you get at the end of the season, there is no remedy except experience. You *must* swing your body in time with the bird and snap at it. If you can shoot that sort of bird consistently, you can shoot anything that flies.

Some birds you meet may be very low-dropping targets because the covey is losing height with the intention of settling in the heather behind. Other coveys may be butt shy and rise and turn as you lead with your gun. A quick snap shot will get this sort of bird, but if you are slow you will be beaten every time by the speed of grouse tactics. If you feel you have remembered everything else I have told you, and you are still missing grouse, you will most likely find that the cause of the trouble is that you are putting your head down to the gun instead of bringing your gun up to the face. This happens so often in grouse shooting because guns get tired with the effort of getting from butt to butt; and I suppose their heads are caught nodding.

Physically, shooting grouse, either walking them up or from the butts, is hard exercise. To shoot consistently well you need to be in first-class condition and first-class practice. You don't want to sit up the night before playing cards or treating yourself too liberally to the local nectar.

IV

How to Shoot Partridges

FOR most shooting men the season opens on September 1st with partridges, rather than grouse on August 12th. I remember a well-known sporting writer, extolling the delights of partridge driving, writing the following sentence: 'When the whistle blows, you instinctively take a firm stance, tightly grip your gun and search the skyline.'

This lyric comment combines so many things you should *not* do that it should become a classic. If you try to shoot like that you would shoot very few birds at all. But, in justice to the writer, it must be admitted that his description of his own reaction is an accurate record of what people, who ought to know better, regularly do.

Let us imagine that we are watching a first-class partridge shot at one of the big shoots in open country where the hedges are low and guns, in order to remain under cover, have to stand fairly close to the hedge. The first thing which should strike you is that the practised shot is *not* in a state of tension. He probably stands quite loosely and unconcerned; but you will also notice that, when he shoots, he is far swifter than the neighbouring gun who, in his anxiety, has braced himself and gripped his gun as he comes on the alert. The expert kills his birds so far as he can 'in front' while his neighbour lets them come too close and so is presented, not with an easier shot, but with a more difficult one.

Partridge coveys do not always come straight. They may swerve or split. But you will notice that the practised shot snaps an odd bird or so as they show for a second above the hedge before they have a chance of breaking-back or flanking. At the end of that drive you will probably find that the experienced man has had 50 per cent more shooting, and killed twice as many birds as his apparently more alert and undoubtedly more anxious neighbour.

Now if we analyse what the expert did we find that in the first place he was completely self-confident; more than that, he was not afraid of missing. I can't emphasize to you enough the importance of not being afraid of missing when you are shooting at partridges. MOST OF THE BIRDS THAT ARE MISSED ARE MISSED BECAUSE PEOPLE ARE SO ANXIOUS NOT TO MISS.

The partridge, by comparison with the grouse or the pheasant, flies comparatively slowly. But, from the flurry that some people get into, you'd think they were moving as fast as jet planes. The trouble, of course, is that a covey of partridges, bursting like shrapnel over a hedge, is in itself a disconcerting experience unless you have trained your eye and your mind to deal with one bird at a time. The most certain way to miss is not to be able to make up your mind which of the covey you are going to shoot at.

Returning to the expert, you will notice that his stance is never a rigid one. He carries himself easily and comfortably in a position which allows him to swing right or left without any constraint of the body. You will probably observe that, before the drive begins, he is practising his gun swing to make sure that he is all set to move sweetly when the birds come into view. He doesn't grip his gun; he holds it lightly and securely with no muscular tension at all. Above all, his eyes are not all over the place 'searching the skyline.'

When I was discussing grouse shooting I warned you of the dangers of searching the heather and wearing yourself out looking for birds long before there is any likelihood of their making an appearance. The rule applies equally in partridge shooting. The partridge shot, who knows his business, isn't rapidly refocusing his eyes here, there and everywhere looking for birds in all directions at once. He is gazing steadily into the 'blue' at the approximate point in the air, not where he thinks the birds might appear, but where he would like to kill them if they do.

Standing there he can see the full field of his zone of fire and consequently he isn't tiring his eyes.* Any birds coming into his field of fire are bound to be seen and, not only is the covey more easily picked up by the gun, but he himself is not surprised by the appearance of the birds. The covey climbs into his view rather than his eyes having to climb to meet the covey. Without having to swing more than a few degrees he can select his bird and kill it before it gets too close or before it swerves. The whole process is relatively effortless, relaxed and easy of timing. The characteristic mark of a good partridge shot is that he never seems to be in a hurry but that he kills his birds yards sooner than the average shot standing next door to him.

* See Editorial notes pages 20 and 117.

The man who is anxiously turning his head to right and left, who is tensed and fiddling his gun with shooting nerves, is asking for trouble. He may even commit the major mistake, and one of the commonest, of being caught watching the next gun just at the unforgiving moment when a covey comes to his own sector. Either he doesn't see it in time, or, if by chance his attention is just returning to that point, he is so disconcerted and flustered in his movements that he misses altogether.

Surprise makes some people jump, whilst the effect on others is to 'freeze stiff.' In either case, the sudden appearance of the birds sets up muscular disturbance; either the shooter is momentarily paralysed and follows the birds with an exaggerated swing or he is confused by seeing too many birds at once and finds himself too surprised to select one to shoot at. If he is the type who 'jumps' to a surprise rather than 'freezes' he is still disorganized and probably blazes away unselectively and far too late.

The shooter who looks into the 'blue' is normally able to cover his whole field of fire without movement of the head. Some look just above the hedge, others look well above it according to where they want to kill their first bird (a matter largely dependent on the distance of the stand from the hedge). With this technique, not only will the covey come into view apparently more steadily, and with no element of surprise but, most important, there will always be one bird which looks larger than the rest.

This is an illusion; but it is the bird the shooter's eye first picked up and focused on which is the easiest bird to 'snap' and the eye should never be taken off it to consider the others. The first shot should be an easy snap followed by a continued swing on to a second bird. A poor shot is sometimes in such a hurry to shoot his second bird that, instead of keeping his gun swinging on to the first bird, until the trigger is pressed and the bird killed, he subconsciously leaves the first bird and begins his swing to the second before he has covered the first.

The 'climbing' effect of driven partridges is largely an optical illusion. If you look at the top of a hedge you are probably centring the pupil of your eye and the hedge itself cuts off half your effective field of 'aware vision.' If you look well above the hedge into the sky you see the birds just as soon as they appear and they remain in vision longer before you have need to move your body or head to readjust to meet them.

At my shooting grounds I have a very difficult driven partridge

PARTRIDGE SHOOTING

'Looking into the blue.'

stand where the birds come forward very fast indeed. I find that if a gun looks at the hill over which the first bird shows it is over his head before he can get his gun up; but, if he looks well above the hill into the sky, he uses the full field of vision effectively and can manage to kill them in time. The diagram shows what I mean.

There are rules for good partridge shooting which can be easily memorized.

1. Choose a flat place to stand on. Flatten out a position, especially if you are standing in a ploughed field.
2. Take things easy, and *relax*. If hares come by it is always safer to wait until they are past the line before shooting.
3. When the whistle blows, remain relaxed. Carry your gun at the ready position, with the barrel uptilted, and look into the sky at the angle which gives you the best view of your field of fire. Do not bother if you cannot comfortably see the extreme flanks. Your concern is with your front, not your neighbour's.
4. Shoot straight at the leading bird as this may split, or turn the covey down the line, and give other guns a chance.
5. Count your kills and remember the spot in the air where you killed your bird rather than watch the bird to earth; except, of course, where you have got an obvious runner.

On the other side, here are some 'Don'ts':

1. Don't count the covey before you shoot. If you waste time doing that you probably won't touch a feather.
2. Don't shoot low into hedgerows. In partridge shooting especially the beaters are very seldom far away.
3. Don't shoot your neighbour's birds. If a covey passes between

you, you are entitled to share the shooting; but you should pick
your bird on your side of the covey and he on his.
4. Don't talk or make a noise. Coveys often settle in front and
break back because of noise.

In recommending you to train yourself to shoot the bird which
looks larger than the rest of the covey and, if possible, to shoot at
the leading bird coming towards you (and the biggest bird to
your eye should be the leading bird), I am also giving you the
advice which your shooting host will be most gratified to see you
carrying out. Normally speaking, when a covey comes over, it is
led by the two old birds. If you can shoot the old ones you will
render effective service in breaking up the covey and increasing
the chances on future shoots of getting the birds over the guns
again. Anyhow, the shooting of the old birds, early in the season,
contributes materially to the improvement of the stock on the
ground. What happens is that the young birds break up and join
other coveys and, when they pair in December or January, there
is a greater chance of unrelated birds mating together. The effect
of this is to produce a stronger stock and to increase the number of
partridges on the ground.

The essential obstacle that the partridge shot must surmount is
to overcome the natural tendency to be bewildered by the burst of
birds. If you are watching a shoot, notice how very seldom the
single 'Frenchman' coming over the guns is missed; and how often
a barren pair is killed cleanly with a right and a left. Birds that
come over in a covey of fourteen aren't travelling any faster or any
differently. Inexperienced guns allow themselves to be bemused by
sheer numbers and, in consequence, commit all the crimes in the
book. They change from one bird to another at the moment of gun-
mounting. They hang about 'poking' the barrels when the gun is
already mounted on the shoulder and, in a sort of panic, they shoot
behind with bodies twisted and leaning on one leg. Much, much
better to attempt to shoot only one bird out of the covey and to
make up your mind which bird it's going to be the moment you
sight it than to rely on pot luck to shoot two in front and two
behind; if you happen to be using two guns.

In fact, to shoot two partridges in front, change guns, and shoot
two behind is an achievement which requires such perfect footwork, timing and gun-handling that it is very nearly comparable
to a century in first-class cricket. In practice it is very rarely

I

achieved; and in practice nobody should really attempt to use two guns until they can fairly consistently get two partridges out of a covey with one.

Anybody who can do that will shoot far more efficiently and kill more birds than another shot with two guns who hasn't the discipline to pick one bird cleanly out of a covey.

There are certain rather special partridge stands where, by means of tall belts of trees or the arrangement of shooting sites in old chalk pits or quarries, really high birds are shown. This makes for rather different shooting than ordinary partridge driving over the stubbles or out of roots. All the rules I have mentioned still apply, but the methods to be adopted are more similar to those applying to high pheasants. It is worth remembering that the partridge, though it may seem because of its size faster than a pheasant, is always considerably slower. Also, on crossing a screen of trees, partridges tend to come down rather lower than pheasants in similar circumstances; that it to say that, where pheasants would make a high glide, partridges tend to dip and swerve towards ground-level more swiftly. By reducing altitude, and offering not the level or rising shot, they present a rather tricky descending one. In some hill drives on downland the same conditions may be noticed but in general, birds driven in hill country tend to follow the natural contours to their jugging place or destination, a point which is often useful to remember when new drives are being discussed.

In general, it is not easy to get partridges to any height without some rather abnormal feature of the ground. All drives have to be planned with reference to boundaries and the seasonal changes in the agricultural crops.

No matter how accurately you shoot, or however well the birds are driven, any day's partridge shooting will be a failure unless you remember the two vital rules. Get quickly to your stand and, above all, *don't talk*. Not even in grouse driving, or in pheasant shooting, is it so vitally important to be silent as it is in partridge shooting. In grouse driving, a little quiet conversation is sometimes permissible because the drives are generally spread over such large areas. The pheasant is a more amenable chap altogether; although you won't be popular, even in the coverts, if you talk too loudly or move about restlessly at your stand. But, in partridge shooting, which usually takes place in circumscribed territory, the merest undertone travels enormous distances. On the downs, where sweeps are made over very large areas, I have literally seen partridges beginning to run, with the old birds giving them the warning call, when the guns were half a mile away. The partridges could already hear them talking. Coveys are lost on every shoot because the guns are unable to resist the inclination to gossip between stands or to make a noise when the drive has actually begun. In roots or potatoes, partridges will often far prefer to face the beaters than to fly over ground where they have heard the frightening clatter of the human voice.

In the early part of the season the greater number of partridges are shot by guns walking-up rather than by driving. In walking-up even more than driving, the shooter has a major responsibility to mark where his birds have fallen and, so far as possible, to help other people to mark and gather their own birds. The majority of partridges are shot when the herbage is very thick on the ground. They are small birds with an excellent natural camouflage in their plumage and it is the easiest thing in the world to lose them because a wounded bird will never lose its skill in finding cover, and even a dying one may have enough strength to travel a few yards to crouch under combined straw or penetrate into a rabbit scratch in the plough. If the shooting party has good dogs the problems of picking-up are simplified. But even dogs are often foxed on the dry, warm and windless days of early autumn. Many a bird drops so far out of range that it is difficult, to say the least of it, for questing dogs to find it without help.

Assume a normal happening on a normal day: a small party of four guns is walking-up partridges in a field of roots. A covey flushes in front of No. 3 gun who kills with right and left barrels, and he and the other guns watch the remainder of the covey disappear over the hedgerow. Probably all concerned are marking where the covey is going to pitch in the hope of getting a chance of shooting into it again. All that the successful shot remembers, or should remember, is that he had one in front, slightly to the left and perhaps forty yards away, and that the other was rather a long shot, slightly to the right. The line moves on until they reach the spot where the successful gun expects to find his first bird. He tramps around until he has lost the line. Then the other guns join him deciding that it must have been a runner. The second bird is searched for, and again the hunt yields negative results. Birds are scarce and the pair would have been a nice contribution to the bag.

That is the sort of thing which is always happening when guns are without a keeper and good dogs. What is the remedy? Of course, the party should have had a dog, but failing that a little more help from the other guns might have resulted in the quick gathering of both birds to the mutual satisfaction of the host and the man who shot them as well. The moment No. 3 fired the line should have stood still. The other guns, who saw one or both birds fall, should have taken the line from some landmark or landmarks. The shooter himself, knowing the spot in the air where he killed the first bird, should note that it was slightly left or right of, say, an oak tree. He should have also noted, if he can, a landmark in his rear; say a church steeple. Having those two landmarks he can always get back to the line if he wanders off it. He now goes forward alone. The birds are not to be seen, so he looks for confirmation from the other guns who are holding their ground. One waves him back. He goes back towards a landmark until the marker signals him to stop, looks around and finds one bird. He then rejoins the line, takes his marks on the second bird, and the other guns, who saw the bird fall, will take their line too. The difference may be too far to hold up the line any longer; but one of the other guns may be able to direct the shooter because he took proper marks when the bird fell. The result is that the second bird is found, too. In the unlucky event that, by taking marks, the gun is unsuccessful in finding a lost bird, it is a very good practice to drop a handkerchief or some other easily identifiable object at the place where it was believed the bird fell. This means that, after the drive is over, it is possible to go back and have a thorough look without disturbing the ground while shooting it.

It is worth remembering that distance along the ground is always misleading. The average shooter's guess of what he thinks is forty yards is in practice probably nearer thirty, and his fifty yards is in practice probably nearer thirty-five yards. We are all poor judges of distance between thirty and fifty yards, so much so that the simple rule of halving the estimated distance and adding ten yards is more often than not the correct answer.

> A guess of 30 yards is really 25 yards.
> A guess of 40 yards is really 30 yards.
> A guess of 50 yards is really 35 yards.

Remember this and try it out in the field.

To underline the system of marking and gathering birds, here is a diagram showing guns advancing in line through a field. The

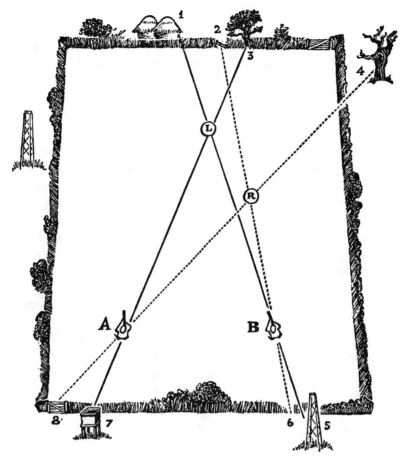

MARKING AND GATHERING OF PARTRIDGES

Gun B walking-up in field of roots gets a Right and Left at covey going away. He marks R on dotted line—*gap* at 2 and *gap* at 6; Gun A marks on dotted line—*blasted oak* 4 and *gate* 8. Second partridge is marked by gun B on line *corner of stack* 1 and *pylon* 5; and by gun A on line *hedgerow oak* 3 and *water tower* 7.

two shot birds are marked by the letters 'R' and 'L'. The plan shows the marks that each of the guns should have fixed their eye on when the birds fell. From it, it is evident to see that the variety of different angles attained by the guns, especially the outside ones, can be invaluable in thick cover.

I repeat that this system, which should always be instinctively applied by every man in a line of guns shooting partridges, needs modification if dogs are present, as they should be. If dogs are working, all the guns, including the shooter, should remain in position, only assisting the dogs by helping them with their own marks to pick up the scent. It is fatal to foil the scent by stamping all round on the ground that a dog is working on. Human scent is very strong indeed and overlays almost any other sort of scent. The scent of a game bird is very finely perfumed, and even dogs are bothered to find it if the conditions are unfavourable. If you have got a runner, or several, and the dogs are unable to find them, very often the best practice is to walk the field again. If you are working in the roots the chances are that you will put out your wounded bird at the end of it. If you have lost a bird, and your best efforts cannot find it, remember to use the trick of dropping a handkerchief or a hat and go back, or get somebody else to go back, and look for it afterwards.

One last warning. When you are shooting partridges at the beginning of September, you are almost certain to find young pheasants flying over the guns. Half-grown pheasant squeakers are just about the same size as partridges and one should always be on one's guard against shooting them. In fact, the mistake, although it is often made, is usually inexcusable. The pheasant has a completely different wing shape from the partridge, the wing beat is much flatter and slower and, apart from other considerations, the call of alarm that a pheasant gives is quite different from that of a partridge. If you do, by chance, kill what is sometimes euphoniously called 'a queen partridge,' don't bury it; just apologize as handsomely as you can to your host.

V

How to Shoot Pheasants

THE pheasant, with the probable exception of the ubiquitous pigeon, is responsible for a higher annual expenditure of cartridges than any other bird. However poor the season may be for grouse or partridges, there are always pheasants; though, in a wet year, they too may be reduced in numbers.

It used to be thought that, without the protection of keepers and the regular introduction of fresh hand-reared stock, the pheasant couldn't hold his own as a wild bird in British coverts. But, during the second war, when sporting estates were necessarily allowed to run wild, when vermin increased, and when food shortages and the high price of game encouraged more ruthless hunting than ever before, it was notable how easily the wild pheasant held his own.

The hens even lived down their reputation of being bad mothers. In places where the hens were spared, the wild stock even increased. Now that hand-rearing, although on a limited scale to what it used to be, has been resumed, the pheasant is now probably the commonest game bird in the countryside. Every shooting man gets a chance to have a pot occasionally, and many enjoy pheasant shooting all through the season, from those pleasant autumn days walking up the outsides in October to the cream of the covert shooting when the leaf falls in November and December, and finally those 'cocks-only' days at the end of the season which so often provide the tallest birds and the best shooting of all.

A pheasant is a larger bird than a grouse or a partridge, presents a more obvious target, gives you noisier notice of his approach and should, in theory, be easier to hit. Yet one so often hears of good grouse or partridge shots who never seem to be at their best at pheasants, even at the beginning of the season or in the first days in the coverts when they are by no means difficult birds to shoot.

It is not always easy to find the exact reason why experienced

shooting men, on occasion, miss pheasants; very often the grouse
shot who has become accustomed to shooting low, fast, incoming-
birds, which have to be snapped very quickly, has also become
accustomed to taking most of his weight on his left leg. Now, if he
snaps in the same fast manner at a rising pheasant as he would at
a grouse, he will almost invariably fire far behind. The reason is
that his rigid left leg prevents him bending his body easily out of
the vertical and slows his whole movement.

The bulk of shots at pheasants are overhead or high angle
shots, and the unconscious habits picked up while taking birds at
low altitudes are likely to spoil precision completely when the
shooter, who has acquired them, is dealing with birds which are
flying moderately high.

Let's put the theory to the test: Take a gun in your hand and
deliberately shift the bulk of your weight on to a rigid left leg.
Make a snap at an imaginary overhead bird and follow the
swing through for a second barrel. I think you will find that the
movement requires a great deal of effort and that, at a certain
point, there is often a perceptible check or re-bound. Fresh effort
has to be summoned up in order to pass what I can best describe
as the 'sticking point.' It is obvious, I think, that in this pose you
are not likely to hit fast high birds or even birds of ordinary
height. Having carried out the experiment which may well reveal
a personal fault of your own, proceed to adopt the proper
position.

Take your gun and hold it in the 'ready position' but narrow
a little your natural grouse stand. With your gun in the 'ready
position,' the whole weight of your body should be on the right
leg, which is stressed but not rigid. This alteration of weight
means that, for overhead birds and birds to the right, all the
weight is on the right leg. Weight is only transferred to the left
leg for shots over the left shoulder.

Now go into the garden and throw your gun at a rook or a
pigeon passing over. Follow it with both hands until you have
picked up its speed. At that point, your left hand should instinctively begin to mount the gun. As the gun reaches eye-level, your
right hand tightens grip a little and a swift final movement of
both beds the gun to the shoulder and completes the action. You
will find that you can carry out the whole of this movement
without constraint, with little effort and yet have freedom to
reach overhead birds. In addition, you have all your time to

devote to the bird and, as a consequence, you won't be flurried; you'll move smoothly and you won't jerk.

With correct gun-mounting, a miraculous improvement in shooting can be brought about simply by narrowing the position of the feet a little and settling yourself so that the body weight can be adjusted easily to either leg with the minimum of movement. If your stance is too wide and rigid, you will find you cannot transfer weight from one leg to the other without losing poise and dropping a shoulder. This in itself is sufficient to make you miss behind your bird.

It is a fact that, on the vast majority of shoots, really high birds are rare. There may be one or more stands where birds come fairly tall, but they are only relative to the average of the day. If a particular stand shows taller birds than the average during a shooting day, you will often notice that these higher birds are missed by men who have been shooting well and consistently at medium-height birds on the other stands. This is a very common phenomenon. But why?

The answer is that the high, fast pheasant is a very difficult bird to shoot indeed, and most of our ideas about appropriate allowances that we should make for him, when he is on the wing, are fundamentally wrong. But if you clear your mind of misapprehensions, you will soon get the hang of the game and find that shooting tall pheasants is a science that can be mastered.

The following diagram helps to explain some of the reasons why good average shots fail on these tall birds. In the first place, the average pheasant, even though he tops well-grown oak trees, is probably not more than twenty-five yards high, while the vast majority of driven birds are barely twenty yards high. A really high pheasant finds his 'ceiling,' or extreme shootable range, at a vertical height of forty yards. Good hillside drives will occasionally produce birds that are really out of range for part, at least, of their journey across the line of guns.

In the diagrams on pages 138 and 139 the squares represent ten yards in each dimension and the line of the angle of vision is taken as 45 degrees. In the case of a bird flying on the twenty-yard height level, it cuts the line of vision about thirty yards from the gun while the bird on the forty-yard height level comes into view nearly sixty yards away. The low bird has only twenty yards to travel before he is overhead, the high bird has forty yards to cover before he is over the guns. The greater

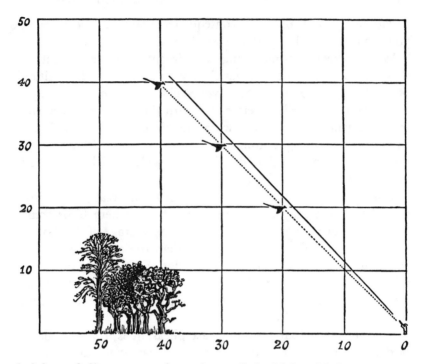

height and distance are deceptive and the higher bird appears to be travelling at half the speed of the lower bird. Distance is easy to misjudge.

In the diagram opposite, we have both birds (who move at equal speed) nearer the overhead position. The lower bird has only ten yards to go before he is vertically over the guns, but the higher bird has still twice that distance to cover. The type of shot who consciously estimates 'forward allowances' now works out his personal equations. The table of allowances gives the approximate allowance for crossing birds at forty miles an hour as thirty-nine inches at twenty yards, and ninety-six inches at forty yards. This would suggest that the shooter must make one-and-a-half times as much allowance at forty yards as he does at twenty yards. This he would presumably do by swinging his gun-muzzle say one-and-a-half times as much forward.

In practice, this means that a movement of two inches of the gun-muzzle will make a difference of forty inches at twenty yards and eighty inches at forty yards. In fact the same relative movement is correct for birds at heights of twenty to thirty-five yards and only the tiniest fraction of extra movement of gun-muzzle will reach the bird at the ceiling limit of forty yards.

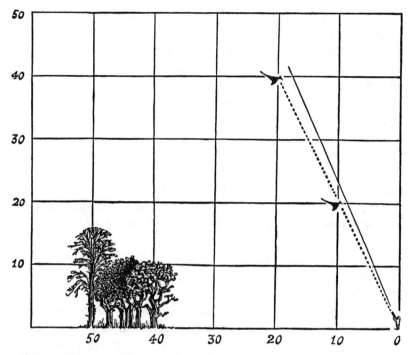

I hope I have said enough to demonstrate once again that the 'conscious allowance' school can only involve you in endless confusion. Forget it. The reason that really high birds are missed is because guns tend to shoot at them when they are too far off, often not really in range, or by missing them in front through trying to put into practice this misleading business of doubling the forward allowance.

High birds are never easy to kill owing to the wide spread of the shot and the decline in pellet energy in all but cartridges specially loaded for this type of shooting. In the ordinary way, the cheapest cartridge should kill at twenty yards, but, when it comes to tall birds, the velocity of the shot pellets is about two hundred and fifty feet per second lower than at twenty yards, and both penetration and pellet energy have declined in even greater proportion.

The indifferent cartridge, which may be quite satisfactory at low birds, lacks punch and driving power at tall birds, while, in addition, the bird itself is well protected by its bones and breast muscles. Weak pellets cannot penetrate to vital spots such as the lungs. The wing bones too are not easily broken or disabled and the main vital exposed area is the head and neck.

Held by the head and allowed to hang there, a pheasant appears to have a very long neck, almost as long as a duck. But contrast the difference in appearance between a pheasant and a duck in flight. The duck flies with the neck fully extended, offering a very vulnerable target, but the pheasant seems to contract its neck or curve it in flight and, as a consequence, the neck itself doesn't attract the eye as a target.

If you look at a real pheasant, not the drawings of pheasant, you will realize how the neck is contracted rather than projected and how very little of the vulnerable part is exposed. On occasion, if the guns are not lined out in an echoing or reverberating valley, you can actually hear the shot patter on a high pheasant, and see him glide on undamaged, undisturbed and giving no indication at all that he has been touched other than a transient flicker or dip that occurs when the sound waves of a discharge that missed him clean, so far as the pellets are concerned, checks his flight in the air.

Nobody knows quite how vulnerable a tall pheasant is to a shot charge. Very, very few birds, even from high stands, are really forty yards high, and of course a drop of five yards means a large increase in the target's vulnerability. The situation is complicated by the fact that, as I said in another chapter, few of us are good judges of height or distance. I have seen celebrated 'high' stands where the average tall bird was thirty yards, yet almost everyone who shot there would have said that the birds were 'out of range.' A few, a very few, 'high' stands exist, and they are almost all of them stands where the face of a hillside drops down in a precipitous slope. The birds, driven-in over the top of it, run downhill a certain way before being flushed by wire or stops, then rise and fly over the guns below. They rise, as pheasants always rise, to clear the treetops, and this height may be (and, on a few downland shoots, actually is) nearly two hundred yards; six hundred feet above the guns waiting in the valley below. This isn't guesswork, you can check it on any ordnance map over the contour lines.

These particularly tall birds are wholly and incredibly out of shot. They fly down over the treetops and break somewhere below the last two contours over the valley below. They will come over the guns at heights which vary from forty yards to about forty-five yards, for very high birds, and twenty yards for low ones. The opposite side of the narrow downs at the bottom is normally steep woodland cover, and the valleys tend to widen towards the low line. Birds at the top end may be very high but, as the valley lengthens it widens, and the last birds beaten out will probably be considerably lower than those at the narrow end. These birds are all birds which are not rising but flying *down* a steep hillside and they are falling, not rising shots. Very few are straight over the guns, and most of the birds plane down with fixed wings at a very high speed and with a most baffling twist or turn on it. The angle of descent is rapid and, if we plot it against our simple diagram of the level flying pheasant, and allow it to have movements in the third dimension as well, it is a very difficult shot for the uninitiated.

If the descending bird flies straight towards you, you are lucky. You should treat him exactly as you would treat a low-driven partridge. Mount the gun with the shortest possible movement of the barrels, snapping at the beak of the bird, when he looks big enough to eat, in front of you. The temptation, when you see a pheasant coming at you from a long way away, is to wait too long. If you fluff about with a bird like this, making up your mind *when* to shoot him, you will find that he is flicking his tail at you and out of range before you can shoot at all. These descending birds coming down hillsides can move as fast as sixty miles an hour. You can swing your gun fast enough to catch them; but it is difficult. The proper moment to shoot your bird is when he is dead in front of you and, momentarily, at what appears to be a standstill. You have only got to move the butt of your gun a few inches from the ready position to your shoulder to kill him.

Once again, let me remind you not to be afraid to miss these fast-moving birds. If you are not afraid to miss, if you bring up your gun sharply and confidently, and choose the right moment to fire, you will have the satisfaction of seeing a real screamer crashing down on his beak. The right moment is when the bird is directly in front of you.

But very few of these tall birds that you will meet planing down hillsides fly straight. The difficulty of most of the shots that they present is that they have a sharp curl on them as well. In that event, if you try to snap at them as they come towards you, you will miss on the right or left according to which way the bird is curling. The way to shoot these birds—and if you can shoot them consistently you can call yourself a first-class shot—is not to shoot them in the nose but on the side of the head as they curl past you. Your gun-mounting must be rapid and you must make sure that both hands are on to him, and the gun-barrels, too, as you mount. In the process of mounting, if you are mounting correctly with your eye on the bird and your whole body moving with him, you will find yourself bending down either to the right or to the left according to the side he curls away from you. If your gun-mounting is true, and your body moves down with the bird, and you shoot the moment your shoulder meets the stock, you will make a clean kill.

I have told you elsewhere that, when you are shooting at driven pheasants, or indeed in many cases when you are shooting at the ordinary going-away pheasant which has been flushed up from the hedgerow by a dog, you have got time to say slowly: 'Come along, my beauty.' But I want to emphasize that that sentence recited slowly is only effective in steadying your shooting if you are making a smooth gun-mounting with your body and hands as you say it and providing, too, that as you speak the last syllable your shoulder has come forward to meet the gun butt.

I know that's not always an easy thing to do. On our off-days the more we miss the more anxious and nervous we become and the more difficult it is to get a sweet gun-mounting and confident trigger pulling. Nearly every experienced pheasant shot knows that there are some days when he can promise with confidence that he will hit the next bird that comes over, however he comes; and other days when, if his life depended on it, he feels that he hasn't got a chance of touching a feather.

On your off-days, which is what I am principally concerned with in this book, it is quite a good policy to get yourself back into form and to re-educate yourself again not to fluff about with your gun, to sharpen your determination by pretending to yourself that you have lost your temper. Make up your mind that you will kill the next bird that comes over because you hate him more than any other bird in the world. Cough up a few choice words and then swing your gun on to him as if you intended to swipe him out of the sky. Suddenly, after all the careful poking which has made sure that you are always miles behind, you may well find that you are killing clean and killing with confidence.

But suppose that even that advice doesn't bring you the right results. Then it's almost certain that there is something wrong with your gun-mounting or your stance. Let's analyse how a really first-class shot at a first-class tall pheasant stand sets about it.

The first thing you should notice is that the best pheasant shots take a rather narrow stance. This narrow stance stiffens the body, which is necessary for high birds because it is important to mount the gun in a very accurate line. There must be no sway or sideways wobble. The least unsteadiness carries the barrels to one side or the other of the bird. As I explained to you in the calculations of allowances, half an inch of muzzle movement means an error of fifteen to twenty inches at the business end. With a thirty-inch killing circle we cannot afford the slightest mistake in centring the charge.

Having noticed the stance of a first-class pheasant shot, watch they way he holds his head. First, he holds it high because naturally he wants to keep his head up to see the approaching target. But holding his head high he brings his eye well above the rib of the gun, thus automatically giving all the forward allowance required. Remember that the eye is always on the bird and only subconsciously aware of the gun-barrels. As the shot takes place, bird and barrel come into view together. If the eye is high above the rib the bird is seen on the barrels before it is really there. But the gun is a fixed affair, firing at the same place. Now as we know, at forty yards we want slightly more forward allowance as the shot takes longer to travel. The attached diagram shows what happens. The eye being held high over the rib the allowance is naturally affected.

You may ask how it is that in the case of ordinary pheasants you're on the target at all if this theory is correct. The answer is that a shot at a middle height oncoming pheasant is fired with confidence, or without conscious calculation, and probably some of the movement is unconsciously quick and exaggerated. The result is that natural overthrow 'picks up' a bird we are 'optically' behind. With tall birds there is usually lack of confidence and the subconscious chuck or overthrow, used in ordinary snap-shooting, is temporarily inhibited.

Just thinking about making the shot slows down the process. There is a lack of rhythmic smoothness in the body swing (which must move in time with the bird) whilst the gun is coming up to make the sudden snap finish on a point of acceleration reached without check. One might describe it as a carefree *accelerating*

THE THEORY OF
AUTOMATIC ALLOWANCE

The shooter's eye sees
the bird but the angle of
the barrels of the gun is
in front of the target at
the moment when bird
and barrels come into
view together. Thus, if
the head is held correct-
ly, the necessary forward
allowance for a moving
target is automatically
provided for.

* See Editorial note page 35.

swing. As the bird comes nearer, the
arc shortens and the apparent movement in time is swifter even though
the bird is really proceeding at a uniform velocity.

In a word, with high birds, the stance
has to be narrow and the shot must be
taken at a point where the body can
still move freely without check. The
shoulder must come home to the gun
and the shot fired before the spine and
muscles begin to offer resistant stresses
to the upward swing.

Try a little more dry practice on
any suitable target in the open. Take
a narrow stance, and with your gun at
the ready position, squeeze the stock*
tightly between your elbow and your
side, holding it firmly so that the inclination to begin gun-mounting with
your arms before your body has begun
to move is mechanically repressed. As
your eyes are on the bird you can,
with your gun so held, point the gun
at the bird whilst the stock is still
under your arm. In fact, if your gun-
mounting is correct, you should be on
the bird from the moment the barrels
start moving and your eye fixes on it.

In the shooting school we are often
able to demonstrate this fact to pupils
in actual practice. When a pupil is
raising his gun to his shoulder and
missing, because he is dwelling too
long on his trigger pull (believing that
he needs time to get the barrels of the
gun on to the target) we instruct him
to pull the trigger on the word of
command. As soon as a clay pigeon
comes over, and before the gun is on
the pupil's shoulder, we order him to

fire. In the end, he cottons on to the idea and does what he is told. With his gun in the half-mounted position he finds, again and again, that he is shattering the clay. The lesson that that teaches is that if your eye is on the bird, and you are mounting correctly, you haven't got to worry about anything at all. All you have to do is to remember when you are shooting, that the gun that fits you is always 'on.' There is no necessity for effort or a duel between arms and body to make sure of it.

Once again:

Don't mount the gun first and swing second. Grip tightly with the left or forward hand, relax the right till the final snap to the shoulder.

Don't look at the gun. If you see the barrels, you have missed.

Don't look ahead of the bird or you will stop your gun swing.

I find that even experienced shooting men have the most misleading ideas of the spread and punch of the shot from a game gun. In pheasant shooting especially it is important that everybody who hopes to kill his birds cleanly and well should appreciate the true state of affairs.

The spread of a normal game gun is approximately an inch to a yard (e.g. forty inches at forty yards), the number of effective pellets likely to penetrate a pheasant are remarkably few. Sir Ralph Payne Gallway in his book *High Pheasants in Theory and Practice* didn't enjoy the modern convenience of a quarter of a century's improvement in pellets and cartridges. But he tells of an interesting experiment. Twenty dead cock pheasants were hoisted by kite to a forty yards overhead position and twenty rounds were fired at each bird. No less than four hundred rounds were fired and 115 thousand pellets expended, yet, on post mortem, the number of potentially fatal wounds on this score of birds was so low as to be calculable on the fingers of both hands. It is an instructive example. But perhaps because Sir Ralph Payne Gallway hadn't my experience of the behaviour of bullets in police work, a misleading one.

In fact the resistance of dead flesh is several times greater than living flesh and the computation of what is a mortal wound and what effect is due to temporarily disabling shot are problems which give rise to a good deal of theory but not one on which any really scientific explanations are yet available.

But that's a side issue for the expert. If you are a good shot,

K

familiar with your ground, you can shoot high pheasants as easily as the ordinary shot shoots the average bird, whatever the cause of their demise. There is no wizardry about it, it is a reasonably easy trick when you get it and there is really no excuse for a man who goes in to a high pheasant shoot continuing to fluff his birds.

With proper cartridges, and proper coaching, any shooting man should bring down anything in range. The eclectic, who desires high birds and high birds only, is not, as he would have us believe, the finest shot and the finest sportsman. He is an addict of the freak shot and, having learnt his freak shooting, may put up a poor performance on lower birds. A snap shot, by a gun walking back with the beaters, may be a far better effort than the shooting of the tallest bird over the stand.

VI

How to Shoot Ground Game

WHEN a young sportsman is allowed to handle a gun in the field for the first time, it is almost certain that he will be given his chance in the type of shooting with the greatest danger factor of all. The ground shot at rabbits* and hares is one in which even the most experienced shot of flying game is tempted to take chances. I don't know what it is about a bolting rabbit, or a hare at full stretch, that contrives to unbalance the judgment of otherwise safe shots; but the temptation to follow through to a dangerous angle and to let fly into a hedge without calculating where the shot charge will finish needs checking with the greatest firmness.

Without exception, the form of shooting with the greatest potential danger is when two or three men stand on opposite sides of a hedge waiting for ferrets to bolt rabbits. The most dangerous form of organized shooting is one of these battues at the end of the season when the farmers turn out to drive the hares.

Any shot made with the barrels of the gun pointing in the air is unlikely to kill anybody; although I think I have said enough to emphasize that an air-shot can be dangerous enough. But the moment a game gun is levelled to the ground, the accident risk is doubled or even trebled. The charge can be placed squarely where it is intended. But a flint on the ground, or the trunk of a tree, can turn the shot in half a dozen directions. There are plenty of cases in which the shooter has killed the rabbit or hare he shot at; but the deflected remainder of the charge has caused serious accident.

In any shoot in which rabbits and hares are shot, with winged game as part of the drive, it is always dangerous to shoot in front unless the topography of the ground ensures that there is no possibility of a ricochet reaching the beaters. The best rule is never

* When there were rabbits!

to shoot ground game during a drive except behind, when the hare or the rabbit has passed the line of guns. And remember not to mount your gun until you have made a complete round-about turn. To pick up the rabbit or the hare in front and follow through is not only abominably bad style (for you'll probably miss) but you needn't be surprised if the next gun in the line is wise enough to throw himself flat on his face as you do it.

Always beware of that tempting shot in roots, when the beaters are closing-in and the rabbits and hares are playing hide-and-seek in front of you. If you will only stand quiet, most of them will come through and you can take them behind. If you miss a chance you can still have the satisfaction of knowing that you didn't take a chance.

Beware of the rabbit that sneaks under the hedge in front of you. You can never be sure what is behind.

Beware of the rabbit, or the hare, that lollops towards you in a covert. Beaters, however often the keeper shouts at them, have a habit of breaking line. When they spot ground game, they are liable to be as irresponsible as you are, and to charge forward through the undergrowth in the hope of knocking a rabbit on the head with a stick.

It is no case for you in civil law that the beater you wounded had no business to be where he was. Always assume, at a rabbit shoot or a hare drive, that the other man is liable to lose his head, and act accordingly. Don't lose yours.

Far better to be one of those shots who complains that he can't hit ground game than make a reputation for hitting anything that moves.

Never go ferreting except with men whose judgment with a gun you can completely trust. Look out on back-end days when the farmers shoot up the hares. Even when you are alone, walking the hedgerows with a dog for rabbits, plodding through the plough in search of a hare for the pot, make up your mind that you are not alone and that the countryside isn't deserted. It is surprising the places that lovers select for their intimacies or that children get into when they are up to mischief.

On the whole, I think it is true that most shooting men enjoy good rabbit shooting and detest shooting hares. Rabbits, in ideal conditions and in safe company, can provide magnificent sport. It is only once in a while that a hare presents a shot which is really worth taking.

Theoretically, hares are usually so easy that a reasonable shot should never miss. In practice, hares are missed—and worse than that, wounded—again and again because (1) the shooter misjudges distance by under-rating the size of the quarry, (2) the shot is made at an angle when it is difficult to make an immediately mortal wound.

A leveret, or a full-grown hare in poor condition, weighs nearly twice as much as a rabbit. A big hare can scale from eight to ten pounds, and hares are shot which are very much heavier.

In advising you on grouse shooting, I have told you to choose the moment to shoot when the bird looks big enough to eat.* In advising you on shooting hares, I must warn you that hares, well beyond extreme ranges, still look big enough to eat. The moment to shoot, and not before, is when you can see the hare's big eyes.

When you are hare shooting, you must adopt a completely different attitude of mind to your attitude when you are shooting winged game in the coverts. As I told you, in the coverts you can generally assume that every partridge or pheasant that comes over your gun is likely to be in fair range, and usually at much closer range than you would possibly believe. In hare shooting, the proper attitude is to convince yourself that the hare is normally out of range until you can pretty well see the whites of her eyes. I want to emphasize that because, as I said earlier, most hare shooting is easy shooting. Once in a while, when a hare is extended at full pace in front of you, you can pull off a shot at forty yards. Fully extended, the vulnerability of the hare is increased considerably. But, normally speaking, you won't get a shot at a hare at full gallop. The shot you will normally get is when a hare comes lolloping towards you, twenty yards at a time, stopping to sit up and look cautiously around her or to crouch down on the ground with ears laid back. Unless you choose to deal with the unpleasant business of wounding her, and hearing her screaming on the ground, hold your fire until she is nearly on top of you.

The way to take the shot at a slowly-advancing hare—the advance will usually be slow—is to shoot the ground from underneath her. The technique is to aim the gun at what amounts to a sitting shot so that the charge blows up like a landmine underneath the target. In that way, you will make a clean kill. If you aim at the head, you will probably do no more than wound the hare in the rump.

* See Editorial note page 119.

Anyhow, if it is a drive, you will do far better to wait until the hare races past you and, on seeing you, increases pace. Under those conditions, you will get a reasonably sporting shot and you stand a very good chance of making a clean kill. The great secret of shooting running hares, as indeed it is the secret of shooting at all game, is not to look at the whole target but to select a part of it. If you try and take in the whole carcase of the hare, the chances are that you will wound her in the hind quarters. If you make up your mind that what you are shooting at is her ears, you'll make a clean kill in the head. The people who have the knack of shooting hares—the shooting of all sorts of game is a knack of one kind or another—are never deceived by the size of the animal. Consciously or unconsciously, they are pointing their gun-muzzles whilst gun-mounting and kill the hare in that clean fashion which makes her turn head-over-heels as she is hit.

But although a great many hares are shot during drives for pheasants and partridges, I suppose the greater number are still killed walking-up and in those sometimes dangerous organized hare drives in which fifty or perhaps a hundred guns push the game from different directions towards a central point. From an agricultural point of view, the destruction of hares at the end of the season is very necessary, especially in downland country. If you take part in one of those shoots, in which most of the chances you get will be hares breaking from their forms under your feet, remember that by the time that the other wing of the party is driving towards you the game will be as dangerous for you as for the hares. The secret of safe and accurate shooting is not to try to kill everything.

Walking up, you may carry your gun in the 'ready position.' When a hare breaks from her form under your feet, come to a halt with feet together. Then, drawing the right foot backwards, mount your gun as if you were taking a normal snap shot at going-away partridges—the easiest shot of all. But, as you fix your eye on the hare moving away in front of you, you will find that your natural inclination is to look at her hind quarters, which is the part of her that you yourself see the largest. You must make a deliberate effort to train yourself to look, not at the hind quarters, which are the least vulnerable part of a hare, but between her ears. From the moment that you can train yourself to plant a charge between the hare's ears, rather than at her rump, you will kill clean again and again.

It is important to emphasize that it is possible to make a mortal shot at a hare only to find that she shows no apparent sign of being hit at all. If you see flecks of down fly off her you can reasonably assume that you've hit her. If she jinks, there's a strong possibility that she is seriously wounded.

In hare shooting, you have a special responsibility to keep your eye on the quarry you have shot at until she is quite out of sight. If you notice that, after a hare has been shot at, she runs about a hundred yards or so, then stops, then goes on again for a short distance and so on, you can be reasonably certain that she will be a dead hare before she reaches the next field. A hare that is un-touched will travel at an even pace until she is completely out of view.

So these are the rules:

1. Don't shoot at a hare at all until you can see the animal's eyes.

2. Don't shoot even at forty yards, except to take a crossing shot when a hare's body is fully extended. In those conditions you will probably make a clean kill or miss altogether.

3. If you are in a stand, or you find yourself in circumstances where the hare is lolloping towards you, resist the inclination, if you can, to shoot her in front when she is crouching. If you must shoot under those conditions, aim the gun so that the charge is placed to lift her off the ground rather than at the animal herself. Alternatively, wait if you can until the hare sights you. You will then get a reasonable crossing shot or, if the beaters are moving up behind her, a going-away shot in which you can kill her under reasonably sporting conditions.

4. If a hare gets up under your feet, and is going away from you, resist the natural inclination to fix the eye on the largest part of her which is her rump. Train yourself to shoot her between the ears. She will give you plenty of time.

5. Above all, remember that a hare is the biggest animal in the shooting field. Just as you will generally over-estimate the range of pheasant or partridges, you will generally under-estimate the range of a hare. If you want to have the reputation for being a clean shot, don't raise your gun to a hare at all until you are sure that you can make a clean kill.

A rabbit is a far more vulnerable target than a hare. Normally speaking, if you centre a gun on him at all, you will be unlucky if he manages to make his escape. Rabbit shooting also demands a higher standard of shooting altogether.

True, in certain circumstance (curiously enough, they are usually the conditions in which rabbit shooting is rather dangerous), killing them can be easy. But rabbit shooting at its best in rough grass, where they have been tainted out of their burrows, or in the coverts where, by clever beating, they can be driven forward across a narrow ride to a line of guns, is often comparable to the best sport that partridges or pheasants or grouse can provide.

The type of shooting that is most likely to defeat you is that best of shooting when you are standing on a corner covering a narrow ride in a covert with thick undergrowth on either side. This calls for snap shooting of the very highest quality. The rabbits are normally running in front of the beaters, so the gun knows from which side to expect them and the directions in which they will run.

It is hopeless, in these conditions, holding your gun pointing at one side of the ride or the other as there is no body swing or carry through.

When you are expecting rabbits in a drive, your first move must be to keep as close into the hedge on their side as possible, so that, as far as possible, the advancing rabbits can't see you. So many rabbits run back, or accelerate, when they see a shooter rushing his gun to his shoulder. The expert rabbit shot stands still and keeps completely quiet, hides himself as much as he can and remains in a constant state of alert. In that way he gets the greater proportion of easy shots, the rabbits are not alarmed and cross the ride at a normal pace; often at less than normal pace.

What the bad shot does is to stand in the middle of the ride jerking his gun at every noise, with his head moving all the time as he searches the covert. Suddenly a rabbit dashes across twenty yards ahead. The unwise shot half-raises his gun, lowers it, looks regretfully at the spot where the rabbit crossed and then curses because another rabbit dashes across the ten-yard mark. He makes a hasty snatch and, of course, his charge is placed yards behind.

The secret of shooting rabbits, when they are likely to pop out at any point around you, is to take a firm stand, keep still and remain in position. The good shot does not shift his head about. He stands there relaxed with his gun at the ready. His gaze is straight along the ride or in the gap where he expects to get the chance of a shot. His eyes are not focused on anything in particular. He is ready to snap at ten, twenty or thirty yards.

In normal shooting, I estimate the average distance at which rabbits are killed is about twelve yards. Pace out the next ten rabbits you shoot and discover if I am wrong. I suggest that 95 per cent of all rabbits shot are killed at twenty yards range and under. A long shot at a wide crossing rabbit that pleases you very much may look like forty yards but, if you pace it out, you will find that it is usually rather less than thirty.

If you miss a rabbit, you can usually assume that you have missed high and behind. High because your hands were in the wrong place and the weight of your legs was out of correct balance, behind because you faulted in concentration and gun-mounting.

In ground game shooting, the gun is held in the ready position with the barrels pointing directly in front of you. But you should adopt the ready position with this difference: You SHOULD SHORTEN YOUR REACH BY DRAWING BACK YOUR LEFT HAND AT LEAST ONE INCH FROM THE NORMAL POSITION WHICH YOU ADOPT FOR WINGED GAME.

At the moment of gun-mounting, you should move the weight of your body forward on the left foot. Indeed, your whole frame should move perceptibly forwards and downwards as you drop the barrel of the gun on to the target.

Try it in dry practice. Shorten your left-hand grip so that you can most comfortably and quickly drop the barrels of the gun for a ground shot. Then lean forward with the weight on the left foot so that your whole body moves sweetly on to the target below you. If you can acquire this movement, so that you adopt it instinctively for ground game, you will pull off snap shots at rabbits, with time to spare, which will surprise you as much as the lookers-on.

(*Norman Clarke's opinion is that the advice 'to shorten the left-hand grip' to take fur is wrong. He himself recommends that there should be no variation in the position of the hands. In his view the forward movement of the body-weight is sufficient. This may well be another case in which a method which suited Churchill's stocky frame and short arms is not right for a taller, longer-armed man. Try it both ways. See which suits you personally the better.*)

If you still miss you can assume that you are making the familiar error of thinking about where the gun is pointing, and not where the rabbit is going. Concentrate not on the whole rabbit but on a part of it; preferably, for a crossing shot, his front legs. *Don't* hold on to the trigger and *don't* make forward allowances which, while you are thinking about them, will ensure you shoot behind. Let the natural overthrow of the gun do its work.

Curiously enough, you will often discover that guns who are completely experienced in shooting winged game will have their eyes wiped by keepers or farmers who probably couldn't hit a crow unless they caught it napping on a tree. The reason is simple. If you adopt the same stance and grip that you are accustomed to for winged game, your shot charge will go over and in the stern of a rabbit or a hare. The farmer, or the keeper, who is accustomed to shooting ground game and has got into the habit of holding his gun a little short, and leaning forward on the left foot to make the ground shot, makes a kill every time. For the reason that he tends to hold his gun short, and to crouch rather than to make a natural upward swing of his whole body to a bird passing over, is why so many good vermin destroyers make a poor show when they are given the opportunity of showing their mettle against driven game. Everything in game shooting is a matter of knowing how to deal with different targets in different conditions.

VII

How to Shoot Wildfowl*

HOW NOT to shoot wildfowl might be a more suitable title for this chapter. There is a tendency in the many excellent textbooks on wildfowling practice to put almost too much emphasis, if that were possible, on the necessity for personal camouflage; on ways of building hides and digging-in, and the choice of clothes to face the rigours of the hardiest sports with a gun that a man can choose.

But the dawn excursions and night attacks, the waiting hours in freezing weather, the muddy discomfort, will be all to no purpose—however tough the fowler and however effectively he sinks himself into the background of the mud flats and the salt-ings—if, when he hears at last the whistle of pinions and gets a fair chance at a duck, he fails to make a successful shot.

Fowlers miss: (1) Because they tend to over-gun themselves with weapons which are too heavy or too long in the barrel for the job; (2) Because they often conceal themselves so efficiently that, when the unforgiving moment comes, they haven't allowed room for themselves to swing a gun with comfort; (3) Because they completely misjudge distance.

Let's take the last first. I have emphasized that, in driven-game shooting, the tallest and widest birds are seldom out of range of the guns in the line. In inland shooting, the only variety of game which is consistently and regrettably shot-at at outside ranges is the hare. The reason that inexperienced sportsmen shoot at hares at sixty yards and more is because they uncon-sciously assume that because a hare looks as big as a rabbit at extreme ranges, it's shootable.

Wildfowlers consistently shoot duck, geese and other fowl at wild ranges because:

* Rightly, I think, this chapter has been described as inadequate. Although Churchill shot more wildfowl than most it was usually in spectacular battues on the marshes of Holland and Turkey. He preferred 'big bag' shooting to a dawn patrol in the hope of a snap shot at a curlew. The value of this chapter to wildfowlers will be simply in the context of the rest of the book. It shows how they can modify Churchill's method of straight-shooting to their own tough sport. For the latest word on modern wildfowling, see 'The New Wildfowler' (Herbert Jenkins, 1961).

1. They get trigger happy after a long wait.

2. The absence of landmarks in typical wildfowling areas makes every object that appears seem nearer than it actually is.

3. The variation in the size of different species of fowl is such that a Brent goose crossing at one hundred yards looks as big as a mallard at twenty yards; and a mallard at sixty yards looks as big as a teal at twenty yards.

4. On the morning and evening flights the duck move most freely in the deceptive half-light between daylight and darkness.

The cure for the wildfowler who continually commits the crime of pricking birds at extreme ranges—and, incidentally, pushing them well up and out of range of any other fowler who happens to be on the saltings—is to give up shooting until he can identify pretty well any species of fowl by silhouette and characteristic flight. It is unforgivable to go flighting without that ornithological wisdom. The best wildfowlers are always first-class naturalists.

To be a first-class shot at wildfowl calls for many qualities besides sheer gunmanship; for that reason alone, wildfowling has an appeal which, when it gets a man, usually grips him like a fever. The successful wildfowler must be ornithologist, astronomer, meteorologist, commando, and longshoreman, too.

But what I am concerned about is what is called in another place 'the end product.' Assuming that you do everything else right; that you choose the right creek on the right morning; that you establish a good hide and that you have that mixture of good luck and good judgment which puts you on the flight line the ducks are using, you must still shoot straight.

To what extent is the drill given in this book going to help you in successful shooting at wildfowl? What modifications are necessary?

Let it be said at once that whether you are lying on your face or on your back, whether you are crouched in a hole in the ground or down at the bottom of a creek, you will miss if your gun-mounting is at fault. But it is evident that, in the conditions in which wildfowling is usually carried out, you won't be in a position to give attention to pieces of finesse like footwork and body movement. WHAT YOU MUST DO, IN EFFECT, IS TO LEARN TO SWING YOUR GUN WITH YOUR HANDS AND SHOULDERS ALONE.

You won't do that unless you are the complete master of gun-

INCORRECT METHOD

The right hand is too far over the top of the stock. The knuckle of the middle finger is hard against the gun. Faulty gun-mounting will result.

The gun cannot be mounted without raising the elbow, thus causing head movement. Finger and arm are likely to be bruised on recoil.

THE CORRECT METHOD

The right hand is well under the stock, thus straightening the trigger finger and clearing the knuckle. The shooter is balanced to meet recoil.

The gun is mounted without head movement. Note that the trigger finger is extended protectively along the guard until the actual moment of firing.

If the muzzle of the gun is held too high in the air . . .

. . . the barrels usually drop below the mark on gun-mounting.

If the muzzle of the gun is held pointing to the ground . . .

. . . the butt reaches the shoulder before the muzzle is on the target.

THE CORRECT READY POSITION

The adoption of this position in readiness for gun-mounting is one of the basic rules of sound, safe shooting. The stock is pressed tight under the right arm. The muzzle in the left hand is pointing towards the target. Note carefully that the gun is *not* held across the body. The left hand holds the barrels on a line with the right shoulder, and at a right-angle to the torso of the shooter. To hold a gun across the body in the 'ready' position is dangerous. Like a cross bat in cricket, it is also bad style.

Note the position of the right thumb as it releases the barrels which are held with the muzzles pointing at a safe downward angle.

Take two cartridges out of bag, or pocket, between the fingers so that the case of the lower one extends about $\frac{3}{4}$-inch.

Insert the nose of lower cartridge into the right barrel. Don't let go of it. Continue to hold both cartridges in your fingers.

Using the right cartridge as a pivot make a twist of the wrist which will bring the upper or second cartridge into alignment with the left barrel.

At completion of move-ment, both cartridges are held together over the chambers. The action is smooth and unfussy.

The process is com-pleted by releasing the rims. The lead in the heads of the cartridges weights them into the gun.

Before shooting, the cartridge bag should be thoroughly shaken. The effect of this is that most of the cartridges in the bag settle with the lighter brass ends upper-most. In consequence, they come more readily to the hand for quick reloading. Attention to this detail is worth many birds in a 'hot corner.'

If the left hand is too far
forward . . .

. . . . the barrels will mount
earlier than the stock.

If the left hand is not forward
enough . . .

. . . the stock will mount earlier
than the barrels.

Correct reach is found by balancing the gun between the two hands.

THE INCORRECT METHOD: The fingers of the left hand encroach over the rib, causing the gun to cant or throw too high on the object. The right finger is bent in an unsafe position over the trigger guard.

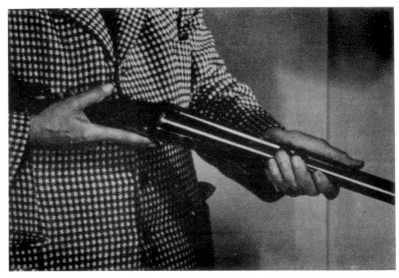

THE CORRECT METHOD: The left thumb, lying along the left barrel, encourages a pointing movement; it checks 'up-jump'; effectively stops the finger-tips covering the rib; and allows the ball of the thumb to stand out prominently, thus blocking the gun sight from the sight of the left eye and ensuring right eye domination.

Everyone knows that, with every kill, the gun-muzzles must have been pointed correctly at the target as it moved through the air.

But many people fail to realize that, as the barrels lie in the left hand, the left hand must also have been pointed in the right place.

The left hand must not be considered simply as a lifting lever. You will shoot just wherever you put it. Therefore, the left hand must point the barrels at the target during the whole movement of gun-mounting and trigger-pulling. If you misuse your left hand simply to lift the gun and then, in a separate movement, try to poke it at the target, you will miss. If the left hand is moving continuously on to the mark as the gun is mounting, the barrels will be on the mark too.

IT IS UNSAFE to shoulder a game gun with the trigger guard resting on the shoulder and without taking proper care to see that the barrels are held pointing skywards.

IT IS UNSAFE to nurse a gun across the forearm in the style of the man on the left. Between drives, a gun should be carried open at the breech and unloaded.

When you are walking-up game, it is a most dangerous position to carry a gun across your body instead of pointing the muzzles straight in front. If you hold a gun in this fashion . . .

. . . what happens is that every time you put the right foot forward the muzzle of your gun will swing and point directly at the next man in the line. The left hand should push the muzzles to the front.

As you wait on your stick for driven birds to come forward, it is correct to carry your gun loaded with the safety catch engaged. This is an excellent and safe rest position in which the weight of the gun is so distributed as to be almost unnoticeable through a long day.

Another safe method of resting a gun during a drive. Note that the finger is guarding the triggers. This is a useful position to adopt when quick action is likely to be called for. The ready position is smoothly assumed as the shooter rises to his feet to take his shot.

This is the most dangerous way of holding a gun during a rest period in a drive. The barrels are pointing straight at the next stand. It is a regrettable fact that even experienced shots are occasionally guilty of resting a gun on their knees in this hazardous fashion. A gun should never be held across the body, but always at a right angle to it.

From this natural and relaxed stance the shooter is in position to take any flying shot that offers.

The left heel is lifted and the gun-barrels move smoothly to meet a middle height incoming pheasant.

The left heel is well up and the weight of the body on a stiff right leg to take a tall pheasant.

The shooter is well back, with his weight on the right leg, to take a high pheasant overhead.

A pivot on the right foot and the weight on the left leg to take a partridge on the left in front.

A pivot well round on the right toe to take a partridge behind. A typical second barrel shot.

With a pivot of the right leg, the shot is taken on a firm left leg at a high pheasant on the left.

With a pivot of the left toe, and the weight on the right leg to deal with a back partridge, right.

The shooter prepares to fire as the loader stands with the second loaded gun held by the small of the butt and pointing skywards.

The shooter has fired. The loader pushes forward the second gun, taking over the emptied gun by the fore-end. Note safe muzzle angles.

The loader turns and, bending so as not to impede the shooter's aim, takes the fired gun and re-loads, with down-tilted barrels.

Still bending the loader holds the gun with muzzles uppermost and checks the shooter's position before returning to first stance.

DRY PRACTICE: PARTRIDGE SHOOTING: 'FIRE'

(Starting from the ready position, the exercises on these pages should be followed, gun in hand, in dry practice with snap caps.)

Turn, with a pivot of the right toe, to take a forward partridge, left.

Make an almost complete turn to take a back partridge, left.

Make a reverse turn to take a forward partridge on the right.

Swing round as far as you can to take a back partridge on the right.

The weight is on the right foot to take a high pheasant on the right.
Note that the whole body shapes like an additional stock behind the
gun. Further, that the body is balanced so that recoil is taken by the
whole frame. In tall pheasant shooting, you should present the actual
physical appearance of stretching to stroke your bird out of the sky.

A rabbit breaks out on the right. The shooter, in the ready position, leans forward on his right leg to decline his body for the shot.

As you take fur on the right, your whole body should cant forward to take the shot from a natural position as the gun swings.

A rabbit on the left. The body sways forward and the weight is taken on the left leg as the gun lifts from the ready position.

'Fire' at a rabbit on the left. Compare this forward position for taking a ground shot with the stance assumed for high pheasants.

A back view of the moment of firing at a high pheasant on the left. The inset reveals the problem of guessing the height of tall pheasants. The three posts are erected ten yards distant from each. The first or lowest board is 1 yard in length, the second or middle one 2 yards in length, the third 3 yards. To the eye they all look alike (see pages 65–66).

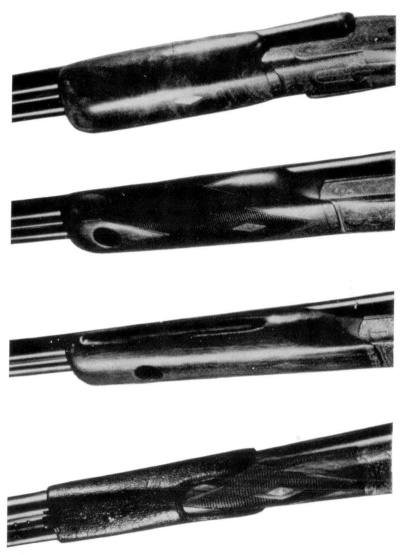

The three upper photographs show variations of the American beaver-tail grip, which is probably the most satisfactory fore-end so far devised (*see page* 197). The lower photograph illustrates the metal leather-covered handguard which can be slipped on to any double-barrelled gun. The handguard assists gun-mounting and protects the fingers when the barrels get uncomfortably hot through constant shooting, or uncomfortably cold in hard weather. The ordinary handguard is inclined to slip unless fitted to the barrels with a special clip.

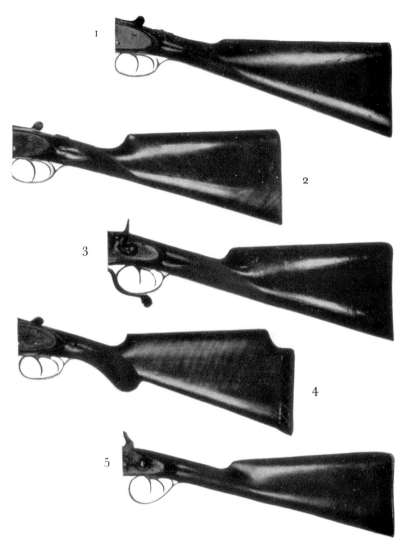

1. The grip of many modern guns, although graceful, is too straight for practical mounting. 2. The grip of Churchill Short-Barrelled Guns is designed to preserve a graceful design but to keep the eye parallel to the line of sight. 3. The 'roach-bellied' shape is copied from the old muzzle-loaders. It has a pleasant contour and a comfortable grip. 4. This is the notched stock of a trap-shooting gun specially adapted to the needs of competition shooting. 5. A traditional stock which is handsome but impractical for modern driven game shooting.

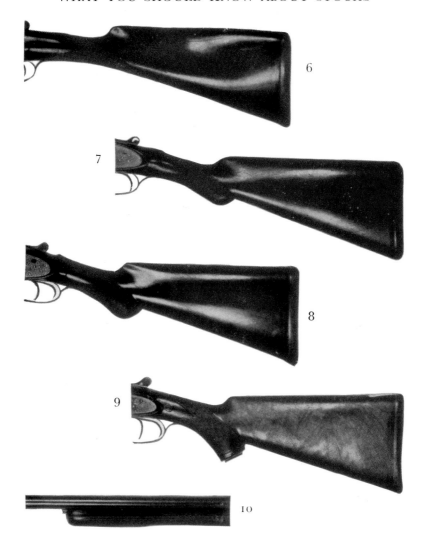

6. An example of a full left-eyed gun stock which is often the most suitable stock for a man with abnormal sight. 7. This is the pistol grip which, in its various degrees, is very suitable for single trigger guns. 8. The half pistol grip is suitable for the trap gun or for walking-up game. 9. The full pistol grip is another form which is favoured for specialized shooting but which is normally unsuitable for ordinary driven game shooting. 10. An example of a gun with a deepened fore-end. It is sometimes a palliative for bad gun-mounting.

(*Gun-stock variations are discussed in greater detail under the figures in the chapter 'The Measurements of a Gun.'*)

EVERY SHOOTING MAN SHOULD RECOGNISE THESE MARKS

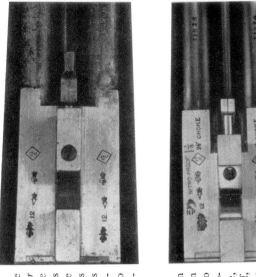

THE LONDON PROOF HOUSE

These marks show that the gun has been proved *for black powder only.* They are found on guns made as late as 1925; but if you see them it generally means proof before 1896. It is dangerous to shoot cartridges loaded with nitro powder through these barrels.

Guns carrying these London marks were proved between 1925 and 1955. From left to right, the marks read: Provisional proof, bore size, view mark, definitive proof, nominal bore size, chamber length, nitro proof mark, maximum charge of shot in ounces.

The London marks (under the 1954 rules) introduced on February 1, 1955. From left to right they read: Provisional proof, bore size, nitro proof, nominal bore size, chamber length, highest mean service pressure for which gun is proved.

THE BIRMINGHAM PROOF HOUSE

Marks which show that the gun is proved for black powder only, and is therefore unsafe under the additional pressure of modern nitro powders. Guns carrying these marks date to 1904, when the crowned mark changed, to the BV. BP. NP. type below.

This is the most common type of marking found on used shotguns. It shows the nitro proof marks which became compulsory in 1925, and includes details of chamber length and shot load. This gun is safe for use with modern powders.

The series of marks introduced in February, 1955, which gives details of service pressure to the square inch. The mark at the bottom left corner—in this case LBI—is the private viewer's mark which in code gives the name of the viewer who passed the gun and the year in which it was proved.

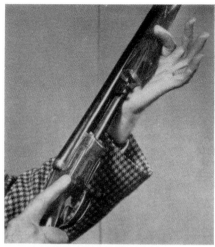

Far too many shooters handle their guns any-old-how. Mounting and dismounting a gun should be carried out as a drill. To dismount, remove the fore-end and place it forward of the barrel-loop. Grasping the fore-end over the barrel-loop, bend the breech of the gun and remove the barrels.

When, the barrels are removed, hold the stock under your arm and replace the fore-end on the barrel-loop. This is how the gun should be put away. It is also the manner, with the fore-end attached, in which the barrels should be held when cleaning the gun. Assembling the gun, the drill is reversed.

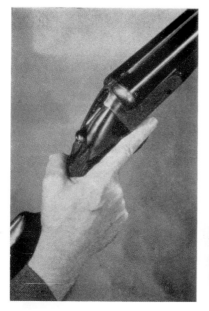

This is a gun designed to enable a one-armed man to use it with comfort, ease and confidence.

The lever that releases the barrels is twisted to give complete one-handed control of his weapon.

Without altering grip, the shooter can control the movement of the safety catch with his thumb.

Without altering grip, he can also use his thumb to operate the lever releasing the easy-opening barrels (*see pages* 230–231).

handling and gun-mounting in the natural standing position, when all the conditions are in your favour. In other words, even though you may find yourself crouched against a sea wall, you must still mentally think of yourself as if you were handling your gun in the most comfortable and natural position. Your body, from the waist upwards, must still move with the bird and you must be more careful than ever, in a cramped position, to check that you are not bringing your cheek to your gun but bringing the gun to your cheek. Head movement is the besetting sin of wild-fowlers who have had to wait a very long time for the chance of a shot.

To check on your personal style I recommend you to assume the sort of position you will probably have to assume in a hide, when you are after wildfowl, with your gun in your hand in front of a mirror. Pick a point on the ceiling well over your head and try swinging your body as smoothly as you can from the waist at the same time mounting the gun until you come on to your target.

As you practise, watch your head. If your head is coming down to the gun or going back too far, as it often does in wild-fowling, you have discovered the reason why you are missing. If you feel that you are not following your bird with your chest, in the same way that you should feel you are following your bird with your whole body when you can assume a natural stance, you can be sure that, on the marshes, you will be missing behind. Notice, as you squat in a cramped position in front of the mirror, how important it is that when your legs are immovable, you should have complete freedom of your arms.

Remember that point when you make a hide. No matter how cleverly you fool the fowl, you are wasting your time unless you settle yourself in a position where you have got this freedom of arm and chest movement which is so important. It is possible in a completely restricted position to make a going-away snap shot, but very few shots at wildfowl are going-away snap shots. Most of them are crossing shots and straight-on shots and in most cases the birds are moving fast. Always try to shoot at the beak and trust your eye to make the necessary overthrow.

The greatest problem of the wildfowler, whose game is often scarce and, on so many morning or evening flights, not even existent at all, is that, when he gets a chance, he commits all the crimes of over-anxiety. If you try and make too sure of your bird you will inevitably hang on the trigger and start poking the gun about making wild and incalculable 'forward allowances.' Your gun must sweep the sky on to your bird in the same way, and at the same pace, that the birds sweep over you. I am only too well aware that it isn't easy; but that's what you've got to do.

Apart from the necessity of making sure that your hide is not only a good hide, but that you yourself are established in a position in which you can swing your arms with comfort, the consideration of the clothes you wear is of major importance. Too many wildfowlers dress exclusively for the weather. You must take care to put on only enough sweaters, coats and scarves to keep warm. If you put on too much you will inevitably sacrifice the freedom in your arms and pad out your shoulder to such an extent that, even a gun which fits you in normal conditions, may be as much as half an inch too long in the stock. Wear loose-fitting clothes for preference, rather than clothes that hug on to your body like thick wool sweaters and heavy tweeds. The secret of keeping warm, and still remaining active, which the bomber pilots used in the war should be noted by everyone; wear thin silk next to the skin and a layer of wool on top of that. It is surprising how the combination of the two will keep your body warm and your muscles active while, at the same time, giving you plenty of freedom to swing your gun. Alternatively, if you must pad yourself out against the weather, it would be better, when you are wildfowling, to use a shorter stocked gun than you normally use on the inland shooting field.

Traditionally, wildfowlers have a tendency to use the heaviest calibred guns they can carry. In the old days anything less than an 8- or 10-bore would have been called a toothpick and, even in these days, I am surprised by the number of wildfowlers who still prefer to go out shooting with old heavy 12s and antique weapons of various kinds which must reduce the performance of even the best shot considerably.

No gun that you take out can possibly be ideal for all purposes. A modern 10-bore probably has a range of at least ten yards better than the 12, and they can be built as light today as the heavy 12-bores of yesterday. But very few men can afford to have a battery of guns for all sorts of purposes. In most cases the wildfowler wants a gun which will serve him reasonably well, and in all sorts of conditions, from the beginning of the season to the end, and from the stubbles to the widgeon grass. From every

point of view I believe that the best 12-bore you can afford,
even with normal loads, is in the long run likely to be just as
efficient as the most arm-breaking 8- or 10-bore cannon such as
our forebears favoured in the past.

The reason is simple. Ease of handling, in the difficult conditions in which wildfowlers have to shoot, is far more important
than the capacity of the gun to push a charge a few yards farther
or throw up a pattern with a few more shots. More than that, I
believe you will get twice as many shots with a 12-bore as
you will with an 8-bore because, with the latter gun, so many
chances are missed through slow gun-mounting. Further, I
would recommend you to use a gun with short barrels. The
increase of the speed that it will give you in your gun-mounting
will make yards of difference to the range at which you are
usually able to take your bird. Nevertheless the powerful charge,
and the longest possible range and the greatest penetration, does
seem to have an effect on the morale of the average wildfowler.

The man who cannot afford a battery of guns and to whom
the cost of cartridges is a serious consideration, should try to own
a long-chambered 12. It is handier than the heavier guns and,
although there is a slight loss of range, you have still got a powerful
charge and, in addition, you can get on to your bird more
quickly and in a long day you won't find it so tiring carrying it.

Remember that, with ordinary game guns, and ordinary game
cartridges, birds can be killed up to sixty yards. Wildfowl in
winter plumage need a greater penetration of shot than inland
game birds, but you can overcome this very largely by increasing
the size of shot. If you get yourself a long-cased 12-bore
firing two-and-three-quarter inch or three-inch cartridges I don't
think you will ever regret it. Besides being an excellent all purpose wildfowl gun, it is also a valuable gun for shooting high
pheasants and big hares. Bored right half choke and left full
choke, short cases *can* be used provided care is taken to clean the
chambers as well as the barrels at the end of the day.

Whatever gun you take out on the marshes, remember that the
action of the sea air is such that you must take far more care of
it than is necessary if you are only using a gun for inland shooting. Personally, when I am flighting, I wipe the whole of the
actions over with oil before going out. Other wildfowlers even go
so far as to have their barrels painted, partly as an extra protection from the action of the salt, but also to reduce the glint of the

barrels which might turn the duck; although, in practice, by the time the duck sees the barrels of your gun coming up, he ought to be dead. Every wildfowler should be even more particular than most shooting men to see that his gun is completely overhauled by a competent gunsmith at the end of each season.

To sum up:

(1) CAMOUFLAGE. In your anxiety to camouflage yourself so that the duck can't see you, don't restrict your movements to such an extent that you have very little chance of bringing your gun to bear in time on a fast-flying duck at all.

(2) CLOTHES. Don't muffle yourself up to such an extent that you restrict the freedom of your arms or pad out your shoulder so that you artificially make the stock of a well-fitting gun too long for you. Either have the stock shortened or, better, wear silk against the skin and only thin wool or cloth on top of that.

(3) GUN-MOUNTING. In dry practice learn to swing your gun from the waist, keep your head still and sweep your birds out of the sky.

(4) DISTANCES. Generally speaking wildfowl tend to look bigger and seem nearer than they really are. Don't make yourself a reputation as a man who pricks his birds. You must learn the hard way to gauge the relative ranges of game which, in a morning's shooting, may range from a jack snipe to a wild goose.

(5) THE GUN. Although you may be tempted to carry as heavy and powerful a gun as you can, remember that you need to be a very strong man indeed to carry a calibre as large as 8-bore. In most cases you will do much better with a 12-bore with short barrels, preferably chambered for magnum cartridges. What you lose in range you will gain from the fact that you will bring up your gun quicker; you will get on to your bird when he is ten yards nearer; you won't tire so easily; and, if you have got a long drag home when half a pound can make a difference, a light gun will be on your side.

(6) CARE OF GUNS. A wildfowler should bestow far more care on his weapon than a man who only engages in inland shooting. The action of the salt can do terrible damage in an incredibly short length of time. Wipe your gun with Rangoon oil when you go out and, when you come home, clean it in every corner patiently and thoroughly. In addition, always remember that one of the many hazards of wildfowling is the hazard to the gun

itself. Setting out before dawn, fumbling with cartridges in the half light, you may well get careless. Whatever you do, never load your gun without holding up the barrels to what light there is and making sure that you haven't scooped up a lump of mud or got some other obstruction into the tubes. Indeed, whenever you are shooting, it's a good habit to adopt the mannerism of many experienced shots who, before they load their gun, will peep quickly up the barrels and give a sharp blow. The blowing through the tubes is, of course, quite unnecessary; but, somehow the habit comes easily and it is an extra guarantee that you are keeping your eye on what you are up to.

In certain conditions, you may have the opportunity to shoot duck from a punt or on marshes where the sport so closely resembles normal driven game shooting that it is unnecessary to give different advice to that I have given for shooting pheasants, partridges and grouse. All it is necessary to say is that, if you have the good fortune to attend one of those magnificent shoots, where the duck come as thick as pheasants out of the coverts at Holkham, it is of the greatest importance that you don't start shooting except at a pre-arranged signal by the host or the keeper. Nothing will make you more unpopular on an organized duck shoot than if you start blinding off at tall birds when the first few wisps of them come over. Duck can very easily rise out of range. The moment to begin shooting is when the guns are in position and the duck are coming over at heights when they present reasonable shooting for the whole party.

When duck are plentiful the golden rule is to resist with iron will the temptation to open fire at the very high overhead birds you sight first; even if you calculate that they are within killable range. If you do that the duck that follow will swing skywards and fly still higher; probably out of range altogether. The shooter's reward for resisting a fancy shot at the start of the morning flight is that the duck that follow will all come down to normal range and, if they really want to come in, will give you good shooting over a long period.

Shooting from a boat has problems of its own. Some men prefer to shoot sitting down. But, if you can stand steadily in a rocking boat without falling over, you are more likely to shoot better that way than otherwise. It's all a matter of personal taste. The best position for you is the one in which you feel you can shoot

L.

most comfortably against the rock of the boat. In specialized shooting of this kind, it is always well to remember that it is certain that there will be local rules as to the time to shoot, the technique of picking up and the exchange of signals, usually by whistles, between guns. Make sure, if you have the good fortune to be invited as a guest to a shoot of this kind, to learn precisely what the local rules are.

Shooting as I do in various parts of the world, I am never ashamed, not only to speak to my host privately, but to get him to explain to all the guns present exactly how the shooting will be conducted. Sometimes guns are too shy to admit that they don't know the form. Sometimes hosts are too polite to say in advance what the form is. You will be popular with everybody if you see to it that the position is crystal clear.

VIII

Various

'VARIOUS' can include an odd partridge in the bag at a covert shoot or, as I once remember, an odd pheasant when we were reducing the population of moorhens in an East Anglian duck decoy. But, generally speaking, 'Various' means the odd and interesting additions to the main bag such as woodcock and snipe, wood pigeons, jays, grey squirrels and other vermin.

Some shoots make a practice of having a forfeit of a few shillings from each gun for every head of vermin that is shot; the spoils to be proportionately divided among the guns who killed them. It's good fun if you are in company where the guns can be trusted not to take chances in their anxiety not to miss the chance at a jay, a magpie or a grey squirrel leaping across the tree branches. It can be very dangerous if guns get over excited, crouching down, as I have so often seen them, go snap at a jay switchbacking with its rising and falling flight just over the heads of the beaters. Better to lose five bob and let the next man take the risky chance.

Never forget the story told of the head-keeper who, on celebrating his hundredth birthday, was interviewed by the press. Asked to what he attributed his great age, he replied that it was because he had never failed to throw himself flat on his face at the cry of 'woodcock.' I hope that that anecdote sticks in your mind as a reminder that, at the call of 'cock' from the beaters, the vital thing is to keep your head. It's a great pity that woodcock have a false reputation that they are difficult to shoot and, further, that they carry those pin feathers which shooting men are so anxious to put up in the ribbon of their hats.

Woodcock have a slow and easy flight, and when they give a chance of a shot it is usually at close range. But they tend to fly low and to weave their way through woodland where every branch can deflect a shot charge. In their anxiety to bag one shooting men constantly forget every basic rule they have learnt. They shoot on sight, and they snap without consideration. I don't think it would be an exaggeration to say that somebody takes a chance nearly every time a woodcock flits down the line.

Let the other man have the cock if he must. If he misses, you yourself can have the satisfaction of wiping his eye after giving yourself time to make sure that you take the bird in a safe arc of fire. The crossing shot is the one to watch; that's the dangerous one. The bird that flies straight over can, and should be, snapped like a partridge in front.

Don't hustle. There is no need. I repeat that woodcock are slow fliers and, in woodland when they zigzag between the gaps in the trees, the gaps are usually even helpful in concentrating your eyes on the bird. Notice how often you will make a clean kill at a pheasant, hustled up by a spaniel in thick woodland when there is only one narrow area of sky in which you get a good sight of him. In fact, the cloaking of trees has the effect of forcing you to concentrate on looking at the bird. And if you look at the bird, and only the bird, you'll always be on him with your gun-barrels.

Snipe are far more difficult to shoot than woodcock; but there's a knack to snipe shooting, too. When a wisp of snipe blows off a marsh in the wind you *must* be quick. Your gun should be at the 'ready position' whenever you expect snipe and you should shoot at the moment when the bird turns in the air after its initial spring from the ground to show you the white of its rump. It's the same moment that the snipe drops a spot of lime as it throws-over to settle into its characteristic zigzag flight. If you wait until the bird settles on its course you will be just plumb lucky if you make a kill. To be certain, you must catch it when it hangs momentarily in the air between the lift from the ground and the going-away flight.

Experienced snipe shots count it so important to kill their bird at the psychological moment that many of them will shoot before their gun is properly settled to the shoulder. I don't recommend the practice (nor do I think it necessary) but it emphasizes the necessity of shooting at snipe at the right time rather than at the moment when you yourself have had time to get ready for it. When you are snipe shooting you must be on your toes. Within a fraction of a second of the bird breaking out of the marsh, with its characteristic scauping call, your gun-stock should be on its way to your shoulder.

Finally, you will always make incalculable misses at snipe if you shoot with shot larger than number seven. Number eight is preferable if you are out on a day when you are concentrating on shooting snipe and snipe only. But number seven is the minimum if you want consistent results. The pattern thrown by number five or number six, if it is the slightest degree off centre, has gaps in it which are well within the bulk of the target.

Throughout this book, I have deliberately refrained from discussing naturalist's lore and the artifices of getting up to game which are the essential corollaries of good shooting. Unless you are something of a naturalist, unless you know how to find game and get within range of it, half of the sport will be lost and, apart from driven game, you will only get in range of half the potential targets. But that can be learnt and it has already been widely discussed in many admirable textbooks. I am concerned with helping you to shoot straight.

For that reason I am assuming that, if you go out after pigeons, you will know how to pick a flight line, how to build a hide, how to set up decoys, and how to pick the crops that the 'woodies' are likely to be feeding on at different seasons. The shooter who doesn't study the habits of pigeons had just as well not go out after them at all. And shooters who haven't learnt how to get among them usually reveal it by declaring that pigeon shooting doesn't provide first-class sport.

If you know how to set about it, pigeon shooting, which anybody with a box of cartridges and the confidence of a friendly farmer can enjoy, offers one of the finest sports with a gun a man can have. More than that, if you are a good pigeon shot, and that also implies that you know how to get among them, and to judge the proper moment to shoot them when they are coming in to feed or roost, you can shoot anything that flies.

Not long ago, when one of the Government Research Stations wanted wood pigeons to make post-mortems with a view to finding out whether they were in any way responsible for carrying disease, I remember they offered three cartridges for every bird brought in. In my view any man who can kill on an average of one wood pigeon to three cartridges must be a first-class shot.

Wood pigeons have the reputation of requiring a heavy charge of shot to kill them. That's not strictly true. What is true is that pigeons have such a loose plumage that they bulk twice as big as they are. When you shoot at them, and they leave a puff of feathers behind them, you may think to yourself as they carry on, what a lot of punishment they can take. The probability is that you haven't touched them.

Pigeon feathers are so loosely attached that a soft-mouthed gun dog will collect an inconvenient bunch of them all round his jaws and tongue just from carrying a dead pigeon twenty yards or so. For that reason, many dogs are reluctant to retrieve pigeons at all. For that reason, when a few feathers fly on charge, shooters get the notion that the birds they are shooting at are hard hit and are surprised when they carry on.

If you hit the breast of a pigeon, or break a wing, he will come down quick enough. But remember that he is half the size you think he is and you must shoot twice as accurately.

If you can put up a good performance with pigeons, you can take it from me that you can put up a good performance at every game bird that flies. From a hide among the wheatsheafs, from the stand on the edge of a covert when the birds are coming in to roost, you will get every sort of shot you are ever likely to meet in the shooting field. Indeed, with pigeons you will be lucky if you get a straight advancing bird. They nearly all have a curl on them. They can gain height quicker than any of the game birds and, on the wing, their aerobatics are quick enough to defeat a hawk. If you make the slightest mistake in gun-mounting, if the alignment of your gun is to the slightest degree out of the true, if you drop your head, if you don't swing your gun sweetly in pace with the movement of the bird, you will miss them. If you kill a fast oncoming pigeon cleanly you can congratulate yourself that you have brought off a shot in which the slightest fault in gun-handling would have beaten you.

It's true that, in certain conditions, pigeon shooting can be relatively easy; personally, it's not the easy shooting that I would have for choice. But, if you are shooting over a field of cabbages in hard weather, if you have got a hide under a skeleton tree which is the sort of observation-post pigeons always favour in the harvest field, the chances are that in addition to flying shots you will get a lot of chances at birds when they are roosting or on the ground. Theoretically speaking, nobody should miss a sitting bird. In practice it is surprising how often people do. But there is a simple trick to remember. If you are firing at a roosting pigeon don't shoot at his head, shoot at his pink legs. If you put the charge into his legs you will kill him through the head. If he is sitting on the ground, in the stubble for example, treat him as I told you to treat a crouching hare. If you shoot at his head your charge will go over him. The secret is to place your charge so that it lifts the ground from under his crop.

If you want to become a good pigeon shot, and assuming that you take the trouble to place yourself where you stand a good chance of getting at them, it's not much good going out with the notion of being over economical with cartridges. The secret of mastering pigeons is to keep on shooting at them. The shots that are really worth taking are the shots which the miserly cartridge user wouldn't dream of wasting sixpence on. True, you can kill pigeons with comparative certainty by knocking them out of the trees where they are at roost, or off the stooks when they are feeding on the corn. The sport is to try and shoot them when they are flying past and wild.

Indeed, the all-round shooting man is one who can kill all varieties of game in all sorts of conditions. And, if you master the drill in this book, you ought to be able to do so in all conditions pretty well anywhere.

In fact, I am well aware that men who can shoot quite brilliantly when they are walking by themselves along the hedgerows fold up completely when they are invited to an organized drive through the coverts. That is largely a matter of nerve; but it is also an indication that the drill of gun-mounting and gun-handling has not become the habit it ought to have done.

When you miss a bird or a rabbit or a hare don't be content to say 'damn.' You shouldn't be satisfied with yourself until you can say to yourself. 'I was behind that bird about one foot. The reason I was behind was because I dropped my head as I mounted the gun and I think that I held my trigger just a fraction too long. I think I missed, in fact, because I was a little over-anxious. Next time, I'll bring up my gun smoothly; I'm not going to worry whether I hit or miss but I am going to make up my mind that, whatever else I do, I'm going to keep my eye on the target.' You will find that this personal reasoning with yourself, whether you are at an organized shoot or walking alone over the stubbles, will help you to shoot better.

When the Metropolitan Police are training the drivers of police cars, they teach them, as part of the drill, to say out loud all the thoughts that come into their minds as they drive along the road. For example, the driver will say: 'There's a child on the pavement in front of me who might easily cross the road without warning. There's a lorry there coming out of that side road which may or may not halt as it should. I'll act on the assumption that the driver won't halt. Look out, here's a pedestrian crossing.'

You couldn't do better than to apply the same technique to yourself when you are shooting. Think all the time what you are doing, and tell yourself what you are doing right and what you are doing wrong. Above all, remember that there is a great deal more to first-class shooting than straight shooting. The men who bring in most of the bag are not necessarily the best shots. They are the men who anticipate before the drive begins where and how, in the light of the conformation of the ground, and the state of the wind, birds are likely to fly. They are the men who seem to know instinctively when something is going to show.

I remember a great partridge shot saying to me that, when he was walking-up, he could sense when he was drawing close to a covey of partridges and when it was likely to get up. That was simply another way of saying that he had become so experienced that, as he walked over the ground, he could calculate where partridges were likely to be in different conditions and at different times of the day. That knowledge enabled him in most cases to kill two birds before the next man down the line had realized that a covey had been flushed at all. You can learn this field know-how far better when you are walking out with a gun by yourself. Learn to consider the possibilities of every tree, of every patch of bramble. Learn to read by the behaviour of your dog what he smells moving over the ground. Learn which way the fur and feather is likely to run, or fly, in different conditions. If you know that, you will make up for many faults in shooting. If you don't know that, however excellent a shot you are, you will be shooting at a disadvantage. And you won't have a fraction of the fun you will if you learn the subtleties of the great sport of game shooting.

PART THREE

TRAP SHOOTING

I

How to Shoot Clays

THERE is a great difference between trap shooting and pigeon shooting. Trap shooting or, as it was originally called, clay bird shooting, is the direct descendant of the old practice of pigeon shooting. This, in its turn, is a direct descendant of the pastime of popinjay shooting, still practised in Flanders and of such antiquity that it is mentioned in the *Iliad*. The popinjay was a pigeon tethered by a short length of cord to the top of a tall mast and capable of restricted flight. With bow and arrow a material amount of skill was needed to hit such a small moving target.

The development of the art of shooting on the wing, subsequent to 1760, and the gaming tendencies of the Waterloo period, led to matches between sportsmen in which live pigeons thrown by hand from a pit or from behind a wall furnished the target. Towards the middle of the nineteenth century, rules regulating pigeon shooting contests and the guns and loads to be used were more or less codified, and collapsible boxes known as traps were introduced.

During the late Victorian era live pigeon shooting enjoyed a certain social recognition; but during the present century, it passed out of keeping with social taste in this country and is now no longer legal in Britain, though it is still very popular abroad.

Modern trap-shooting employs discs made of a mixture of pitch and pulverized limestone, and known as clay targets to distinguish them from live birds. Primitive traps, or throwers, designed to eject either clays, or hollow glass balls stuffed with feathers, were introduced during the eighties of the last century. These early devices were not very good. Largely owing to their mechanical imperfection in use these did not achieve immediate popularity. During the past generation very important developments have taken place and the modern automatic clay target trap has brought about an astonishing change in the sport. Clay bird shooting clubs are increasing rapidly, the number of local clubs being a noteworthy feature.

Independently of their value as one of the most pleasant of summer pastimes, and the opportunity they afford for keeping in shooting practice during the close season, they are excellent schools for the novice who wishes to learn how to handle a gun. Clay bird shooting is the most valuable approach to the senior sport. Its educational value is so great that it was adopted during both wars as part of the essential training of the fighting services.

Game shots ask: 'Are the conditions of clay bird shooting any use to me as practice for actual game shooting?' The answer is that they certainly are.

Good shooting depends on a co-ordination of muscular effort, correct stance, correct movement and automatic adherence to certain rules. Trap shooting gives you this practice in a very close approximation to natural conditions. The double rise events, particularly, afford excellent training, whilst the string of successful shots at clays gives one a thrill closely allied to a fine pick-up after a drive. The two are not strictly comparable in all respects but one may safely say that the 'quantity' element in scoring hits on clays is almost as exciting as the 'quality' element in game shooting. In addition, there is the spur of the competitive element and the pleasure of outdoor recreation in company with those of kindred interests.

Though a shooting man may have ever so much sport of a regular kind he would do well to take part in trap shooting meetings when he can conveniently attend them. I have often seen really excellent shots seriously perturbed by the presence of a stranger, perhaps a friend of one of the farmers who has come out to see the sport and, in all innocence, has placed himself behind the one member of the party who is easily put off. Public shooting contests help you to overcome the nervousness of being watched. You learn that you can't shoot your best unless you concentrate. And, having once adopted this attitude, you can obliterate the onlookers from your mind.

Trap shooting differs from game shooting because game rises slowly, gains velocity rapidly and maintains or accelerates speed until out of range. Trap shooting reverses this sequence, the clay being projected at a high velocity which gradually lessens as it reaches the crest of its rise. In practice, we remedy this difference by adopting a different technique which meets the conditions inseparable from artificial targets.

THE POSITION IN WHICH THE GUN IS HELD IS DIFFERENT.

Indeed this section might just as well be entitled 'How to shoot at moving objects with the gun at the shoulder' because this position—with the gun ready mounted to the shoulder—is now universally adopted by the best competition shots. It is quicker, and quickness is the essence of modern trap shooting.

Stance, grip and the technique of gun-mounting are exactly as previously outlined in the drill section and in the field notes on game shooting: with the difference that you mount your gun AND POINT IT AT THE TRAP. You do not shoot at the trap, and you do not keep your head down to the stock. You remain aiming at the trap. The trap is about to throw a target to a known height but at an unknown angle and projection. Thus, if your head is down to the stock, you will not have adequate freedom of movement for the eye to follow the bird, and the gun to follow the eye with accurate alignment in the time.

A close study of the best European and American trap shots reveals systematic head movement as the basis of their skill. If their procedure were analysed by a slow-motion film we should see: (1) the gun is mounted to the shoulder and aimed at the trap; (2) the head is then very slightly eased off the stock; (3) on the appearance of the target the head moves to it first; (4) the gun remains pointed at the trap almost until this head movement is completed and is then raised rapidly to the target which it rapidly overtakes. Discharge occurs on the instant that alignment is obtained.

The whole art of trap shooting is comprised in the ability to take instant aim and pull the trigger practically without visible swing. Speed is all essential. The quick shot has a very marked advantage over the slow shot where clays are concerned, for his speed gives him what is for the moment an apparently stationary target.

If we examine the flight of a clay target we find that it is thrown off the trap to the distance of fifty to fifty-five yards. At about fifteen or twenty yards from the trap it reaches the zenith of its curve. For the next ten yards or so it travels a practically horizontal course. Viewed from the gun stand it appears to be hovering although, in point of fact, it is still moving rapidly away from the shooter. This is the position in which the quick shot takes the target. At the end of its horizontal flight it loses momentum and begins to fall earthward with a pronounced dip. The slower shot, who only comes into action at this stage, has thus a more difficult target to tackle than that of his swifter competitor, independent of the fact that targets that have lost their spin are harder to break; also, at the increased range, a target may pass unbroken through the gaps in the pattern, by now become wide.

The quick shot has the choice of any relative point during the transit of the target over the latter portion of its curve of flight. An expert selects the precise point where he knows his gun will give its best killing pattern.

When you are shooting clays, remember everything in the instructions regarding stance, grip and gun-handling.

Don't put your left hand too far up the barrel, because this makes you shoot behind your right-hand target.

The eye must never be brought down to the rib; the rib should be brought up to the eye.

When mounting a gun at the trap, bed the butt in the right part of the shoulder and do not shift it again.

See that the trigger pull of your gun is both quick and sweet. It must respond instantly. For most people, a bad trigger pull is fatal to good trap shooting.

Apart from practice shooting at clays in the shooting school, the game of trap shooting takes the form of either what is called 'Down the Line' shooting or Skeet.

'Down the Line' trap shooting is the earliest form of clay target shooting. It used to be much more popular than it is today when there were many clubs around London. The reason that it has decreased, rather than increased in popularity in recent years is, I think, largely because the best performers of 'Down the Line' shooting became so monotonously consistent that the novices gave up all hope of trying to compete. This in spite of the fact that in 'Down the Line' shooting a system of handicap is normally employed. The fact is that a man, equipped with a gun specially made for the job and keeping in constant practice, can give the average game shot twenty-five in one hundred and beat him at 'Down the Line'; although the same trick shooter at clays probably wouldn't do much better than the next man at a shoot in which live game were the targets.

The trouble with trap shooting is that it is largely trick shooting. And, although it is great fun when you can hold your own, it is essential that you should study the very special technique which is required. The man who is keen should first get himself a gun which fits him and preferably with a raised ventilated rib. The reason is that trap shooting is so fast that, on a hot day, a mist can form along the rib of an ordinary gun and so obscure the target. Further, a special trap-shooting gun should be laid to shoot level or even slightly below the mark.

In shooting the weight is always on the left foot and the eyes should not be focused on the trap house but just over the top if it, ready to pick up and snap the target as it rises whether right, left or centre.

Many years ago I was a very keen trap shot myself, and it was in competition with me that Frank Troeh, the American champion, first shot 'a hundred straight.' The second 'hundred straight' was made in similar fashion by Alec Maunder. And, subsequently, astonishingly long runs have been made over automatic traps. A few of my American friends have each made runs of over five hundred. And one of them never missed for a week, breaking 1,500 clays straight. I mention that to emphasize how important it is to master the trick of trap shooting. If you want to excel at it it is essential that you perfect your style until you can break the clays with mechanical precision, something that you can never hope to do, however fine a shot you are, in the real shooting field.

The champions at 'Down the Line' shooting adopt many and varying methods. One will hold his muzzles high, another drop them below the traphouse; one keeps his head erect and snaps as the gun touches his cheek, another 'rides' his target; but all follow the essentials of successful shooting at inanimate targets. They don't look for the bird until they see it. When they see it they keep their eye on it. And then they make a smooth swing and a snap finish.

The clay target can be likened to a window-pane. Fire a high velocity bullet through a window and it leaves a neat hole. But take the bullet and throw it with your hand and you will shatter the window. Therefore pattern and not penetration is what is required of the trap-shooting cartridge. You should use one with a smaller charge of powder and a heavier charge of shot. If your cartridge has too high a velocity the pellet can actually go through the target without breaking it.

SKEET

In 1927, I myself introduced the game of Skeet to England. I had seen it at the Western Plant at East Alton at Illinois and was immediately attracted by its possibilities. I still think that Skeet is the best form of competitive clay target shooting for the ordinary game shot. A special gun is not required for it. It lends itself to many variations, and it provides far better practice for live game shooting than 'Down the Line' events.

The technique of shooting at Skeet has been developed by American experts. The basis of their method is that they 'point out' their target; that is, they hold their guns ahead of them in almost the position they intend killing, and, with a barely perceptible movement, yet perfect timing, snap their birds. But I wouldn't advise a beginner to try and begin that way. Although Skeet shooting is not as widely practised here yet as it is in America, here is a description of the various targets and the methods to get good results and good practice (*see diagram on page 178*):

THE FIRST BIRD AT NO. I STAND. You are alongside the High Trap and, from the diagram, you will appreciate that the target is coming from overhead and is going away; but, to your eye, it is flattening out and beating down whilst your gun is coming up in a contrary direction. For this bird only you should hold your muzzle high, put plenty of weight on your left foot, look well ahead and take care not to shoot over the top of it.

THE SECOND BIRD FROM NO. I STAND. This is an easy left incomer from the Low Traphouse. Keep your eye on it, and put a little of your weight on your left foot, don't try and shoot too quickly, yet at the same time don't let it get too close. That sounds a difficult instruction, but if you get the opportunity to shoot at Skeet you will very quickly realize what I am getting at.

THE FIRST BIRD FROM NO. 2 STAND is an away bird from the High Traphouse. Put your right foot forward and put most of your weight on it. Don't look at the Traphouse. Look midway between the Traphouse and the centre and shoot off his 'front leg.'

THE SECOND BIRD FROM NO. 2 STAND needs another change of stance. Draw back the right foot slightly, put a fraction more weight on the left foot, face the centre but swing the body back towards the Low Trap. As with every other bird at Skeet, take care to make a snap finish.

AT NOS. 3, 4 AND 5 STANDS, as you can see from the diagram, we have wider crossing shots. A change of stance is necessary. Put your weight on the right foot for the High Trap bird, on the left foot for the Low Trap one. Don't look at the Traphouse but look at the centre. If you find that you are shooting behind your bird, turn your body a little more towards the particular Traphouse that individual birds are coming from to encourage you to make more body swing.

AT NO. 6 STAND we have what is a fairly easy incoming bird from the High Trap, but it is a really tricky target from the Low Traphouse which is often missed by the slow shot because he is deceived by its direction. If you watch the bird leave the Trap, you can easily be fooled into believing that it will eventually cross your front and end by overshooting it. In fact it doesn't cross your front but rather fades away to your right. You can turn this otherwise difficult target into one of your easiest by putting all your weight on your left foot, looking towards the centre and making a very very fast shot AT THE BIRD'S TAIL. Don't worry to shoot in front of him; your natural overthrow will give you all the necessary lead.

AT NO. 7 STAND we have a couple of easy targets. Put all your weight on your right foot and raise your left heel slightly to the income. Reverse the process for the away bird.

NO. 8 STAND which is situated between the Traphouses can be a difficult one if you don't know how. But High and Low Trap birds are trick shots which require that knowing how to look and how to stand is a matter of the utmost importance. If you look at the Traphouse the bird will come at you like greased lightning and will pass overhead before you can get your gun up. Yet, if you will only look well into the blue, putting your weight on the right foot, raise your left heel bending the body back for a direct overhead shot, you will find the bird climbs into vision and becomes a quick, but nevertheless a simple shot.*

THE LAYING OUT OF SHOOTING GROUND

It is possible today for anyone to make his own shooting ground at very little expense. If it happens that you have only got one trap, a single stand can be erected to match either the low or high Skeet tower and pegs put all over the place exactly as if it were a clock-golf layout.

Hitherto it has been customary to stand alongside a single rise

---

* *There have been changes in the rules of skeet-shooting since this was written. But, as the game is only practised on a limited scale in Britain, Churchill's instructions remain as he gave them.*

M

trap, and blaze away at targets thrown at a known speed, height and angle. This isn't bad practice for the novice but, as soon as possible, he should get more variety into the shots he presents himself. The following diagram is one of many of possible variations:

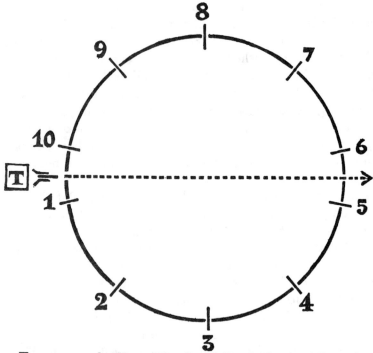

T represents the Trap. The dotted line is the fixed line of flight. The circle is a 30-yard one drawn 15 yards from the trap.

In the diagram, ten different stands are shown. The shooter must always face the Trap; therefore the Trap itself must be shielded. No. 1 Stand is alongside the Trap and gives the straight-away bird. No. 2, ten yards to the left of No. 1, gives the wide left-hander. No. 3 may be released whilst on the walk from No. 2, and gives the shooter an away bird flying slightly to his left. No. 4 is a wide left crossing shot. No. 5 is a fast bird over the left shoulder that needs a quick turn to be killed behind. Nos. 6–10 Stands are the reverse to the above.

The rules should be that all competitors and spectators should always stand at the rear of Nos. 2 and 4 Stands when the shooter is on that side, or at the rear of Nos. 7 and 9 Stands when shooting for the right field.

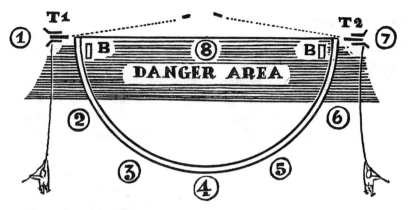

Above is a double Skeet layout to enable the shooter to practise for the whole of the Skeet round. T1 and T2 represent the Traps, B the Blinders.

These layouts are only suitable for sites three hundred yards from tracks and buildings. In other more restricted conditions the Trap must be removed or set to throw targets in a safe direction.

An ideal sporting ground can be made out of a disused chalkpit as these are generally cut out of the hillside and I have seen many where a single Trap can give a variety of incoming high-driven birds from stands in the 'basin' and difficult crossing shots while walking up and around the edges.

If the cost of cartridges is a serious item, competitions may be at five or even at three birds and handicaps may be by distance. The automatic Trap needs at least twenty shooters to form four teams and so give each other a rest, but with the single Trap a party of four can have a most enjoyable meeting, shooting, three, five, eight or ten bird competitions; taking turns in pulling, scoring or refereeing.

You may put your Trap to throw its targets in the best direction. You may make your own plan of layout to give you the practice you need for your particular sport of rough shooting or for driven partridges, grouse and pheasants. But the rule should be that you must move to another stand for the next shot. This last point is most important as in game shooting you are not allowed a second chance.

The single Trap can be adapted for driven birds by placing the Trap the other side of a low hedge for driven partridges; in a tree for overhead pheasants; or firmly secured to a sort of hobby horse it can be carried anywhere you wish. The 'hobby horse' is a tripod mount with two short front legs and one long back one. The Trap is mounted and the trapper sits on the back leg to steady it.

In my own shooting grounds I have set some morning, afternoon and evening stands so that, in summer time, we can always keep our backs to the sun. The 'hobby horse' has a great advantage in that it can also be moved about to suit the state of the light.

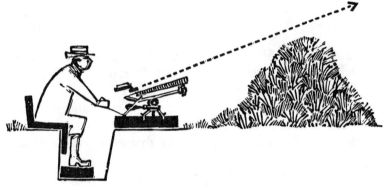

HOW TO SET UP A CLAY PIGEON TRAP

Dig a hole 3 feet deep and wide enough for standing room. A wooden seat with a backboard should be provided for the trapper. Fix the Trap firmly on to a heavy plank to prevent vibration and broken targets. In front of all this, build a protective earthwork low enough to clear the target and high enough to hide the trapper from view.

PART FOUR

GUN KNOW-HOW

I

Game Guns of Today

THERE has been very little progressive development in sporting guns since the modern conventional double-barrelled side-lock ejector became more or less standardized in the last decade of the nineteenth century. There has been a certain amount of detail improvement such as steel barrels replacing Damascus, but to all intent many makers are still regularly turning out a gun with little, if any, variation from their model of a half-century ago.

Most modifications of design have been in the nature of a simplification of lock and ejector mechanisms. New steels have been selected and particular attention has been paid, not so much to reduction of weight as to its better distribution in barrels and action. Coincidentally, there has been an all-round increase in hidden strength to meet conditions liable to be imposed by modern powders. These matters are important but they do not strike the eye; their effect on external appearance is practically nil.

Broadly speaking, the modern gun may be pronounced 20 per cent better balanced, 30 per cent stronger and 40 per cent less likely to fail in functioning details than the guns of our fathers.

Within recent years a certain improvement has been made in barrel boring. Constant experiment has enabled us to evolve methods which give an improved pattern at forty yards. What was unusual in the old days has become common since. For instance, it was exceptional, fifty years ago, to find a gun which would consistently give 70 per cent patterns at forty yards. Today we are able to get this standard of 70 per cent of pellets in the thirty-inch circle at forty yards with absolute certainty. Very often we exceed this average by an additional 5 or 10 per cent. Corresponding improvement has been effected in the lesser degrees of choke now necessary.

This interesting progress in boring is associated with the modern development of the short-barrelled gun. In the matter of shot-gun design, the development of the twenty-five-inch barrelled gun is associated with my name. I regard it as the most significant contribution that I have been able to make, personally, to the improvement of the sporting gun in my time.*

Many years ago, when I first introduced my short-barrelled guns, they aroused a great deal of controversy, and I shall always be grateful to the sportsmen who were the first to take them out into the field and prove, in a practical way, that my theory was right.

When the controversy about short-barrelled guns was at its height it was said that the velocity of the charge would be seriously affected by reducing the barrels from thirty or twenty-eight inches to twenty-five inches. Other older sportsmen, who had been accustomed to using guns with barrels of thirty inches or more, protested that my short-barrelled guns didn't 'look right.'

Today, forty years after, the short-barrelled gun is so widely used in the shooting field that it is the man with barrels thirty inches long under his arm who carries a weapon that looks out of date. But as a well-made shot-gun is an arm which will last a generation or more, a great many people are still using the twenty-eight and thirty-inch barrelled guns which were in fashion when I introduced my own shorter and lighter model. For that reason, it may be as well if I state, once again, the reasons that led me to introduce the short-barrelled gun and the advantages in shooting which this type of shot-gun design affords.

Modern conditions call for maximum strength and shooting qualities, minimum weight compatible with low recoil, perfect balance and something beyond the poise and ease of manipulation characteristic of the best examples of ordinary guns. The old thirty-inch barrel is a relic of past ages and is purely a survival from the black powder period. It has long been common knowledge that smokeless powder will permit a very radical reduction of barrel length, but conservative tendencies amounting to prejudice suggested that this reduction could only be made at the expense of pattern and penetration.

In point of fact, almost all velocity is generated in shotguns with smokeless powders within a few inches of the chamber and is not materially increased as the charge approaches the muzzle. The shooting or pattern is regulated at the muzzle-end of the barrel, independent of length. It does not matter whether the muzzle is thirty or twenty- five inches from the breech; velocity

* See Foreword.

of the charge is not affected and the pattern has to be regulated by the usual methods of control.

A century ago, a barrel of less than thirty-six inches long would have been derided. With the establishment of the early breech-loaders, firing the same charge of powder and the same kind of powder as the old muzzle-loaders, barrels shortened to thirty inches. At the close of the century, the demand for light guns for driven game reduced the length to twenty-eight inches. Today, the modern twenty-five-inch is as good as the longer barrels; it shoots as strongly and gives as good a pattern. In addition, the short-barrelled twenty-five-inch gun shows an improvement in weight, in balance and in ease of handling. The reduction of effort needed in gun-mounting allows steadier yet quicker shooting.

It is self-evident that you can bring the muzzle of a gun which is only twenty-five inches long quicker on to the target than you can barrels of twenty-eight or thirty inches long. And, in fact, what we have learnt from experience is that the shorter barrel tends to have an upward flip on delivering the charge just as thirty-inch barrels have a definite downward flip as they are fired. As the commonest error in shooting is to miss behind, it follows that the short-barrelled gun is more likely to make you lift up your charge to meet the target and the long-barrelled gun more likely to cause you to miss behind.

There is a very slight difference in the velocity of the charge from a short-barrelled gun and a longer one. But shot-gun velocities are never taken as muzzle velocities. Over twenty yards, the commonly occurring difference between twenty-five and thirty-inch barrels is usually well under forty feet per second. Muzzle velocity cannot be measured, it can only be inferred, but while this inference is exact in the case of rifle bullets, the changing form of a shot charge of a column of shot that it throws forbids calculation. But these are technicalities you need not be concerned with.

As I have cause to explain, in many places in this book, most game gun shooting is carried out well within the potential striking range of the gun. As any loss in the velocity of the charge between short-barrelled and long-barrelled guns is quite insignificant, the matter is a purely theoretical one for ballisticians and firearms experts. You can take it from me that the speed at which you can bring a short-barrelled gun to a target far, far outweighs any theoretical loss of striking range.

It was tentatively suggested, many years ago, that short barrels
are more difficult to align and that the sportsman using them
missed the guidance afforded by the extra barrel length. This
argument, even if it were true, would only hold good in the case
of those very rare shots who actually aim their guns as a rifle is
aimed; who shoot, in fact, in the very manner which I advocate
that the shooting man should avoid. But even people who
'aim' their guns are not so much influenced by barrel length
as by 'apparent barrel length'; they are victims of an optical
illusion.

When the controversy about short-barrelled guns was at its
height, shortly after the first World War, Major Hugh B. C.
Pollard summed up the situation about barrel length in an article
in *Country Life*. I cannot do better than to quote him here:

'The most effective ground for criticism of a short barrel is
that the eye, accustomed to guidance along the top rib to the
foresight, so to speak, misses the customary extra five inch of
barrel, and that the short gun gives "a sense of something missing." This is very plausible but I am not altogether certain
whether it really means anything.

'The game shot is seldom conscious of his foresight at all. His
eye is on the bird, and it is only after discharge that the muzzles
lift momentarily and give him a glimpse of half a foot of barrel.
He certainly "sees" the barrels as they come up to the line of
sight, but he should not have them in focus.

'I am inclined to believe that the "sense of something missing"
is purely psychological and entirely illusory. Whether it is visual
illusion is open to doubt, for, if a large foresight, improvised out
of a bead of sealing wax, is applied to a standard game gun of
twenty-eight- or thirty-inch barrels, the barrel appears short, and
a twenty-five-inch barrel with a small foresight appears comparatively longer than the other.

'It follows that if a "sense of something missing" is due to an
optical illusion, a small foresight to a short gun compensates for
it. If, on the other hand, it is, as I suspect, psychological rather
than actual, and due to the unanticipated swiftness of response of
the shot-gun, it will vanish as soon as the new gun is used in the
field or at practice at clays, and is a testimony of the handiness of
the new type. After all, driving a different kind of car for the first
time often produces a feeling of strangeness, but it has never been

suggested that progress in car development should be restricted because of this transient feeling of difference.'

This elucidation by Major Pollard not only explains the point at issue but will interest many of the earlier users of short-barrelled guns. These, as originally built, have the usual wide shot-gun rib with the ordinary foresight, and, in consequence, gave a noticeable impression of shortness until the eye became accustomed to them.

Today the later short-barrelled guns are made with a special form of rib and sights in strict proportion. The rib taper is specially designed to harmonize with the perspective effect of the barrels, as seen by the eye, when the gun is mounted to the shoulder. The result is astonishingly effective, for a twenty-five-inch barrelled gun is thus made to convey to the eye the effect of a full thirty inches. It can easily be made to appear longer.

The optical illusion is so complete that, if a man mounts one of my own twenty-five-inch guns to his shoulder, with his eyes closed, and then opens them to look along the rib, he will find it impossible, except as guesswork, to measure the barrel length with his eye.

But, although the modern short-barrelled gun is now an accepted improvement, many sportsmen who read this book will themselves be using guns of an older and, in many cases, more cumbersome pattern.

What I teach in this book about gun-handling applies equally to any sportsman whatever weapon he uses; but I want to emphasize that I hope all who can will, sooner or later, adopt the more modern type of short-barrelled gun. The many years of my life that I have devoted to giving instruction in shooting have clearly shown that it takes approximately four times as much ammunition and four times as many hours of practice to enable the average individual to attain a modern standard of efficiency with the long barrel as to reach the same stage with the twenty-five-inch barrelled gun.

Years are necessary to learn the really perfect handling of the old long gun. Today the short gun, with its far, far better balance, becomes 'part of yourself' in a quarter or less of the time. The first season or so with the old guns was always a matter of 'chance it.' With the new type, 'sense of direction' is quickly achieved; success with it is not empirical but logical. The twenty-five-inch gun is easier to shoot with—best of all to shoot really well with—and not less effective in pattern and penetration than any of the old long-barrelled types. Essentially modern in its adaptation to the modern cartridge it dismisses the obsolete parts.

Just as we now find it more convenient to live in smaller houses, and use lighter and shorter fishing rods, so in the matter of guns the most convenient gun is the modern lightweight twenty-five-inch. It has been redesigned in every detail, re-balanced, fined down and perfected during forty years of careful critical and invariably progressive work. It is harmonious within itself and in tune with its partner, the modern cartridge.

The gun-maker, who knows no better than to supply his customer with the old standard fowling piece, having barrels shortened to twenty-five inches, is bound to meet with disappointment; and I must warn any sportsman who, reading this, thinks that, by carving a few inches off his own barrel, he can bring his gun into line with modern practice that that policy won't work. Apart from the fact that he will interfere with the choke of his existing gun he will also be using a weapon which isn't designed overall for the shorter barrel length.

My short-barrelled guns are not a wedding of old and new, they are something quite new altogether. I claim for them that they handle like a 20-bore, shoot as hard as a 10-bore, look as long as thirty inches when aligned on a bird and, most important of all, that they quicken the faculties of the shooter and reduce fatigue because they are twice as comfortable as the old heavy guns to carry. Lighter weight and increased strength, better functional design and better handling qualities are the chief characteristics of the best modern shot-gun. Indeed the improvement has been so marked that one effect is that, these days, all bores except 12-bores are virtually obsolete.

I suppose that practically all guns made in London and Birmingham today are in fact 12-bores of one kind or another. The popularity of 16-bores, 20-bores and 10-bores all date back to a time when the larger calibred guns were much too heavy for many people, and the smaller calibred guns suited sportsmen who through physical disability or personal taste, preferred not to carry a gun weighing 7 lb. or more.

Today the modern 12 weighs as little as the 20- or 16-bore of half a century ago. The 16 and 20 have been replaced by the light 12-bore chambered for 2-inch cartridges.

(At the time this text-book was written, Churchill was enthusiastic about light 12-bores chambered for 2-inch cartridges. In his latter years he used a pair himself. None of us who saw him shoot with them considered that the guns were adequate to kill tall pheasants. We suspected that the only reason he used them was because he was beginning to feel the weight of the flying years. There is no sign yet of such guns supplanting the 16 and 20.

It is important to remember that the London gunmakers, having developed a near-perfect implement for its limited purpose, have always inclined to exaggerate the importance of minor modifications. In the first edition of this book, Churchill enthused over a new type of under-and-over gun he had developed. As it was a flop, in this edition I have excised the reference to it.

But his 25-inch barrelled guns have stood the test of time. While they don't suit everybody, as I have pointed out in the foreword, they are a boon to many, especially to middle-aged men and those with physical disabilities who think their day is done. I can't honestly recommend them to a big-boned tall man (although I've seen Lord Rank using one).

It's amusing to recall that, at one time, Churchill toyed with the notion of making guns with shorter barrels still. Major Hugh B. C. Pollard demonstrated to him that, below 25-inch, the crack of the report is unpleasant to the ear.)

At the other end of the scale the 10-bore wildfowling gun of our forefathers has been succeeded by the more heavily built 12-bore wildfowling guns made to take 3-inch and 2¾-inch cartridge cases.

There is, of course, every reason why sportsmen should take advantage of the change whenever they can. First, the variation of cartridge sizes is an inconvenience. Second, the 20-bore is always a dangerous gun to keep in the same house as the 12-bore because the 20-bore cartridges just stick in the top of a chamber cone of a 12 gun. In the event of a 20-bore cartridge being accidentally loaded in front of a 12-bore a burst or perhaps a serious accident is almost unavoidable. The same danger exists in the case in which a 28-bore, or a 16-bore, is kept in the same house as a 20-bore. The answer these days, if you want to have a range of guns, is to have a very light 12-bore chambered for 2-inch cartridges; a medium weight gun which, these days, shouldn't weigh more than 6 lb. for the standard game gun cartridge; and, finally, a magnum short-barrelled gun, full choke if you like, for wildfowling.

All I need add to these comments on the development of the

game gun, as it exists today, is to excuse myself for not referring to the modern automatic or pump gun. These are admirable and cheap weapons for a man who wants to use his gun to keep down vermin or to make an occasional expedition to collect a bird for the pot. But any man who tries to shoot with an automatic shot-gun under the test conditions of driven game will never be able to compete with a first-class shot with a properly measured and properly balanced double-barrelled game gun in his hand. For that reason, automatic guns have never been popular and, in many places, actively unwelcome in the English shooting field.

I know that some men can use them with considerable efficiency; but I often wonder how much better they would shoot if they had a gun of lesser weight, better balanced and more pedigree construction in their hands.

This textbook is directed to the sportsman who wants to get the best out of himself under test conditions. Even the idea that the automatic gun, pumping up to five cartridges into the breech one after another, is more deadly than the ordinary double-barrelled shot-gun is an illusion. It might be advantageous for pumping lead into a cloud of pigeons on a wheat field but, in ordinary sporting conditions, it is a slow-action, ill-balanced and ugly weapon.

So far as the actual range of the charge is concerned, the effective punch of any gun, even the cheapest mass-produced object, is just the same as the range of the best shot-gun that money can buy. In spite of the fact that sportsmen persist in speaking of their own guns as particularly hard-hitting guns the truth of the matter is that all guns hit more or less the same. All that the gun does is to explode the propellant inside the cartridge and the shot travels just as far as the propellant pushes it. Why you should buy the best gun that you can possibly afford is because:

1. The boring of a best London gun will present the charge in a pattern which is, on average, 30 per cent better than the pattern you will get from a mass-produced weapon.

2. The difference between a good gun and an inferior one is the difference between a thoroughbred horse and an old nag. Both will go; but the way a thoroughbred handles is a pleasure and a source of pride to the owner in itself.

3. An inferior gun has a comparatively short life; in some cases limited to a few hundred days of hard shooting. A good gun

will fire hundreds of thousands of round, and like it; and last not for one lifetime but for several generations.

4. You can never get the balance and the tailoring in a cheap gun which a gun built for you will give you. In consequence you can never hope to shoot so well with a gun 'off the peg' as with one that has been bespoken for you.

Those are the reasons for buying the best gun you can afford; and now I will give a warning. Just because a gun has a famous maker's name on the barrel it doesn't follow that it is just as good as it used to be. Even the best built guns in the world wear out some day and, although it may look in good condition, an expert will be able to tell you that the barrels are paper thin and completely shot out. The moral, when you buy a gun, is to go to the maker. If he sells you a second-hand one, he will still pass it over to you with the hall-mark of his judgment and the pride of his reputation, which is the best guarantee that you will be well cared for.

II
The Components of a Gun

EVEN grandmothers know that this means 'Lock, stock and barrel.' I have no intention of explaining in detail how a gun is built or, least of all, encouraging the average sportsman to pull his own to pieces. Leave that job to the gun-maker. He will do it far better than you ever will.

But there are aspects of the Mystery of Gun-making, as it is called, which shouldn't be a mystery to any shooting man who is really keen on his sport. Gun know-how can be an assistance in good shooting, in the same way that a study of natural history is not only one of the greatest charms of the shooting field but a positive aid to good marksmanship. Know the habits of the game you are hunting; know the animal's ways, and you will be more successful in pursuing it. Know also the subtleties of the arm you are handling, and in consequence you will undoubtedly handle your weapon with greater skill.

I am dealing with the stocking of the gun in the next chapter, rather than this, only because the shape of the stock is the most important factor in gun measurement. Gun measurement is a subject sufficiently important to be treated on its own.

THE BARRELS

The barrels of a gun are simply smooth tubes which are roughly measured for size by the number of lead balls made to the diameter of the barrel which will add up to a pound weight. So, in general, a 12-bore barrel is one in which twelve lead balls of the same diameter will add up to a pound; a 20-bore one that will take twenty lead balls to the pound; a 16-bore, sixteen balls to the pound, and so on.

What distinguishes the barrel of one gun from another is the degree of choke. Choke is simply a restriction in the metal at the muzzle end of the barrel to hold the charge of shot together more tightly as it leaves the gun. The degree of choke in the individual barrels of every gun should be a matter of considerable personal concern to its owner. Very many shooting men have only the vaguest notion of the effect of choke in actual practice.

Here is a table, based on a 12-bore gun with a standard cartridge, to assist:

Super choke should put 75 per cent or 225 pellets of a 300 pellet charge within a 30-inch circle at 40 yards.

Full choke should put 70 per cent or 210 pellets within a 30-inch circle at forty yards.

Three-quarter choke should put 65 per cent or 195 pellets within a 30-inch circle at 40 yards.

Half choke should put 60 per cent or 180 pellets within a 30-inch circle at 40 yards.

Quarter choke, better known as Improved Cylinder, should put 50 per cent or 150 pellets into a 30-inch circle at 40 yards.

One-eighth choke should put 45 per cent or 135 pellets into a 30-inch circle at 40 yards.

True cylinder should put 40 per cent or 120 pellets into a 30-inch circle at 40 yards.

After studying that table, don't jump to the conclusion that the super choke, which puts the greatest number of pellets into a 30-inch circle, is the most satisfactory barrel for you.

It is very unlikely indeed that it is. But, as a general rule, if you are ordering a new gun and deciding how much choke you think you will need, it is just as well if you have the slightest doubt, to err by having too much choke rather than too little. If you want to reduce your choke later it can very simply be bored to a larger size; but if once the choke is taken out and you have got a true cylinder gun you can't put it back again into the barrels. Apart from that, my general advice to you is not to handicap yourself with too close a pattern. The correct boring for you is the one which will enable you to put the largest majority of the shots on to the target.

The following tables gives the diameter of the spread of shot with normal loads to the nearest *inch*.

DISTANCES IN YARDS

Boring	5 in.	10 in.	15 in.	20 in.	25 in.	30 in.	35 in.	40 in.
True cylinder	8¾	19	26	32	38	44	51	57
One-eighth choke	7¾	17	23	29	35	41	47	54
Quarter choke	6¾	15	20	26	32	38	44	51
Half choke	5¾	12	16	20	26	32	38	46
Three-quarter choke	5½	10½	14	18	23½	29	35	43
Full choke	4½	9	12	16	21	26	32	40

N

Having given you those figures, it is worth noting that, in the shooting of driven birds, you will shoot in the ordinary way nearer with the second barrel than the first. For that reason, guns bored both barrels one-eighth choke are most likely to give satisfaction. Remember that it is a tall tree in Britain which is fifteen yards high, and very many driven birds are shot at that distance. The shooter using a full choke, with a correspondingly smaller spread, would need to be very accurate indeed and, even then, there would be a serious possibility that he would badly damage his game.

For walking-up game, a second barrel bored one-quarter choke would give an almost identical pattern of spread at five yards greater distance if the first barrel were bored one-eighth choke. The man who is slow with his second barrel would get a similar pattern at ten yards greater distance by having half choke in the second barrel. For rough shooting at all distances, the combinations may be quarter and half choke; quarter choke and three-quarters; or half and full choke for long-distance shooting.

The ideal killing spread is between thirty-five inches and forty inches. If all shooting were at forty yards then full choke would be the ideal choice. As it is, a great deal of shooting is well within the forty yards range. For that reason, modified choke will suit the vast majority of sportsmen and the greatest variety of shooting. And the modifications for individuals, who are characteristically slow or characteristically fast on their targets, should only be decided after a good deal of practice either at the shooting school or in the field. So, if you are ordering a new gun for yourself, err on the side of too much choke but have no hesitation in having it reduced if you are not getting the best performance.

Apart from the control which choke exerts over the pattern of the shot, it also serves the very useful purpose of checking the wads from scattering the shot. Some form of choke in a modern game gun is clearly desirable.

I ought to add, for the benefit of the experts, that the Belgians make cartridges with square pellets which increase the spread of shot at different ranges. These square pellets are not available in this country now. Designed to give a quick spread for shooting rabbits at short ranges, they ensure that the game isn't shot to pieces by the full charge. Using this square shot the spread at fifteen yards is fifty-one inches with cylinder bores; forty-four inches with quarter choke; thirty-eight inches with half choke; and thirty-two inches with full choke.

THE BODY OR ACTION

Apart from the action of fully-automatic guns, all game guns are built either with what is called the sidelock action or the box lock.

Years ago, it was truly said that the sidelock action handled more sweetly than the box lock, then more generally known as the Anson and Deeley, after the two great craftsmen who designed it. But it must be remembered that, in those days, all best quality guns were sidelocks and all cheap quality ones were box locks. The best sidelocks, at that time, were better than the cheaper box locks.

The box lock has always been a cheaper action to make because it is simpler to work and contains fewer parts. The side lock has a larger body and is the heavier of the two actions. The box lock not only has the lightest possible body but, further, the triggers are nearer to the breech of the gun, thus saving woodwork and, in consequence, saving also the weight in the gun-stock. Indeed, it is probably true to say that, if there had never been any hammer guns, there wouldn't be any sidelock guns at all made today; for, in fact, the sidelock is purely the old hammer lock with an internal tumbler instead of an external hammer.

In fact, some sidelock ejectors should be treated with even greater suspicion than some box locks. There is the type of side-lock, which has an overdraught on the ejectors, causing the gun to run back after ejection. The barrels have to be pulled down again against the weight of the spring whilst fresh cartridges are inserted. A gun should always stay wide open after ejection. Then again, we have the action which does all this but is very hard to close, a further handicap to quick shooting. The trouble is often due to bad positioning of the limbs and the excessive strain of main and ejector springs. All these actions I am talking about are of nineteenth-century vintage; but, unfortunately, some of them are still turned out by conservative gun-makers. Sportsmen should be on the lookout against them.

In spite of what I have said about sidelocks—that the best sidelocks are more expensive to make and, in some ways, more reliable—I admit to a personal prejudice in the matter myself. Personally, I normally shoot with sidelocks and so do most other sportsmen who use 'best' guns. But, in fact, the matter is one of personal taste and prejudice; and no sportsman will go wrong, whichever action he uses, provided he buys the best.

Whichever action you choose, the important thing is to settle on a gun that is easy to open and easy to close. In most of the normal game guns, the opening of the breach cocks the locks and the closing of the gun cocks the ejectors.

The ejector springs should not be of such strength that they throw the fired cases great distances. All that is needed is an ejector which is certain in action. With a good gun, the ejector hammer gives a direct blow, instead of a glancing one, and springs of mild strength are quite sufficient and, in handling, much easier to compress.

You will find that there are some 'easy-opening models' which are easy to open and hard to close. I personally disagree with this type of gun as the dropping or throw of the barrels on opening helps this first operation. Further, I find myself, and I think most other sportsmen will, that I can pull far better than I can push, and I would rather have a gun which is easier to close. If a tired loader has one of these guns in his hands he is inclined to lift the barrels instead of lifting the stock to close the gun.

Of other easy-opening types there are those that fly open at the touch of the lever whilst they remain unfired, but once the trigger is pulled, the extractors which previously free the opening are held and the gun is hard to open. Another fault with them is that they all need a lighter spring and shorter rebounding strikers; but that is a technicality.

Today the strikers of some 'easy-opening models' have a measure of rebound; a good feature because a striker which indents the cap of the cartridge and stays there is making a grip on the indentation of the cartridge which is a check to easy opening.

So, on the whole, there is a lot to be said in favour of choosing an easy-opening type of gun. The tension, when the gun is closed, stops vibration and tends to check barrels from shaking loose from the face of the action. Further, when shooting with one gun, you can open and reload without altering or bending the body.

With the old type of breech opening, you have to bend down to reload and then stand upright again to fire. That doesn't sound much of an effort but I estimate that, in a hot corner, you can shoot 25 per cent more game with greater accuracy thanks to the absence of this bodily effort.

THE FORE-END

To a sportsman who only handles guns' casually, it may seem surprising that the mere choice of a fore-end offers such a tremendous variety, from the American beaver-tail, as it is called, to the hump-backed and raised fore-end which some trap shots prefer. Actually, it is my opinion that this is a part of the modern game gun which has not yet been perfected. Let me do no more than to put down what is needed in a well-designed fore-end in the hope that some clever gun craftsman can solve the problem.

In the first place, when we are shooting, we are constantly varying our forward grip on the fore-end of the gun; not only in accordance with our build and the length of the gun-stock, but also according to whether we are shooting ground game, grouse or pheasants. I should like to have a fore-end which was adjustable for all three conditions, or long enough to allow me to trombone my hand up and down it at will.

Second, the ideal fore-end should not be too smooth of surface. It is very important that the hand should grip the fore-end and not slip. On the other hand, the checkering must not to be so rough as to injure or bruise the hand on recoil.

The third requirement of a fore-end is that it ought to be of sufficient size to fill the hand and yet prevent the fingers of a large hand encroaching over the rib. In addition, it ought to be a non-conductor of heat so that we can shoot a great number of rounds very quickly without discomfort.

On aesthetic grounds, it ought not to be too large or conspicuous and it ought to be at least as light as the standard fore-end which is in use on game guns now. It is very important that we should not start adding to the overweight of a gun.

So much for the ideal. Here, for the interest of sportsmen, are a few of the many notions which have already been tried out towards the achievement of the objective:

The 'Colley' fore-end is simply a deepened one which certainly has the merit that it keeps the fingers off the barrel; but I dislike it because it encourages the left or forward arm to lift the gun upwards instead of to point it forwards.

The Hump-backed fore-end also keeps the fingers off the

barrel, but the hump-back encourages the shooter to pull in with the forward hand instead of pushing out and, as you will remember from the drill, that is bad style.

The beaver-tail is a great favourite with Americans, and, to my mind, it most nearly fills the bill; but it is just too much of a handful and adds rather too much to the weight of the gun for an ordinary shot.

On balance, the nearest we have got to the solution of the problem so far is the leather handguard with fastener. The ordinary handguard, which is a metal sheath encased in leather, is a most beneficial accessory which can be fitted on to the barrels of any gun. It has the three advantages that (1) it improves the variability of the handgrip on the fore-end considerably, (2) it effectively protects the hand from heated barrels when a great many rounds have been shot off in succession, and (3) it provides a warm and pleasant grip in hard weather when the metal of the barrels becomes almost as uncomfortably cold as in hard shooting it becomes uncomfortably hot. The objection to the handguard, if it is merely sprung over the existing fore-end and not fastened with a catch to the barrel itself, is that it has a dangerous habit of slipping forward in shooting, unless the spring steel is squeezed really right on to the barrel. So, if you use a handguard, either have an attachment put on by your gun-maker to hold it in position or squeeze it on as tightly as you can. If you don't, you will find that, one day, you will pick up your gun by the handguard and have it slip through and fall to the ground with frightening results. Further, you will find that it is not very pleasant when it shifts its position as recoil is taken.

As a substitute for the handguard, the ordinary glove is no protection from a heated barrel, and I am still looking for the ideal glove, one that buttons up the back. The objection to the ordinary glove is that it exposes the disc of the palm just where it touches the barrel. The glove I want would be thin and flexible, with finger-tips and ball of thumb reinforced with some material which would protect the side of the thumb and the first finger which touches the barrel, in addition to the other three finger-tips. In fact, the hand actually touches a very small area of the barrel. As an experiment, wipe the barrel dry and then grasp it in normal fashion. The thumb and finger-prints that are left behind will show you just how small is the area of surface which is touched.

TRIGGERS

If you are not a very keen shooting man indeed it is possible that it has never ocurred to you that trigger pulls, or the shape of triggers and trigger guards, should be a matter of any significant importance at all. I can only tell you that first-class shots can become so sensitive about the trigger pulls of their guns that they can notice a difference of half a pound or less. They won't be satisfied with their guns until the maker has adjusted them exactly to the comfortable pressure.

The weight of trigger pull depends on the weight of the gun. For instance, if you are one of those sensitive shots accustomed to putting on exactly the same amount of pressure every time you fire, you will probably require that your 6½ lb. guns should have pulls of 3 lb. right trigger and 3¾ lb. left trigger. But if you use a lighter 12-bore, or even a 20-bore weighing perhaps only 5½ lb., you will find that, although the lighter weapon may have exactly the same measurements as your heavier gun, the pull you require will have to be altered.

As a rough guide, the weight of the first or right trigger pull shoulder be approximately one-half of the weight of the gun. A 6-lb. pull on a 13 lb. 8-bore feels just as light as a 3-lb. pull on a 12-bore of 6½ lb. or a 2½-lb. pull on a 20-bore weighing 5 lb.

Generally speaking, the left pull should always be about 25 per cent heavier than the right because the greater leverage makes it feel proportionately lighter. Of course, the man with only one gun is not likely to be such a sensitive judge of trigger pulls as the man who uses a pair of guns. The latter always has the comparative pulls between number one and number two to contrast, and he can immediately detect differences between his two guns; for instance, that one responds instantly and that the other drags and causes him to pull on his birds. The man with fingers as sensitive as that must use 'best' guns with locks which are less likely to vary. But for the general sportsman, it is just as well not to worry very much about trigger pulls. If you are having trouble with your trigger pulls, you can probably overcome it pretty quickly by going back to the drill. Practise gun-mounting with a slightly relaxed grip. If you do that, all the little troubles of varying pull will inevitably disappear. If you are throwing your shoulder forward and making your trigger pull with a rigid finger a light pull isn't really necessary; and, in the interests of safety, a pull on the heavy side is even desirable.

Many years ago, I used to have a pigeon gun with a $1\frac{3}{4}$ lb. right pull. As there was no safety catch on the gun, I had to be very careful indeed not to jar it as I closed it, because that alone was enough to make it go off. I now use a $2\frac{1}{2}$-lb. pull on a 6-lb. gun; but I cannot even recommend this pull to anyone who has not a very sensitive touch, or who wears gloves, or who shoots in a very cold climate. In fact, gamekeepers and other shooting men with strong muscles who are accustomed to hard exercise or hard manual labour are more often inclined to put on a pound or so of pressure on their triggers before being aware of it. If you are a strong man, accustom yourself to a heavy pull.

The basic disadvantage of a heavy pull is that it causes one to drag off the target. On the other hand, the danger of too light a pull is that the gun goes off before you are 'on.' Don't be ashamed to have a heavy pull yourself. Many good shots prefer it. One of them, for example, was Frank Troeh, undoubtedly the greatest trap shot ever born.

The American trap-shooting records show that he started shooting in 1912 and, in registered shoots, broke between the years 1912 and 1938 the huge total of 129,603 targets for the expenditure of 132,970 cartridges for a liftime average of ·9746 in all sorts of weather. He is also an all-round game shot. I remember him asking me to try his gun, a graceful compliment. I eagerly accepted. But, on calling my target, I could not fire it. I examined the breech for the safety catch whilst he looked on with amusement. There was no safety catch. I tried again without success and then discovered that he used a pull on his gun of over 8 lb. weight.

The expert is not only concerned with the weight of pull but also with its crispness. Here again, the best lock (another argument for the best gun) can alone give a never varying safe, crisp and light pull. The cheap lock, owing to the irregularities of its component parts, cannot fail to vary; further, the shaping of the sears and the bent of the tumblers is cruder and only too often the pull is a long drag.

More sportsmen are troubled by the fact that when they make a bad trigger pull they imagine that the trigger pulls themselves are at fault. Sometimes the consequences can be blamed on the shape of the trigger itself, but more often the trouble is that the shooter has taken an uncomfortable grip.

Basically the trigger is the lever which raises the sear nose, **and** thus releases the tumbler. If it is so shaped that the fingers slide upwards during the effort to pull it backwards, then the nearer the finger moves towards the point of axis the more effort will be required. On the other hand, of course, the greatest leverage is obtained near the extreme tip.

Assume we have a gun with one of those small grips which allows the hand to get anywhere. When our hand is on the top of the grip and the shortened finger can reach only the top of the trigger, the weight of the pull is apparently much harder than when we try again with the hand placed more firmly underneath the stock. The extra reach allows us to pull at a lower angle with the first joint instead of the finger-tip. As a matter of fact, there are not so many bad triggers about today as there used to be; but there are still bad trigger guards.

In choosing a gun you should look for a trigger guard which is sloped to allow sufficient escapement for the finger. It was how the great nineteenth-century gun-maker, Joe Manton, solved the problem over a hundred years ago.

Finally, very large hands need large trigger guards and a greater width between the triggers. The super-sensitive shot, who requires a very light trigger pull, should have his trigger blades checkered to prevent his finger slipping.

THE FORESIGHT

Some shooting men will tell you that they never see their foresight, others doubt whether it is of any importance and the great majority, I suppose, agree that a foresight is necessary.

The expert shot is at all times most particular as regards its composition, colour and shape. At various times foresights have been made of gold, silver and other metals, porcelain and ivory. When I was a boy, the pigeon shots of the period generally favoured an ivory sight because, against the dark background, it showed up white, and, against a light background, it showed up dark. But they were all undecided as to the best size and shape. I remember that one well-known shot had a wide flattened blob on the end of his gun and argued that the fine pinhead sight he had discarded caused him to look at his gun too long, whereas his 'billiard ball' sight was always in vision and helped him to focus his eyes on the bird instead of on the gun. There was something in what he said.

The Hon. Seton Robert Beresford who, in his book *Beresford's*

Monte Carlo, tells many interesting tales of the old days when Englishmen went out to shoot live pigeons from traps there, records that he himself used different foresights for different occasions.

As regards colour composition, I prefer a white metal to ivory on my gun because the latter can be so easily broken. As regards shape and size, I think it is important not to have so fine a sight that it is difficult to find without looking. Again, the sight should not be so large that it distracts the eye. Let it be a medium spherical sight such as is normally fitted today.

True, most of us only use the sight, or rather I hope that most of us only use the sight, for sitters and target shooting. But it does help to show where we have been pointing after we have missed.*

THE TOP RIB

The top rib of a side-by-side double-barrelled gun may be concave or flat in varying widths at the breech and the muzzle end of the gun; also it may be plain or engraved, file cut or engine turned, and so on, in endless variety. In my opinion, the worst rib of the lot is the concave or half hollow rib which is unengraved. It reflects the sunlight and, when swamped in the centre, it acts not so much as a guide to the eye as a distraction for it. A perfectly flat and wide rib, although file cut or engraved, still occasionally catches the eye and looks humped up in the centre.

Long experience has convinced me that the ideal rib is one that is narrow and flat and is also cut up by file or engraver to show a dead black surface. The narrower a rib is made, the longer it seems. When I was working on the development of my twenty-five-inch gun, I also evolved a special rib for it, which is now known as the 'Churchill quick-sighting rib.' This rib, when properly fitted and file cut to show a thin dead black line, is an enormous aid to shooting. Of course, it deceives the eye and makes the barrels look much longer than they really are. But that's the purpose of it. As I have said so often now, I don't want you to see the gun-barrels but to look at your bird, and I don't want the rib on the top of the gun to distract your eye either. My quick-sighting rib appears as a dead black line which never has to be looked-for because it is in the shooter's field of vision just before a gun reaches his shoulder It encourages him to do the right thing. Second, the rib shows up

* You will do better if you forget that your gun has a sight at all!

clearly in the shooter's eyes as the gun kicks backwards on the recoil. In other words, it helps him to see where he has been pointing.

On all short-barrelled guns, the Churchill quick-sighting rib is really a necessity; on barrels of any length it has material advantages.

SHAPE OF THE BUTT

We have now covered all the components of a gun except the stock, which I shall deal with in greater detail in the next chapter. The butt, of course, is the further extension of the stock; but it calls for some general comments which are outside the major consideration of the stock itself.

The expert always demands that the butt of his gun should fit the shoulder perfectly. The very tall thin man may need a prominent toe to check too high a gun-mounting and to prevent the gun turning or canting. But any fully-chested person needs a normal toe which means a stand or drop or two inches from the upright.

Personally, in my own workshops, I have always concerned myself very deeply with the matter of settling the width of the butt. I have learnt how important it is through shooting guns in their rough state with huge blocks of wood for butt ends; and I have learnt that, if a stock is narrow enough, it can be bedded into the fleshy part of the shoulder; but if it is too wide then it comes on to the bone.

A flat American ventilated recoil pad with slats is my own preference; not so much for saving recoil as for the purpose of fitting the shoulder perfectly and holding there at the instant of recoil. A square and wide wooden butt is inclined to slide instead of to give. When this happens the second barrel is fired with the butt on the shoulder bone instead of against the flesh.

Anatomically, the vein which carries blood down to the arm runs in front of the shoulder bone. When this vein is sandwiched between bone and butt, then a bruise extends far down the arm and leads the unfortunate shooter to believe that he has been firing with the butt on the muscle of his arm. The normal depth of the butt should be five-and-a-half inches. The normal stand in gun measurement is two inches off the upright.

III

The Measurements
of a Gun

THE shape of stock which fits one man is not necessarily
the best for another man of similar build. A great many
factors influence the selection of the best shape of stock for
the individual.

The tendency of many modern guns has been towards a grip
which is too straight for practical
mounting. The line is graceful, and
looks well in an illustration, but it is
a handicap in use. (See Illustration 1.)

The natural stock developed in my
short-barrelled guns is the same in bend and general measurements as the last named but with very material alterations to
the grip. The tang of the action and
trigger plate curve down so that the hand
moves naturally parallel to the line of
sight without enforcing a strained position to the right arm. (See Illustration 2.)

The third model is a return to a pattern over a century old.
This is the keeled or 'roach-bellied' shape shown in Illustration
3. It was copied from an old muzzle-
loader and possesses a peculiarly
pleasant balance, as well as proving
not only a pleasant contour but a
comfortable grip.

Trap-shooting guns for competition experts need special
adaptation to the needs of their specialized shooting position.
The 'Monte Carlo' (Illustration
4) is the basic model. It is also
very valuable for game shots
with long necks or those who
find difficulty in mounting an

ordinary stock to the face without the butt rising half above the shoulder.

Illustration 5 represents the old flintlock stock which is occasionally preferred but presents a return to a gun shape not particularly practical for modern shooting conditions, driven game in particular. The  hand and grip is small and comfortable but is likely to slip through the hand on recoil of stock.

Illustration 6 shows a full left-eyed gun-stock which is occasionally necessary.

Illustrations 7, 8 and 9 represent the development of the pistol grip in its various degrees of quarter, half and full. The most appropriate 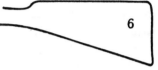 form for the individual depends not only on arm length, width of body and size of hand, but also particularly on the type of gun and its special use.

Full pistol and half-pistol grips are more suitable for single-trigger guns than for double triggers, as with the latter there is always a  slightly different position of grip with each barrel. A pistol grip also checks overhead swing. The full pistol grip, therefore, is more suitable on the special trap gun or for walking-up game and it is seldom seen on the modern game gun.

The half-pistol grip is more common. It is preferred to the straight stock (Illustration 1), but the special stock (Illustration 2) has all the advantages of the low-curved hand of the half-pistol grip without any of its disadvantages and would be more likely to suit the majority of sportsmen.

Illustration 10 represents a gun with deepened fore-end. This hardly concerns stocks, but, with certain individuals, is a palliative for bad gun-mounting. Except in the case of a man who is disabled or limited in his freedom of physical movement, the need for this amendment suggests that the gun is either badly balanced or does not fit.

The fitting of the stock of a gun to an individual is one of the highest arts of gun-making. The length of stock necessary depends not only on the length of the shooter's arms, the breadth of his body and the length of his neck, it also depends on the position of the left hand, the position of stance and finally the weight of the gun.

Weight of gun.—The general rule is that the heavier the gun the shorter the stock, and vice versa. To go to extremes, the man who shoots well with a 12-bore weighing 6 lb. with a fourteen-and-a-half-inch stock would probably need a fifteen-inch stock if he was shooting with a ·410 and a stock as short as fourteen inches if he was shooting with an 8-bore wildfowl gun. The reason for this is that the shooter hugs the heavier weight and extends his arms with the lighter one.

Position of Stance.—If the body is turned too much sideways the shooter needs a longer stock than if he normally stands squarely to the target and puts his shoulder forward into the butt of the gun as he fires.

Position of Left Hand.—If the left hand is held too far back the result is that the shooter can handle a much longer stock. In reverse, if he over-reaches with the left hand, the tendency is that any stock will become too long.

To the many keen sportsmen who read this book and who have not the means or the opportunity to have a gun specially made to measure for them—and to those, too, who on occasion have to shoot with any odd gun they can lay their hands on—it is worth emphasizing this point that the shooter can, to a certain degree, control the length of the stock by regulating his grip on the gun. It is by no means an ideal state of affairs and, in driven game shooting, with really fast well-presented birds, no sportsman with a gun which doesn't fit him can hope to put up his best performance. But, if you are using a borrowed gun, or you have got a gun which is too long or too short in the stock for you, you can overcome, to a large extent, the problem of fit by drawing your hand back on the forehand if the stock is too long and extending it if necessary right up to the barrels if the stock is too short. In fact, His Late Majesty, King George V, was one of those who adopted what is called the straight-arm stance. He invariably moved his left hand forward during gun-mounting until the left arm was fully extended up the barrels. I don't recommend the practice to the majority of shooters, but George V, as is well known, was in his prime one of the greatest shots of his day, and the straight-arm grip on the barrel may be an unusual style, but assuming that everything else is all right, it is still good style.

The man who is away from civilization may feel doubtful about the fit of his gun and wish to test it. To do this, he should cut a finely pointed piece of paper and shove it in the breech absolutely central with the rib, so that the point stands up about three-eighths of an inch above the barrels. This point is the temporary backsight, Next, with equal care, fasten a precisely similar point at the muzzle end to serve as a foresight.

Then, with both eyes open, and holding the gun in the 'ready' position, look at an object and mount the gun at it.

Close both eyes a fraction of a second *before* the gun is home to the shoulder. Then, *before* you pull the trigger, open the eyes and observe where your sights are really pointing.

Practise this at various objects or points of aim and you may find that, though you may be 'dead-on' for straight-away shots, and, say, shots to your left, you will yet find that you aim over or behind in the case of shots to your right or overhead.

In order to avoid false stance, move the feet after each shot, and above all avoid adjusting yourself to an artificial and temporary fit to the gun, the idea being to take these snap shots as naturally as possible. The information to be gained from this experiment is limited to the discovery that your failure of certain shots is, in all probability, due rather to the poor fit of your gun than to any other cause.

For a more critical analysis, an outdoor shooting test can be made without the paper sights. If a whitewashed steel or iron target, about three feet square, is available, this is best; but, if it is not, you can extemporize an adequate test by sticking double sheets of newspaper on a wood frame or on a hedge. See that the print is the right way up so that you will know afterwards which is the top or bottom of the pattern.

In the centre of the target make a big ink aiming spot; then measure off—do not pace it but measure it exactly—a firing point at sixteen yards.

Assuming the eye is thirty-six inches from the gun-muzzle, also that the gun shoots with true elevation and that the two barrels are in the same line, then errors in bend and cast-off will be magnified sixteen times on the target.

Fire several snap shots at the target with your normal stance, then take the centre of your composite pattern as the average. If your charge is centred two inches *below* the point of aim, the stock certainly needs straightening one-eighth of an inch. A group two-inches high represents a nicely placed pattern. If higher, for every two inches surplus elevation the stock should be bent down one-eighth of an inch. A group one inch to the left would involve an increase of cast-off of one-sixteenth of an inch, while three inches to the right would involve reduction of cast-off by three-sixteenths of an inch.

There is always the possibility, of course, that the shooter rather than the gun is at fault; hence any consistent error should be further tested not only in terms of the gun but in terms of gun-mounting as well. The following rules apply:

POSITION OF THE SHOTS ON THE TARGET
AND EXPLANATION

Shooting on the right.—Causes may be: (*a*) too much cast-off; (*b*) head too far forward with eye too far over the stock; (*c*) stock too short; (*d*) incorrect stance.

Shooting on the left.—Causes may be: (*a*) not enough cast-off; (*b*) stock too long; (*c*) pulling in of the left hand; (*d*) stock on the arm instead of into the shoulder.

Shooting low.—Causes may be: (*a*) too much bend of stock; (*b*) too heavy a pull; (*c*) flinching; (*d*) left hand not far enough forward or a badly balanced gun that is heavy forward and shoots low.

Shooting high.—Causes may be: (*a*) stock too straight at the bump; (*b*) too light a pull; (*c*) too long a stock; (*d*) too much 'toe' to stock.

If you want to make a quite simple experiment to test whether the length of stock on your gun suits you, the overhead shot is the best test. For the going-away shot, whatever the size of the gun, the shooter can extend or shorten the reach of the left hand to make the gun fit. But in the overhead shot, if the gun doesn't fit really well, you will recognize that something is wrong. If the stock is too long, you may well find that your swing is checked. You may indeed find that you can shoot more easily by using the second trigger. If the stock is too short, you will notice that you have to push your left hand up the barrel to make a smooth and natural follow-through.

If the stock is finally proved to be at fault, it should be altered by an expert who has seen you shoot. Self-gun-fitting is very much like self-doctoring; not by any means a certain cure. Nevertheless, to suspect a malady is the first step in locating it, and putting yourself in the way of a cure.

IV

Cartridges

DON'T blame your cartridge if you miss. Once in a thousand times, it might happen that you mounted your gun correctly, placed the charge correctly, and the column of shot misbehaved itself to the extent that the bird slipped through the gap in a bad pattern. But, for practical purposes, you can assume, if you miss, that it was your fault.

Don't become a 'size of shot' fanatic either. Fifty years ago, shot was either as soft as putty or as hard as steel; there was no happy medium. Cartridges were not of the quality that they are today and guns did not shoot such regular patterns. For that reason, No. 5 shot was the most popular size. But, as cartridge manufacture improved, the 5½ or 'medium game' (often labelled M.G.) ousted No. 5, and, latterly, Nos. 6, 6½ and 7 have gained popularity.

Today, if you have never shot with anything else, in inland game shooting, except No. 6, it wouldn't make any material difference to the results.

In fact, I know that many sportsmen like to use No. 6 at the beginning of the season and change to No. 5 at the end of it. Others, when they are shooting on the marshes, put No. 8 in the right barrel to deal with snipe and No. 4 in the left barrel against the chance of a possible duck. What so often happens, in practice, is that they miss the duck with the No. 4 and bring him down, to their surprise, with the No. 8 and vice versa.

On this subject—size of shot, types of powders, various loads— I probably know as much as anyone. A well-known writer, many years ago, used to call himself the 'twenty-thousand shot man' which was the number of rounds he claimed to have fired at testing plates. I wouldn't like to estimate how many tens of thousands of rounds I myself have loaded and shot at plates. I am still at it. And, after a lifetime with a gun in my hand, I assure you that I can quote you figures to prove pretty well anything.

It is self-evident that big shot has greater energy, at a given range, than small shot; but, when it comes to penetration, we

o

know that the fine-pointed gimlet penetrates better than the blunt-pointed one. Generally speaking, the more pellets there are in a cartridge, the better chance there is of hitting a vital spot and bring the game down. A No. 7 in the head is much more likely to kill a bird than a No. 5 in the body, although pellet energy is less.

In the days of muzzle-loaders, when the argument about shot sizes was even more clamorous than it is among shooting men now, experts like General Hangar recommended 2 ozs. of No. 2 shot over a charge of little more than a dram of powder for all forms of inland shooting. At the same time there were other shooting men who preferred to put in a couple of drams, or more, of powder with about ¾ oz. of No. 6 shot. In those days, there was some reason for the variation of opinion, because the shot was soft and the powder was not as efficient as it is now. In our own time, cartridges are so standardized, and patterns are so regular, that it won't help anybody to shoot straighter to worry about cartridges, powder and shot at all; except perhaps over the price of them.

Nevertheless, I am quite aware that nothing I say will stop keen shooting men from regarding the matter as of major importance. I remember one renowned shot who always used to insist that his cartridges should be loaded with No. 4; but marked with No. 6 top wads. Another sportsman swore by 5½ shot and, if circumstances necessitated his using shot of another size, such was his conviction that, by a natural reflex, he never shot so well. So, if you have a taste for different types and different sizes of shot in different loads for different game at different seasons, I certainly don't want to persuade you to change. You will always shoot best with the cartridge you trust best and, if you feel happier with a pink cartridge than a brown one, you *will* be happier; and shoot better accordingly.

The only circumstances in which the size of shot can be a matter of importance is in shooting heavy fowl like geese, where No. 3 is probably the best size. And, if you happen to be shooting driven snipe, or on a marsh where snipe represent the larger proportion of the game, I would recommend you to use cartridges loaded with No. 7 or even No. 8 shot.

But, for all general shooting purposes, you won't improve on No. 6.

If you want to satisfy yourself with a personal test, and nothing

will satisfy you so completely as a personal test, get a piece of old
sheet iron and wash it over with white distemper or whitewash.
Then, at the standard distance of forty yards, which should give
you a thirty to forty-inch pattern on the plate, fire a number of
test rounds with different sizes of shot; remembering, after each
shot, to wash over the plate again with whitewash so that you get
a clear silhouette of each individual pattern.

Experts, when they are testing cartridges without the aid of a
proof gun and a chronograph, distinguish by ear the quick
cartridge from the slow one. By looking at the cap indentation,
and the case expansion, they can judge pressure and, by studying
the pellet marks on the plate, they can gauge whether the
charge is hitting hard or not. In your own case, you may find this
more difficult. But, if you examine the pellet marks on a steel
plate after they are fired, you can judge by the size of the marks
whether the pellets were hitting hard or not. Make a close examination, and you will discover that the marks on the plate vary in
size. If you find pinhead marks, it means that the pellets that
made them were useless so far as penetration was concerned. But
a strong bruising mark on the plate indicates that your shot was
hitting well. Alternatively, if you want to test penetration, there
is no better subject than a London telephone directory. You can
simply measure penetration by the different letters to which
different parts of your charge have penetrated.

If you make this experiment carefully, with all the different
sizes of shot, you will find at the end of it that you have learnt
precisely nothing at all except that modern cartridges have a
standard steady performance and that, if you hold your gun
straight and pull the triggers at the right time at the right range,
anything you shoot at must be killed.

(*I have taken out a passage here in which, in earlier editions, Churchill
expressed the view that hand-loaded cartridges by a gun maker are fraction-
ally better than standard ones; and that it is fun to have your cartridges
loaded with particular powders and shot charges to suit your own taste.
So was the matter up to the end of Churchill's days. He himself believed
that the cartridge should have a metal case rather than a paper one. Time
has overtaken his opinion.*

*Today, only one or two gun makers load their own cartridges. Although
you will still buy cartridges with the gun maker's name on the case, they
are nearly all manufactured in this country by Imperial Metal Industries, in-
corporating the old names of Kynoch and Eley. And all the better for that.*

The new cartridge is waterproof, non-corrosive, and consistent to a degree that no hand-loaded cartridge could ever be. Churchill, aggressive and idiosyncratic as he was in his opinions, could scarcely have failed to admit that, at forty yards, only a few pellets fly out of a thirty-inch circle. The powder is as consistent as the firm shake of a friend's hand.

Churchill, criticising the paper case, wondering whether metal might be better, did not anticipate the advantages of plastic.

In truth, even the plastic case has its snags. Convenient as it is for the shooting man, the expended cartridge is virtually indestructible. Paper cases rotted into the ground. The plastic ones, as they are manufactured now, are likely to survive like the flint arrowheads of our ancestors.

Nevertheless, I am conscious that paper cases, with corrosive powders, are still common in shooting bags in many gunrooms. There are still plenty of them in the stock of country ironmongers. For that reason I have not changed the text in the latter part of this chapter.)

Worrying about your cartridges won't help you to shoot a fraction straighter. If you master the drill, you will kill your birds with anything in the way of powder and shot you can buy at the gunmakers today.

True, you will occasionally come across a bad cartridge. The usual trouble is that, in manufacture, the turnover hasn't been made strong enough. Just as a squib will fizzle off ineffectively if you don't put your foot on it and the harder you tread on it the better the bang, so the turnover of a cartridge builds up pressure according to its strength.

A good tight turnover holds until the cap ignites the powder and the powder combustion forms the propelling gases. You can test turnover yourself by the very simple method of taking a cartridge in your hand with your index finger pressed on the top wad. Tap the brass end of the cartridge sharply on the table. If you can move the top wad with the pressure of your index finger, it means that the cartridge isn't packed strongly enough.

Even so, it will probably shoot well enough to kill your bird at normal ranges. It is a very bad cartridge indeed, and a very rare one, which won't kill at twenty yards.

But I realize that everything I am saying is militating against one of the favourite discussions at a shooting lunch. Every keen shooting man likes to believe that his cartridges make a difference. In an attempt to co-operate, on pages 215–217 I give tables, if only for the record, of the bores of gun and the number of pellets in game gun cartridges.

Just to emphasize the relative unimportance of these tables to the average shooting man, let me reveal to you that many years ago I built some double-barrelled weapons which were designed to fire only one pellet at a time. They were constructed with the same care and precision, and attention to the shooter's measurement, as a first-class gun. But they weren't shot-guns. They were double-barrelled ·22 rifles.

With these guns, in the hands of a good shot, it was possible, again and again, to smash a clay pigeon. Subsequently, I supplied some of them to American sportsmen who were keen to pull off long shots at duck. In practice, what we found was that these ·22 rifles, tailored to fit the user, had an effectiveness comparable to about 33 per cent of a shot-gun in the hands of the same man, but, of course, they were killing game well outside the extreme ranges of a smooth-bored gun.

One very fine American shot, who had one, told me that, on several occasions, he had succeeded in pulling off a right and a left at mallard at over a hundred yards.

The moral is simply that, if you are using a gun properly, time and time again you would hit your bird if you only had a single bullet in your gun. In fact, the shooter, who is on his day, is doing this consistently. And, if you hit a bird with any size of shot from BB to No. 8, in the centre of the pattern, you will kill him as certainly as if you had hit him with a ·22 bullet because the concentration of the pattern is always at its greatest in the dead centre of the charge.

(I can confirm Churchill's assertion that, on his day, any average shot would kill with only a single slug in his cartridge. The story is, to a certain extent, at Churchill's expense. Immediately after the war, when cartridges were difficult to get, he bought back millions of rounds of ammunition which he had supplied to the Services. They were loaded with ball; but he found a way of removing the solid lead charge and replacing it with shot. Under the trade name of Hercules (not a bad name in the circumstances) he flogged them to sportsmen at reduced prices. I had some.

One day when we were walking pheasants through the kale on the Berkshire Downs, a cock curved back, and flew high and straight over me. When I upped my gun and shot, I was astonished to see the bird's head separate from its body in mid-air. The carcase came down in two parts. Obviously, I had got hold of one of the cartridges in which the ball hadn't been replaced by shot. Others, at the time, had similar experiences.

On the other side of the coin, every shooting man should know that there are times, comparatively rare, when the gun is correctly mounted and aimed, but the bird flies off unscathed. If you are sure of yourself when that happens, the explanation is almost certainly that the charge 'cartwheeled'; in other words, it went up like a smoke ring instead of a concentrated puff. But if it happens to you, don't tell the other fellows about it. They're sure to think you're covering up.)

By all means, use the cartridge as a convenient excuse to explain your misses. Surprisingly, it is an excuse which is often accepted by even experienced shooting hosts. But, privately, don't believe a word of it. When you get home, go through the gun drill again. Practise, if you can get the opportunity, on clay pigeons. Practise, practise, practise . . . and you will never have a dud cartridge again.

In fact, you may get so good that your shooting friends will ask you what cartridges you use with the notion of adopting the same brand of straight powder that you yourself favour.

(Some keen shooting men 'hot up' their cartridges by warming them in a low oven or on the kitchen range before shooting. It is not to be recommended. If cartridges are stored in an even temperature in a dry place, they will do everything required of them. If the cases of cartridges stored in a damp place swell, it is possible to get a reamer to make them usable. But they should be reserved for pot-shots and vermin days.)

BORES OF GUN

Description	Approximate Shot Charge oz.	Approximate Weight of Gun lbs.
4-bore 4 in.	3–4	$14\frac{1}{2}$–$18\frac{1}{2}$
8-bore $3\frac{1}{4}$ in.	2–$2\frac{1}{2}$	$10\frac{1}{2}$–$12\frac{1}{2}$
10-bore $2\frac{7}{8}$ in.	$1\frac{7}{16}$–$1\frac{5}{8}$	8–9
10-bore $2\frac{5}{8}$ in.	$1\frac{1}{4}$–$1\frac{3}{8}$	$7\frac{1}{2}$–8
12-bore 3 in.*	$1\frac{3}{8}$–$1\frac{1}{2}$	$7\frac{3}{4}$–$8\frac{1}{2}$
12-bore $2\frac{3}{4}$ in.*	$1\frac{1}{4}$	$7\frac{1}{2}$–$7\frac{3}{4}$
12-bore $2\frac{1}{2}$ in.*	1–$1\frac{1}{8}$	$6\frac{1}{2}$–7
16-bore $2\frac{3}{4}$ in.	1–$1\frac{1}{16}$	$6\frac{1}{2}$
16-bore $2\frac{1}{2}$ in.	$\frac{7}{8}$–$\frac{15}{16}$	$5\frac{3}{4}$–6
20-bore $2\frac{3}{4}$ in.	$\frac{7}{8}$–$\frac{15}{16}$	$5\frac{3}{4}$–6
20-bore $2\frac{1}{2}$ in.	$\frac{3}{4}$–$\frac{13}{16}$	$5\frac{1}{2}$
24-bore $2\frac{1}{2}$ in.	$\frac{11}{16}$	5
28-bore $2\frac{1}{2}$ in.	$\frac{5}{8}$	$4\frac{3}{4}$
32-bore $2\frac{1}{2}$ in.	$\frac{1}{2}$	4
.410-bore $2\frac{1}{2}$ in.	$\frac{7}{16}$	$3\frac{3}{4}$

* Churchill 'XXV' guns with 25-in. barrels are built approximately 8 oz. lighter.

PELLETS IN GAME CHARGES

oz. of Shot	Size of Shot			
	4	5	6	7
$1\frac{1}{2}$	255	330	408	510
$1\frac{7}{16}$	244	316	391	489
$1\frac{3}{8}$	234	303	374	468
$1\frac{5}{16}$	223	289	357	446
$1\frac{1}{4}$	213	275	340	425
$1\frac{3}{16}$	202	261	323	404
$1\frac{1}{8}$	191	248	306	383
$1\frac{1}{16}$	181	234	289	361
1	170	220	272	340
$\frac{15}{16}$	159	206	255	319
$\frac{7}{8}$	149	193	238	298
$\frac{13}{16}$	138	179	221	276
$\frac{3}{4}$	128	165	204	255
$\frac{11}{16}$	117	151	187	234
$\frac{5}{8}$	106	138	170	212
$\frac{9}{16}$	96	124	153	191
$\frac{1}{2}$	85	110	136	170

TRUE CYLINDER (= 40 PER CENT) PATTERNS

oz. of Shot	Pellets in 30-in. circle at 40 YARDS for different SIZES of Shot			
	4	5	6	7
1½	102	132	163	204
1⅜	94	121	150	187
1¼	85	110	136	170
1⅛	76	99	122	153
1 1/16	72	94	116	144
1	68	88	109	136
⅞	60	77	95	119
¾	51	66	82	102
11/16	47	60	75	94
⅝	42	55	68	85
9/16	38	50	61	76
½	34	44	54	68

IMPROVED CYLINDER (= 50 PER CENT) PATTERNS

oz. of Shot	Pellets in 30-in. circle at 40 YARDS for different SIZES of Shot			
	4	5	6	7
1½	128	165	204	255
1 7/16	122	158	196	245
1⅜	117	152	187	234
1 5/16	111	145	179	223
1¼	107	138	170	213
1 3/16	101	131	162	202
1⅛	96	124	153	192
1 1/16	91	117	145	181
1	85	110	136	170
15/16	80	103	128	160
⅞	75	97	119	149
13/16	69	90	111	138
¾	64	83	102	128
11/16	59	76	94	117
⅝	53	69	85	106
9/16	48	62	77	96
½	43	55	68	85

HALF CHOKE (= 60 PER CENT) PATTERNS

oz. of Shot	Pellets in 30-in. circle at 40 YARDS for different SIZES of Shot			
	4	5	6	7
$1\frac{1}{2}$	153	198	244	306
$1\frac{7}{16}$	146	190	235	293
$1\frac{3}{8}$	140	182	224	280
$1\frac{5}{16}$	134	174	214	267
$1\frac{1}{4}$	128	165	204	255
$1\frac{3}{16}$	121	157	194	242
$1\frac{1}{8}$	115	148	148	230
$1\frac{1}{16}$	109	140	173	217
1	102	132	163	204
$\frac{15}{16}$	95	124	153	191
$\frac{7}{8}$	89	116	143	179
$\frac{13}{16}$	83	108	133	166
$\frac{3}{4}$	77	99	122	153
$\frac{11}{16}$	70	91	112	140
$\frac{5}{8}$	64	82	102	127
$\frac{9}{16}$	58	74	92	115
$\frac{1}{2}$	51	66	81	102

FULL CHOKE (= 70 PER CENT) PATTERNS

oz. of Shot	Pellets in 30-in. circle at 40 YARDS for different SIZES of Shot			
	4	5	6	7
$1\frac{1}{2}$	178	231	285	357
$1\frac{7}{16}$	170	221	274	342
$1\frac{3}{8}$	163	212	261	328
$1\frac{5}{16}$	156	202	249	312
$1\frac{1}{4}$	149	192	238	298
$1\frac{3}{16}$	142	183	226	283
$1\frac{1}{8}$	134	174	214	268
$1\frac{1}{16}$	127	164	202	253
1	119	154	190	238
$\frac{15}{16}$	112	144	179	223
$\frac{7}{8}$	105	135	167	209
$\frac{13}{16}$	97	125	155	194
$\frac{3}{4}$	90	115	143	179
$\frac{11}{16}$	82	106	131	163
$\frac{5}{8}$	75	97	119	148
$\frac{9}{16}$	67	86	107	134
$\frac{1}{2}$	59	77	95	119

V

The Shooting School

IF anyone asked the ordinary shooting man if he could see shot in the air his reply would probably take the form of an impolite negative. Yet it is quite easy to see shot in the air once you get the knack of it. It is the trade secret of most shooting school coaches. They can *see* where you are shooting.

During the war, it was fairly commonplace for people behind a big howitzer to see the shell in the air and trace its track. A howitzer shell is a big object and its initial velocity is not very much higher than a shot-gun charge. Airmen have reported that they have seen artillery projectiles from the cockpit, and there is every reason to suppose that their claim is sound.

It is not yet established what degree of perception the human eye can undertake in terms of time. Some people take a long time to focus their vision on an object; others see it and recognize it as quick as thought; far quicker than speech. It is largely a question of knowing what you are looking for. The mind may be slow to interpret the unexpected; but as swift as the eye to mark an object once the strong factor personal disbelief is removed.

You think you cannot see shot in the air because you have always been told that you cannot. You can. And, with a very little practice, you can pick up the trick. I don't suggest that you will see the shot charge as a swarm of individual pellets; but what you *will* see is a sort of 'aerial disturbance.'

At 25 yards range the human eye cannot discern differences if these are less than a certain minute of angle. Two bullet holes on a ·22 range target are not visible as separate holes unless the difference of centres exceeds one-tenth of an inch. A double is only visible without glasses, as a double, if the degree of separation exceeds this. In the same way a definitive line on a landscape target, shot at 25 yards, has to be one-tenth of an inch or over before it is effective, and it is not effective then with thin shading lines near it. In fact, the behaviour of our eyes is something which it is very difficult to calculate exactly.

Although we think of our cartridges as smokeless and flameless

there is actually a fair amount of smoke and quite a big handful
of flame at every discharge. If you are shooting at dusk you will
see the flame. If you are shooting on a still day, with a damp
stagnant atmosphere, you will see the smoke. As the shooter, you
may not notice it; but, if you look down the line of guns, as a
spectator you will.

The shooter himself cannot see his own shot because the flame,
smoke and hot gasses get in the way; but any ordinary individual,
having been told where to look, will soon pick up shot in flight
and follow them to the target. At first, what you will see is only
the wad; but, very soon, you will learn to disregard the wad
altogether.

I need hardly say what a valuable asset a well-trained loader
who has been taught that trick can be to any sportsman. The
loader can say *where* you are shooting and with that information
you can, or you ought to be able, immediately to correct your
shooting instead of getting flurried and blundering about in your
anxiety to discover what you are doing wrong.

Muzzle blast means a flame of two or three inches and a gas
disturbance nearly as big as an orange. It is because of this that
the shooter cannot see the shot that he fires himself. If you can
imagine an air gun firing a 12-bore load with equivalent velocity
it is possible that one could see the effect; but with powder it is
impossible for anyone, except an observer behind the gun who
looks, not at the gun-muzzle, but at a point in the air on the
line of shot and forward of the gun.

The observer should stand behind the gun and his eye-level
should be about three inches above the gun-muzzles. To begin
with, it is wise to stand on something like a soapbox which gives
adequate elevation; but, once the trick has been acquired, this
additional height is not necessary.

This is the way to make a practical experiment. Choose a safe
level site. The shooter kneels down and shoots parallel with the
ground. The observer stands a foot or two behind the shooter's
shoulder. Unless the observer is a very quick learner it is quite
possible that he won't see anything at all for the first dozen rounds
or so; but, if he studies the matter carefully, and sets about it in
the knowledge that he will see the shot if he concentrates he will
pick up the trick in well under 60 rounds. There are, however,
several requisites which are necessary.

Most people are inclined to jump, start or flinch at the report of a gun. Even experienced Bisley rifle shots sometimes find adjoining rifle fire disconcerting. It is only with practice that they become almost unaware of it. Shooting school coaches, of course, never notice gunfire at all, but the shock of constant explosions can be a little trying to an individual who is not at it all day and every day. A plug of cotton wool, or better still cotton wool kneaded up with a pinch of plasticine, forms a very good 'shock stopper' even if it checks conversational exchange. Make no mistake that this is an important requisite of learning to see shots in the air. 'Observer's jump' has to be overcome. But once the shooting becomes mono- tonous, 'observer's jump' vanishes and you can employ your ears to be as dead to the gun as many listeners seem to be dead to the background of sound provided by the radio.

The kneeling position is a very good one for the shooter to adopt. In the learning stage, it gives an observer altogether better angle of vision. In fact, proof guns are normally mounted about two feet from the ground and fired over open country; and most proof attendants can see the shot charge every time on its way to the twenty-yard target. Indeed, background is very important and even the expert coach and gun-fitter prefers certain weather con- ditions, such as a slightly overcast sky to a cloudless sky, or the glare of brilliant sunshine. But, even so, the expert coach can still see the shot in the air and tell from it where the gun-muzzles are pointing at the instant of discharge. That is something which comes from experience; yet, once the loader has got the knack of seeing the shot in the air, he is able to tell the shooter exactly where he is shooting even though he may not be able to locate the error.

But the trained coach sees a great deal more than merely the flight of the swarm of projectiles. He sees the flight of the charge with the centre of his eye but he is also aware of the gun-muzzles on the outer edge of his field of view. He is looking ahead to the shot pattern and he is literally watching the gun-muzzles 'out of the corner of his eye.' He sees how the gun comes up, whether steadily or jerkily, whether it checks or wavers, how true the alignment on the target is, and whether the barrels are level or canted to the right or left. He is also able to detect, from the muzzle movement, errors of gun-mounting. Some people, for example, tend to bring up their gun out of parallel with the axis of vision; that is to say, the barrels are dipped or pointed. The barrels come up before the stock, or the stock comes up with the lift of the right hand quicker than the left hand, and the fore hand pushes out the barrels.

From this, the trained coach can also judge whether the gun comes up in front or behind the bird. From the level of the muzzle he can gauge whether the left-hand grip was correct, or over stressed, or whether the right elbow was properly kept down. 'Lifting the elbow' is not a gesture which makes for clean shooting. Lastly, in that fraction of a second when the skilled coach sees the barrels at the same time that he sees the shot in flight, he gets an impression of the shooter's behaviour at the instant of firing. He can tell if the trigger has been snatched, or pulled with too great anxiety, or whether, as he hopes, properly and automatically pressed as a sort of reflex of gun-mounting.

Every shot makes occasional errors; otherwise none of us would ever miss. But the coach is not dealing with an occasional fault. He is searching out and trying to remedy a consistent one.

I think it very unlikely that an amateur, or even a regular loader, can be trained to make the all-round assessments of shooting as a professional can; but anybody who shoots with one man regularly would be well advised to have him taught to see shot in the air. It may well be that, if he gets to know his master well, he can even help him to diagnose his errors. But, even if he can't do that, he can very quickly learn to explain where the charge went.

What the layman can do, as distinct from the coach, depends a great deal on personal intelligence. There is probably a limit to the groom-chauffeur-loader-handyman's capacity; but, if *two* sportsmen get together to practise gun drill and to help each other by marking shot in the air, they will be able to do a great deal to help each other's shooting.

The preliminary instructions are simple. Plug your ears if you jump at a charge. Stand behind your fellow shooter's right shoulder as he kneels and look in line with whatever stationary target you have erected. Incidentally, it is a good idea to test patterns on sheets of paper at the same time. When you are observing, fix your eye in the first place about a couple of yards in front of the barrels. If you don't see anything, increase the distance shot by shot, a yard at a time. The distance that accommodates itself most easily varies with different individuals. You can only find out what personally suits you best by experiment.

Your first impression, on seeing the shot, will be a kind of 'flicker' as a ghost of a shadow passes. In a few more shots you will be able to pick up the line and follow its course to the target.

Actually, it is doubtful if we really see the shots themselves; but the turbulence is enough. When a few pellets are very close together you *may* see them but only as a part of the general disturbance. What you see is perhaps closer to a heat effect, but it is nevertheless a substantial visible entity. In a very short time the knack is acquired and you can follow shot from gun to target as easily as you can a golf ball from tee to green.

All good shooting is really synchronization in timing. Most good shots say frankly that they 'do not know how they shot.' This is true: but if we use the slow motion cine camera we find that, quite unconsciously, arms, body and gun move at the same speed whilst picking up the bird. The gun is for the time a rigid member of the body, not a movable projection free to move in arcs of the body as centre or pivotal axis. In a word, a good shot doesn't move his gun on to a bird; he turns the whole body and head, the gun moving rhythmically *with*, not independently *of* the body. In fact the secret of good shooting is to point yourself, not the gun, at the bird.

When shooting clay pigeons some indication of imperfections in shooting can be inferred from the way the pieces fly. A perfectly centred hit usually means a cloud of dust and no big pieces: but a clay hit at nine o'clock will usually throw off its bigger pieces in a direction opposite to the point of fracture. That is to say that, if you hit a clay at nine o'clock, or on the edge, the bigger bits will fly towards three o'clock. The rule is that where you hit the clays will be revealed because the larger pieces will take the opposite direction to the side hit by the charge. Clays which are hit, but not broken, are an indication that you are shooting too high.

I can imagine a keen shooting man thinking, as he reads this, that it might be much simpler to use tracer cartridges. Tracer cartridges have been in existence in various forms for nearly half a century but they fail in their object because, in nine cases out of ten, the shooter cannot see the trace until too late, owing to muzzle blast. It is visible to others and may cause interest and hilarity; but it also distracts them from the job of looking after their own shooting. In practice, tracer cartridges are little used, but I understand that the latest examples are non-poisonous and not likely to start moor fires. If you kill a bird with a modern tracer, it will still be edible.

But there are other objections to its use. The unskilled observer can see where the trace goes but he sights it rather late and only after recovery from blast dazzle and recoil. He cannot gauge where it is in respect of range and the apparent tracer line may be sixty yards high. As the bird (at thirty yards) has gone on, the impression is that the shot was behind. An individual observer might have seen it pass in front of the bird whereas the gunner himself, seeing it later in relation to a bird which has gone on, sees it behind. It is a misleading affair and even well-skilled and well-placed observers can tell little from a single tracer shot. In brief, tracer cartridges are on the whole best avoided. Much better to learn to see the shot in the air and use ordinary shooting school methods rather than spectacular but misleading pyrotechnics.

Let's assume that you have now mastered how to see shot in the air. And that, with the aid of a friend, you are beginning to learn where you are with your shooting—right or left, high or low. But, so far, you don't know the reasons which lead to the misses. You know that you are shooting in front or behind, too far to the right, too far to the left, but you don't know why.

Years of coaching lead me to some useful and helpful generalizations. Admittedly, what I can tell you is not a complete explanation of every shooter's behaviour with a gun; but, for practical purposes, the advice I can give you is likely to be correct in the case of ninety-nine people out of a hundred. So let's diagnose the symptoms of the most common disorders among shooting men.

I think you can learn from what I tell you. But I do want to remind you again that the advice of the written word, however invaluable as a record or a foundation, does not replace, and never can replace, the personal contact. You can get help from this book for it will show you where you are wrong; but, even if you can diagnose your own faults and perhaps partly cure them, it is still better to go to a specialist for treatment, for self-diagnosis often overlooks other faults in its eagerness to cure one. Doctors, in the ordinary way, don't try to physic themselves. But I realize that this book is likely to be read by many people who are denied the opportunity of being able to go to shooting schools where there are first-class coaches. For them, the written word from me will have to be enough. For the rest, they will have to do what they can to experiment with the means available.

Perhaps you are reading this in a place where there isn't a clay pigeon trap within hundreds of miles; but you can devise a moving target which is better than nothing at all. All you need is an old inner tube out of a bicycle tyre and a supply of empty tin cans or other projectile. If two strong tall stakes are driven into the ground and the inner tube used as a simple catapult you will find that you will be able to throw empty food cans, or even some easily obtained local produce like a gourd, or a melon, with considerable effect. Alternatively, of course, you can get a strong-armed human being to pitch for you, but you will be well advised to see to it that he is standing behind a protective sheet of metal or an earth butt. Now, with an experienced friend who has learnt to see shot in the air, start shooting.

My advice now is to the observer:

The most puzzling shooter to help is the really *inconsistent* shot who seems to miss birds sometimes in front, sometimes behind, sometimes to the right and sometimes to the left. Watching him shoot you fail to find any rhyme or reason in what he is up to. In that event you can be practically certain that, in ninety-nine cases out of a hundred, he is letting his eye leave the bird and shooting at some point in front where he thinks his shot will intercept it. This is not always a conscious process; it is a sort of half memory of loose advice about 'shooting in front' and 'forward allowances.' What is really happening is that he is not firing at the bird at all but at a vague point on space somewhere on the bird's line. Even if he judges it fairly well, in terms of relative speed and range, a quick snap shot sometimes puts him ahead of the bird but more often he momentarily pauses with the idea of letting the bird get to the place that he expects to meet it and, in consequence, shoots behind. This is a very common type of error, typical of the man with quick reactions who tends to anticipate the bird rather than travel with it.

In fact, you can learn a great deal about a man's shooting without looking at the target he is shooting at. Look out for the case of the man who is so hypnotized by the appearance of the bird that he mounts his gun slightly behind it and then has to make a terrific heave with his arms and body to try to recapture the line of flight. The fault of this type is that he always looks at the muzzles of his gun instead of concentrating on the bird.

These, of course, are fundamental errors. They overtake a man who has shot fairly well in an untutored sort of way all his life, and they are responsible for half the disappointments of middle age and nearly all the disillusionments of the youthful shooter.

In both these cases the remedy is that the offender must be taught the only sound basic method of shooting. He must master the gun drill and be trained to look at the bird, pick it up with his eyes, body and hands and mount the gun without any special effort. It is a matter of controlled rhythm.

If you want to help a man who is making the sort of mistakes that I have described, it is paradoxical, but true, that if you tell him to 'try to fire behind the bird' he thinks to himself that that will be rather easier than trying to hit it in the beak. At once, he relaxes and unconsciously falls into the correct rhythm of movement of body, gun and eye. It does not follow that he will begin to hit his bird; but he will begin to shoot with the same degree of relaxation and he will begin to *shoot* consistently. Consistency is the hardest thing to attain in shooting; consistency in performance, even if the performance is in error. Once you have nailed an error, and the man keeps on making it, it is relatively easy to put him on the straight road. It is invariably the emotional man, with his quicker reactions and inconsistent stresses, who is the most difficult to train.

It would be easy, indeed, if every error of shooting behind or in front of a bird could always be related to human emotions, but we must also look for physical bad habits.

A common error among many shots is to 'trombone' the left hand up and down the fore-end. Sometimes the shooter grips the fore-end at one point and sometimes another. If his hand is too far forward he will tend to shoot to the left (i.e. behind a right-hand crossing bird) and when the hand is back towards the breech he shoots to the right (i.e. behind a bird crossing right to left).

A hand guard is usually an immediate cure. It tends to place the grip.

Once you have overcome some of the commoner errors in shooting you will still find that there are some angles of shot that you can take successfully every time, and others which continually beat you. Normally speaking, it is easier for a right-handed man to take a crossing bird moving from right to left than it is for him to take a crossing bird left to right. The reason is simply that the body movement in taking the right to left bird comes naturally and he does not usually swing as well in the reverse direction. There is also a very great difference between low birds on the left or high birds on the left; and, in the same way, low and high birds on the right.

P

A man who is fairly good at pheasants, however they come, may find himself shooting high and over low birds such as grouse and partridge. The reason appears to be that, for the low shot, he bends his neck too much and gets his eye down to below his *normal* for his gun rib.

If you are shooting with a friend, arrange it, if you can, so that you get the largest variety of shots possible. It is only in that way that you will find out your weakness. The same oncoming bird presented to you again and again may become so easy that shooting is automatic. You will know its place in the air before it reaches you. In the actual shooting field you never know what is coming or at what angle it is going to approach you. We have a phase in the shooting school where we shout out to the boy in the trap: 'Vary them.' There is no surer way of finding out a sportsman, who is feeling a little above himself; and there is no better way either of really shaping him up into a first-class shot.

Don't be content, when you are shooting clay pigeons, to shoot them somehow or another. Concentrate on style and the finesse of gun-mounting and anticipation. Try too, if you are taking the same shot again and again, to improve your performance by killing your bird earlier and earlier. Within a few rounds at the shooting school we can tell the difference between a first-class shot and a good average performer by the fact that the first-class shot will always break his clay, or almost always, ten yards ahead of the middlingly good man.*

In the case of a man in good physical condition, a natural flare for athletics and the keenness that goes with it, what I have said in this book can scarcely fail to benefit him if he follows my advice carefully. But, in the course of a lifetime of intensive work as a gun-fitter and coach, I have learned that there are many cases where special treatment is called for. Many of them are related to physical handicaps of one kind or another; and many of them are cases of an almost melancholic loss of confidence.

The most usual symptom is when a man comes to see me, who, after many years' shooting, complains that he has completely lost confidence in his gun; that there is something the matter with it, and it won't do what he wants it to. Usually, it isn't the fault of the gun at all. Usually, what we find is that we are dealing with a case of nerves, brought on either by ill health or through over-anxiety to do well. The man who is sick dwells on

---

* Before they look 'big enough to eat.'

his trigger and the over-anxious man snatches and fires before his left hand can get to the bird. The result, of course, is always the same: a clean miss.

To shoot well it is extremely important to feel complete confidence in your gun and your cartridge. You must make up your mind that, if you miss, it isn't the gun's fault; once in a thousand times you may pick on a bad cartridge and, once in a lifetime, something may go wrong with the mechanism of your gun. Normally, if you miss, it is your fault. You must believe that. Second, you must count the bird dead before you pull the trigger. I know several good shots who would be really wonderful shots if they could only master themselves and concentrate on the one shot they have to make instead of worrying about the bird they missed or wondering what people will say about them if they don't put up a better show later in the day.

I remember one man who was, I think, one of the worst shots I have ever seen; yet he was by no means a novice. At his first lesson he did everything but kill the bird. He was so slow, even in starting his gun-mounting, that the target would move yards ahead of his gun before he got up to it; and, even then, in many cases, he wouldn't fire at all. He explained that his trouble was lack of co-ordination and that a specialist was treating him for this complaint. It was evident that eye and hand were not working together. I treated it as just another case of nerves.

At the second lesson, I took out the try-gun and a pair of snap caps for practice at ordinary incoming targets. For the first dozen birds or so I also held the gun with my right hand round the action, immediately in front of the trigger guard. As soon as the bird appeared I helped mount the gun to the shooter's should whilst keeping the muzzle on the bird. After a bit of practice he was doing fairly well and I knew I had taught his left hand what to do. As I had also called 'pull' and the trigger *had* been pulled each time fairly consistently, I went on to the next job of teaching his eye where to look. I told the shooter that he was now ready to do some actual shooting, but that all I wanted him to do, at first, was to shoot behind the bird and not to bother about hitting it at all. All I was concerned with was to polish up his style. To his surprise he began smashing the birds at once and whereas, on the previous occasion he had come to the shooting school, the bird was over his head before he could get his gun up, now he was doing much steadier work and banging his gun in front. A little later, I was able to fit him, and to coach him into being quite a reasonable shot.

There was another case of a man who was suffering from severe war wounds which completely paralysed both his legs. He could shuffle along with the aid of a walking-stick, and could stand without its aid; but the recoil of a 12-bore gun would disturb his balance and knock him over. As he was still keen to shoot he wanted me to supply him with a ·410-bore gun. I saw that he was helpless without his stick; he had no body swing. So, rather boldly, because I had never come across a case like his before, I suggested that he should hold his stick at his back with his left hand, using it in effect to help support his legs in the form of a tripod. Then I taught him to shoot with one arm only. He is still using a 12-bore gun.

I had another pupil who couldn't stand at all; but sat on a cushion on the ground. He had no need to turn round as he could lie back and shoot birds that passed well overhead. I remember this very well as he nearly singed my hair off on one occasion when I knelt at the back of him.

The worst case of flinching I have ever come across was a man who, when he fired, would close both his eyes tight, hang on with both hands, and fail to pull the trigger. I decided that this was a case in which the only thing to do was to do the shooting myself and let him watch me. Sportsmen so rarely get the chance of watching anyone else shoot that it is sometimes a lesson in itself just to let them see the instructor polishing off a few clays. At first my pupil even flinched at the noise of my shooting; but, a little later, he wanted to try again. I told him to keep his head and neck very stiff, to sink it in fact, as if he were shrugging his shoulders. I hoped that that device would cure him of flinching. It worked, and he, too, became ultimately quite a reasonable shot.

Another case of a physical disability was a tall man who came to me with such a long neck that, although his stock was sixteen-and-a-half inches, he had to put his head down to meet it. The consequence was that his neck muscles were loosened and his head was jarred back every time he fired a shot. He flinched badly and suffered from gun headache. I built him a stock on the Monte Carlo style (*see page* 204) which would come up to his face instead of his having to put his face down to the stock. By getting him to put his shoulder well into the gun his trouble was cured.

Troubles with the right hand are comparatively rare. But I remember one case of a man whose trigger finger was in good order but whose middle finger was slightly bent and the other two fingers completely doubled up and useless. There was no grip at all in the hand and, on recoil, the gun jumped back and bruised his fingers. After several experiments he found that, first, by pointing the left hand at the bird (in other words, by keeping it firm and not pulling), a certain amount of recoil was taken bodily by this left arm. Secondly, by pushing the right shoulder forward and altering the stance, there was less injury to the right hand. But all was by no means well. I made him a very curved pistol grip, somewhat on the lines of my one arm grip, but very narrow. It was an improvement, but still the shooter could only hold the gun between middle finger and thumb. Finally, I discovered that, although the other two fingers were doubled up and weak at the top joints, yet they could pinch my finger when I forced it between the two knuckle joints. This gave me the idea to fit a small rubber peg on the left side of the grip to fit between these fingers. Finally, this shooter, too, was able to carry on without discomfort.

I wouldn't like to tell you how many people have come to see me who have introduced themselves quite cheerily by saying: 'You have probably met the worst shot in Britain; now you are meeting the worst shot in the world.' There was one man who came into me to confess that he had been shooting ever since the shooting season had begun and that he had not killed one single bird. I am never worried by cases like that very much. In fact I maintain that the very bad shot is a much easier task to pull together than the ordinary shot. The very bad shot is usually doing something consistently wrong and can be speedily put back on the mark. The ordinary shot is usually so inconsistent that he fills the air full of lead and misleads himself and everybody else by the fact that some head of game occasionally runs into the charge he throws up.

Often, when a man finds his shooting going off, he starts worrying because one off-day leads to another and the whole is put down usually to increasing years. I am not sure that this is the cause at all. As a man grows older muscles contract and slight modifications in a lighter gun, refitted for these physical changes, will allow him to enjoy his sport more than ever before. I remember very well when that celebrated farmer and fine shot, Mr.

A. G. Street, came to me to say that he had got to give up shooting because, owing to a couple of crippled arms, he couldn't get a gun up any longer. I fitted him out with one of my short-barrelled guns and, in half an hour at the shooting school, he was bringing down pheasants as tall and partridges as fast as anything he had killed in his life. That was many shooting seasons ago, and most people who know him will say now that A. G. Street is still an outstanding game shot.

To demonstrate how little old age and bad sight is a bar to good shooting, I remember one man whose sight was so poor that he couldn't see a bird in front. Yet he was still very keen to go on shooting. I decided that the only way to deal with him was to tell him that he must rely on his loader's eyes entirely and rest what was left of his own by looking at nothing until his loader said 'Mark' for an overhead bird, 'Left' for a left-hander and 'Right' for a right-hander. He was then to look into the blue at an angle of about forty-five degrees. If the bird came at all into his vision he was to snap at it, but otherwise he wasn't to look for it. As he only shot pheasants we had no low shots to cater for. The improvement was noticeable immediately. An onlooker said that his sight had improved 100 per cent; but what had really happened was that he had stopped staring about, looking here, there and everywhere and so forcing his eyes out of focus. Now he was concentrating on letting the birds come to his eyes.

Whatever your physical disability, I want to emphasize that, if you are keen to shoot, there is usually something that can be done to help you. The one-arm gun, for example, is intended primarily for those who have lost an arm, but men with artificial legs, men who are weak on their legs and men who have a weak left arm might all be better and safer shots for its use.

The late Lord Gough was classed, not as one of our best one-armed shots, but as one of the best shots in the country; so great a distinction that a sporting magazine once published a full-page article entitled 'Are Two Arms Necessary for Shooting?' With the right tools and proper technique a man using a one-arm gun can easily hold his own on the field.

Of course a special gun is needed. The illustration facing page 225 shows my own design. It is based on the fact that, for the one-armed shot, the ordinary gun is too top-heavy. The weight of it causes head movement in gun-mounting and a poking aim which may look dangerous even if it is not so in reality. By twisting the lever and fitting triggers and safety work in a forward position much nearer the breech, the gun balances in one hand. The lever, safety catch and triggers can all be manipulated without shifting the hand or relaxing grip. The photographs show the method of opening, loading and closing the gun, and the technique is to shoot, right foot slightly forward; to keep the gun under the arm-pit in ready position until 99 per cent of the body swing has been completed. Plenty of indoor drill until a smooth effortless action is obtained will allow a man using a one-arm gun to be as quick as anybody on the fast driven partridge and steady on the high pheasant.

VI

The Care of a Gun

THE modern game gun, as made by a first-class London maker, is an arm with an almost indeterminable lease of life. Properly looked after, it will endure year after year without deterioration; but only the very few take the proper amount of care.

The vast majority of sportsmen have indeed never learnt how to assemble a gun properly when they take it out of its case; or how to dismount it when they put it away again. Most second-hand guns carry the scars of brutal ill-treatment. It is to the credit of their makers that, in spite of it, they are still sound if battered weapons.

A gun is normally put away in its case in two pieces: the barrels with the fore-end attached and the stock and actions. Take down your gun case and, without reading further, put one of your own guns together in your usual way.

Unless you have a very exceptional knowledge of gunmanship, I fancy that you began by lifting out the barrels, removing the fore-end and placing it on the table beside you. After that, you lifted out the stock and action and then fiddled about for a few seconds while you hooked the lumps on the barrels into the action of the gun. I shouldn't be surprised if you bruised the metal even slightly as you did so. Subsequently, you picked up the fore-end again and clamped it under the barrels of the gun.

First, the chances are that you did not hold the barrels at the correct angle to the action when you tried to join the two together. Second, you took a considerable risk of denting the barrels, or dropping them, by handling them without the firm grip that the forehand normally gives you. Third, as you attempted to hook the barrels into the action, the probability is that you hadn't pressed the lever completely home.

Let me now describe to you, in detail, how you should have assembled the gun. Taking the barrels out of the case, you should have removed the fore-end and, instead of putting it down, placed it loosely beyond the fore-end loop which normally holds it to the barrels. Then, with a firm grip round fore-end and barrels, you should have taken the stock of your gun under your left arm, forced the lever well back with the point of your thumb and then, holding the barrels at right angles to the action, smoothly slipped the lumps into their seating. It should have been a movement as oily as the movement of a limb. When the barrel was locked on to the gun, you should have then grasped the weapon by the small of the butt and, only then, released your grip on the fore-end and adjusted it in its proper position.

Dismounting the gun, you should go through the process in reverse. First, remove the fore-end and place it loosely above the catch on the barrels. Grasp fore-end and barrels with your right hand, give yourself a comfortable grip, and then, pressing back the lever of the gun to its full traverse, break the weapon in your hand. Subsequently, the fore-end is clicked on in its proper place.

Many shooting men, when they dismount their guns, still believe that they rest the mainsprings by releasing the cocking levers. Don't do it. First of all, the action of a shot-gun, unlike a rifle, can be severely damaged if you release the pins on an empty chamber. If you must do it, make sure that you have got snap caps in the barrels. But, apart from that, releasing the mainspring is quite unnecessary. Whatever you do, the mainsprings in a gun are always under tension and, in fact, the difference in the pressure on the springs between a gun cocked and uncocked is a matter of not more than a quarter of an inch. Put your gun away fully cocked. The springs won't mind and, further, when you come to mount the gun, it will come together that much more easily. ·

When you buy a new gun, you will notice that the gun-maker supplies a cleaning rod, a mop and a wire brush, and little else. The equipment is not really adequate to clean a gun properly or to keep it in the order you should. In fact, any keen shooting man should keep in his gun cupboard not one cleaning rod but two or three all fully assembled. The wool mop, which every gun-maker supplies, is not really an essential, although it is useful for wiping out the barrels with light oil before the gun is put away. The essentials of gun cleaning are a jag, with patches cut to size to fit it, a wire brush, and one of the excellent gun oils like Young's cleaner. In addition, you can treat yourself to all sorts of accessories which are useful but not essential, such as a toothbrush which is really very valuable for brushing mud out of the checkering of the stock, a chamber brush designed for cleaning out the chambers which are larger than the barrel of the gun beyond; some wax polish to keep a shine on the stock; an oily rag and a clean rag for polishing up the stock itself.

Properly speaking, every shooting man, unless he is one of those fortunate individuals, these days, who has a manservant, and a manservant, too, whom he can really trust, should clean his own gun. However tired you are at the end of the day, it is foolish to delegate the cleaning of a weapon, which costs as much as a piano, to a keeper or somebody else who 'couldn't care less.' And, if you clean your gun yourself, clean it properly.

I see so many shooting men whose idea of cleaning their guns is to insert a rod into the barrel, scrub the top fifteen inches diligently and ignore the first ten or fifteen inches of the barrel (which most needs cleaning) altogether, except as they push the brush in or pull it out. They put away their guns with fouling under the extractors and in the recesses of the action. Usually there is wet which will cause rust in the gutters on each side of the rib. There is mud in the checkering and, probably, they have made a dent in the barrel which, through putting the gun away dirty, they have failed to observe.

Before the general introduction of non-corrosive caps, I pointed out that the firing of *one* cartridge creates just as much fouling as five hundred cartridges. Now, it can be said that the residue from the cartridges (make sure you haven't got a batch of the old corrosive sort) won't harm the gun. We're back to the situation which ruled in the old days when sportsmen used black powder and flintlocks.

Black powder was comparatively harmless to the metal and the necessity of cleaning the gun was determined rather by the need that, after forty or fifty rounds, the barrels became so fouled with the residue of the powder that they had to be cleaned in rather the same way that a pipe has to be scraped out at intervals to remove the carbon.

But, in the black powder days, shooting was a sooty business. After a day in the field, men came back with hands and faces greased like sweeps with powder waste. Guns were dirty, smelly things which had to be relegated to the sort of corner in the house where nowadays we leave gumboots.

But, nowadays, many sportsmen like to keep their guns as ornaments, in a rack or behind a glass-fronted cupboard in the study or library. Guns should still be looked after as the ornaments they are. My advice, it's the only advice when guns cost as much as they do today, is to clean them and look after them as religiously as if the non-rusting cap had never been developed. Only in that way can you be sure that hidden enemies aren't damaging your valuable property.

Different shooting men have their own different ways of cleaning a gun, and different accessories. But the principle never varies. When you bring home your gun at the end of a day's shooting, dismount it, not forgetting to replace the fore-end on the barrels; and, if it has been raining during the day, take the stock and action in your hands by the small of the butt and shake it thoroughly. It is surprising the amount of water that can collect in the striker holes in the face of the action. You will do a great deal to keep rust down if you remember to do this after a wet day's shooting. Next, wipe over the action, and the barrels, and set the barrels up in a safe place to enable any water which has collected in the gutters on each side of the ribs to drip away and dry off.

To clean the barrels, begin by pushing through an old rag to get out the worst of the fouling. A good trick is to roll up a tiny ball of newspaper and push that, with the point of the jag, through the two barrels. The idea of getting rid of the worst of the fouling before you start cleaning is to keep the rest of your cleaning gear clean and in decent order. Subsequently, using Young's cleaner, Three-in-One, or better still the solvent of Young's cleaner with three parts of water (because oil alone will not eliminate the chloride), clean the gun thoroughly with a linen patch wrapped round the jag. When I say thoroughly, I mean work the cleaning rod up and down with pushes of about three or four inches at a time from the chambers to the muzzle and back again.

Make a really thorough job of it and put some elbow grease into the effort. Subsequently, hold up the barrels to the electric light and look at it carefully, from both ends, to satisfy yourself that there are no revealing streaks of leading showing. The leading is something to look for. The barrel should be absolutely moon-bright when you have finished with it.*

After making sure that the barrels are quite clean, raise the extractors and poke around to clean out any residue of powder

---

* *This work is not quite so necessary with non-corrosive cartridges today. You can tell at a glance the difference between the residue left behind by a non-corrosive cartridge and a corrosive one just by looking up the barrels. Nevertheless, the principle remains. Clean your gun, which costs so much, as thoroughly as you had to do in other times. You will never regret it.*

which has got underneath them or in the ridge of the chamber which takes the rim of the cartridge. This is a fiddling job but important. Next, with a piece of oily rag, wipe out the gutters on each side of the rib very carefully. Subsequently, wipe the barrels over to remove any blood marks or finger marks which you have left on it.

Then pass on to the stock. Wipe over the metal work carefully with an oily rag. Then, with a matchstick, put the very smallest drop of oil into the cracks where the trigger blades extend through from the action into the two pinholes on the face of the action, on to the safety catch and under the lever of the gun.

If the gun is muddy, clean the checkering gently with an old toothbrush. When it is quite clean, if you are particular about the appearance of your stock, rub it with a little oil; or, better still, polish it up like a piece of furniture with a good quality wax polish.

(*It is a matter of doubt whether there is any real advantage in polishing the stocks with wax polish, or not. It can't do any harm, but it is very difficult to improve on the finish of the craftsman who brought out the figure in the walnut in the first place. Perhaps the best plan is to keep the stocks clean, and return the guns between seasons to the makers to have dents in the wood lifted and the stocks professionally polished. It's miraculous what can be done for a few pounds.*)

Treat the fore-end in the same way that you treat the stock of the gun. Rub the mud out of the checkering and administer a smear of oil to the ejector springs, the joined catch and the flats and face of the action. After that you can put your gun away.

I want to emphasize that it is unwise to use too much oil. Heavy oiling of ejectors and cocking limbs, strikers and trigger blades, is not to be recommended. When a gun is overhauled by the maker— as every gun should be at regular intervals—fine oil is put on the working parts which is sufficient to last the season. Excessive oiling causes the woodwork to swell, locks to get 'gummy,' and pulls to behave irregularly. Oil you must, but the tiniest touch of oil is adequate. Much more important to remember not to put the gun away wet, with drops of water under the cocking levers or water where it will create rust hanging about in the gutters under the ribs.

If you can possibly arrange it so, it is much better to keep your guns fully assembled in a case, or a rack, than to put them away in their cases. If the only place you have got to keep your guns is in their cases, never leave them there for more than a few months without taking them out to have a look at them, and wipe them over. If you *must* put them away for a long period, either send them to the gun-maker to look after them for you or, alternatively, coat the barrels and the actions with the jelly called 'safety paste,' which is made by B.S.A. It is a very excellent preservative. Whatever you do, don't use one of those old-fashioned rods covered with baize inside the barrels. They don't do any good at all and, in fact, encourage rusting.

It is always a good thing to treat your baize-lined gun cases with D.D.T. or some other effective moth spray. Many a sportsman has had an ugly shock when he has opened a beautiful new gun case, which he hasn't looked at since the season before, to find that the clothes moths have cut it to pieces.

If you get interested in taking care of your guns, you will get nearly as much joy out of that as out of using them. I have only given you the bare essentials of gun cleaning here. You will find, if you get interested, that you can buy the most intriguing box of tackle and complete gun-cleaning outfits containing detailed and adequate instructions on cleaning a gun properly.

It is a wise and economical policy to send in your gun or guns for overhaul and thorough cleaning at the end of every season. The owner's cleaning, however thorough, is necessarily limited to externals. The gunsmith strips the locks and action and makes a general overhaul besides cleaning and lubricating all moving parts. In the process, wear and tear are noted and corrected and the gun properly tightened up for the next shooting season. This is much more important than is generally realized, for if there is any undue free play or movement about the action of a gun, and the weapon is fired repeatedly in that state, the hammer action of the firing is likely to exaggerate this small element of wear and tear into a serious looseness.

Further, a great many sportsmen never realize the extent to which in the season they bruise, dent or cut the barrels of their guns. A dropped gun, a hasty scramble into a car, or any of the casual bumps of a day's shooting may account for it. There is only one thing to do; never entrust your gun to a man who may, or may not be, a master of his craft; but send it back to the maker or to a gun-maker known to be reliable. Barrels are sensitive things and, if any accident occurs which dents or bruises them at all seriously, DO NOT ATTEMPT TO FIRE CARTRIDGES

THROUGH THE INJURED TUBE. Rather give up sport for the day than run risks with an expensive gun. The chief causes of burst barrels are as follows: first, the barrel is indented; secondly, a hard tight-fitting wad meets the obstruction and turns it into a bulge; finally, the smallest obstruction to the damaged muzzle will burst the barrel, for the strain flies to the weakest part and that part is already strained to its limits.

Repeated use of a dented barrel tends to wear the internal bulge thin. In extreme cases, it may push it out and so turn the dent into a bulge. Both render the subsequent repair more difficult and involve the removal of important metal in polishing.

There is another reason why you should always send your gun to the maker for an annual overhaul. Apart from protecting the gun for a very small charge, it also does a very great deal to improve it. In fact, it takes much longer to 'run in a gun' than a motor-car. This periodical overhaul and polishing of all the mechanism gradually converts a solid medium-priced article into a better quality machine, whilst the best gun, after a few overhauls, gets even better in its sweetness of opening and closing, its crispness of pull and behaviour under fire. Apart from this, you are neglecting a valuable article by putting it away and allowing the mechanism to rust, as it certainly will.

There are one or two minor mishaps which may occur in the field. A loose-fitting fore-end may drop off the gun while it is being closed. If the ejector hammers are down, it may be difficult to replace. In the fore-end can be seen the projecting hammers of the ejectors. If the fore-end cannot be replaced with the gun in a partly open position (as it was when it fell off), these ejector hammers should be pressed back into the fore-end until they cock. This should not be done except with a blunt tool such as the end of a hard wood cleaning rod. Best of all is to fit the fore-end on to the barrels and push the protruding extractor or extractors back by using a firm pressure against a wooden bench, or its equivalent in the nearest fence or gatepost.

When a single trigger gun jams, and the top lever refuses to operate, push the trigger forward and pull the safety catch back.

The cause of a gun jamming is often to be found in a striker sticking in a cap. The speediest solution of this problem is, if the other barrel is loaded, to fire into the air, trusting to the jar of recoil to dislodge the errant striker. Then hold the lever open with the thumb and give the gun a sharp jerk. This usually puts matters right and, at all events, it cannot damage anything except the striker point.

If the lever refuses to open under ordinary pressure, hold the gun sideways; put both thumbs, one over the other, against the lever and the fingers of both hands against the right lock. The amount of pressure from such a squeeze is ever so much more than can be made with one finger and thumb; after opening look for and remove the cause, which may be either a burst rim or powder residue between barrels and action.

Another embarrassment occurs when a cartridge slips behind the extractor. This is a case when force should not be applied. There is a danger of 'making things worse.' First, dismount the barrels, put the extractor out to its limit and, if the case cannot be manœuvred into position for extraction, it will be necessary to remove the screw holding the extractors; pull them bodily out, remove the case, and replace them. If the arm is an ejector the ejector hammers may need re-cocking in the manner previously explained.

The irregular functioning of ejectors may be caused either by lack of oil and friction from rust, or by use of wrong kinds of oil which gum the cocking and ejector limbs. If a wash-out with paraffin, and a relubrication with good gun oil of the limbs protruding from the action, fails to remedy the trouble, the gun should be sent for adjustment.

Sometimes the gun action cannot be easily closed. This may be due to an unusually thick-rimmed cartridge, a rare but, nevertheless, not unavoidable fault in machine-made factory-loaded cases; or, more often, to a slight deposit of fired powder, fouling or dirt getting between the barrels and the action, either on the flats of the action, the flats of the barrels or in the slots of the action. Clean out any accumulation and see that the extractor screw is right home; if this is loose and projecting, it will prevent the gun closing properly.

When assembling the gun, note that, should the barrels refuse to close long before they are in contact with the action, the trouble is usually due to a projecting striker catching on the base of the extractor. If the latter is pressed back with the finger the gun will probably close.

But, no doubt, the commonest mishap you will have in the shooting field is to find that a cartridge sticks in the chamber, and the pressure of the ejector spring is not strong enough to throw it out. This very often happens with cheap cartridges which have got damp or odd rounds which, for one reason or another, are misshapen. The best thing is always to carry one of the finger-ring cartridge extractors in your pocket. Alternatively, an equally effective method is to carry in your pocket—or see to it that a keeper carries in his pocket—a sausage-shaped piece of lead (an elongated fishing sinker is ideal, about an inch long). If a spent cartridge case gets stuck in the chambers, take out the loaded case and then, with the breech open, drop a piece of lead down the muzzles. Even a fisherman's weight of about an ounce will, in the fall, gather sufficient momentum to remove the most obstinate obstruction.

The sportsman, going abroad, is sometimes induced to take cheap, or machine-made guns, on the assurance that these are quite good enough for the rigours of an expedition where rough usage will be the rule. This is the most fatal of false economies. Generally, it can be said that the better the gun the worse usage it will stand. The metal of which cheap and most foreign guns are made is remarkably soft. As a result, the guns shoot and wear loose with astonishing speed. They are not constructed to last and, though sold at a low price, are not cheap in terms of a serviceable life. They are seldom worth repairing, for they will give out in a fresh place almost as soon as the first source of trouble has been mended. The man, who is away from civilization of any kind can, however, effect temporary repairs if one of these arms 'shoots loose' by simply centre punching the metal at the sides of the front lump beneath the barrel to bring the metal of the hook nearer to the cross-pin or hinge-bar, and thus close the breech of the barrel towards the action face; or, if the bolt is loose, a light hammering up to the back lump will enable the bolt to pull the barrel tighter down to the action. There is, however, neither economy nor reliability in cheap guns. They may not, perhaps, be actively dangerous—they carry proof marks— but they are invariably inefficient and unreliable and always provocative of small delays and embarrassments in the field. Any sportsman who is going abroad should take expert advice from his gun-maker on the care of his weapon in the country to which he is going. In tropical countries especially extra precautions are necessary to protect the woodwork and the action. These are best explained by the gun-maker when he knows the particular country to which the sportsman is going. Alternatively, he should find somebody who really knows what he is talking about on the spot.

Conclusion

I HAVE read somewhere that one-third of the motor cars at present in use in this country would not survive a strict test of road-worthiness (*written before the tests were introduced*). Whether or not this statement is true in the matter of motor cars, I would wager my last cartridge that, if all the shot-guns in regular use in the countryside were submitted to expert examination, at least 10 per cent of them would be condemned as thoroughly dangerous.

It is only necessary to attend an average rough shoot to meet people carrying suicidal antiquities which, by all the rules of ballistics, ought to explode in their hands the moment they pull the trigger. Every farm in the country includes in its deadstock some calamitous fowling piece of a former generation. And there must be thousands of people using soft metal hammer guns, made for a few pounds on the Continent, which are potentially lethal to the holder after the discharge of a few hundred rounds.

Hardly any of these guns, with the problematical exception of the cheaper foreign firearms of recent manufacture, have been proofed for use with modern smokeless powder. If you pick one up, you will find that, in most cases, the barrels fit so loosely to the stock that you can see daylight between the action face and the chambers. Locks are untrustworthy, the barrels pocked with rough holes, and the woodwork swollen from the metal like an old man's joints.

On many occasions, I have seen men out shooting with old hammer guns lashed together with bits of wire and even string. I know a gamekeeper at the moment who is using a gun in which the barrels are punctured like a colander. Every time he fires, puffs of smoke spurt out through the pits in the paper-thin tubes. Yet, if you give the owners of these guns the friendly warning that every time they shoot, they are liable to be blinded by back blast or lose their fingers through a burst barrel, they seem to take a perverse pride in the accident risk. And, invariably, they will tell you that their own gaspipe is the 'hardest hitting gun' they have ever handled.

I often wonder what they mean. Since the punch behind the charge comes entirely fron the combustion of the propellant inside the cartridge, all that any gun can do is to guide the shot in an

Q

even pattern in the direction in which the barrels are pointing. Admittedly, the constriction, or otherwise, of the shot pattern is controlled by the degree of choke in the barrel. Admittedly, too, some guns throw better shot patterns than others. But you only need to glance at the muzzles of those ancient weapons to recognize that the barrels are completely 'shot out.' The charge must spout out of them as erratically as if the shot were thrown by hand.

Nevertheless, I am the first to admit that many of these old guns do, in fact, stand up to considerable use (or mis-use) without serious accident and their owners, on occasion, shoot passably well. The explanation, if you can call it so, is that the men who use these old guns are usually enthusiastic sportsmen with an uncanny skill of their own and the guns themselves are quite often the rusty remnant of the uncanny skill of some great old craftsman. Against all reasonable possibility, the guns hold together, and contain a charge long after the margin of safety has vanished altogether. But it is not good enough.

It was A. P. Herbert, I believe, who, as a subaltern in the first world war, warned his men, when they went into action, 'to treat all Germans with the gravest suspicion.' The same might be said of old hammer guns with Damascus barrels. Some of them, not many, are proofed for standard pressures developed by modern cartridges. But the guns should be checked; and, fortunately, it is the easiest matter in the world to do so.

Any gun made in this country carries proof marks on the flats of the barrels and the actions. If a gun in good condition is stamped 'nitro proofed' or 'N.P.' it is safe to use with smokeless powder. If not, it should be sent to a reputable gun-maker for reproofing at the London or Birmingham proof house. If the barrels burst, as they probably will, under the maximum pressures imposed in proofing, the owner should count himself lucky. It might have happened when he had the gun in his hand. If the barrels stand the test, the owner will have the satisfaction of knowing that he can shoot the gun in perfect safety and that its market value has been appreciably increased by the nitro proofing stamp.

Indeed, whether the gun is old or new, I repeat that it should be sent without fail to a gun-maker at the end of every season for examination and overhaul. It is marvellous how many years a good gun will shoot without the benefit of expert attention. But it is alarming, too, to discover how many little things need seeing to in a gun after, perhaps, one season's shooting.

When you consider that the price of a new gun by one of the top London makers is now as much as the cost of a good car, and that any reasonably useful weapon can't be had much under a hundred and fifty guineas, it is false economy to begrudge a few pounds a year to have an expert keep it in first-class order. A car wouldn't last long if you didn't have it regularly serviced.

But, if my parting words are to warn you about using unsafe guns, I must also add that guns are not only unsafe in themselves. Everybody who keeps a gun in the house has a responsibility. Those who have to keep guns in the same house as children have a very special one.

My own view is that it is useless to hope that a child growing up in a country house, and in an atmosphere of country sports, can be permanently kept out of reach of game guns. The gun cabinet may be locked, but sooner or later any child in the country will get the opportunity to pick up a firearm; if not in his own house, in somebody else's. Neither, I think, is it fair to suppress a small boy's healthy curiosity for an object that glitters and bangs in such a fascinating fashion as a shot-gun.

My own idea is that the most intelligent approach to the problem is to recognize the fact that, to a small boy, a gun is irresistible and to take the earliest opportunity to gratify his hands. Once he learns what a gun is for, it is time to canalize his interests in a similar toy.

I don't want to advise fathers but, when little boys put greasy fingers on the barrels of my own guns, I always make a point of giving them a demonstration of how they work. I make no attempt to move them out of reach. I let them look up the barrels to see that they are properly polished. And, with a pair of snap caps, I let them pull the triggers and watch the ejectors work. That's one way of making sure that guns have no particular mystery for children.

How soon a boy should be allowed the use of a real gun is entirely a matter of individual development. I remember seeing a boy using a ·410 with safety at the age of seven, which is supposed to be the time when children come to the use of reason. But I think that, while seven is about the right age to put a boy on a pony for the first time, fourteen is soon enough to give him a gun. I should be reluctant, even then, to let him shoot without someone to keep an eye on him.

The old rule, to train a boy in the use of a gun, was to start him off on shooting days carrying an empty one; with the promise that if he handled it safely all day he would be permitted one cartridge.

For their first gun, most boys are given a ·410. On humane grounds, I am not an enthusiast for guns of that bore. Four-tens are limited in their effectiveness. In the hands of any but a skilled shot, an undue proportion of game is pricked. Apart from the undesirability of wounding without killing, the ·410 tends to encourage young shots to pop off at song birds.

Personally, I would always give a boy the largest bore gun he is able to handle with comfort. These days, what I usually recommend is a light 12-bore chambered for 2-inch cases.* Twenty-bores are going out of fashion, largely because 20-bore cartridges have a way of accidentally slipping into the top of the chamber of a 12-bore gun.

In my opinion, people who give boys the use of hammer guns, especially old ones, are bad parents.

I would also like to repeat what I have already said in the chapter on how to shoot rabbits; that rabbit or rat shooting to ferrets, which is usually the kind of shooting that most boys are first introduced to, is almost certainly the most dangerous form of shooting there is. Boys should not be allowed to ferret without the most careful supervision.

Finally, the day that any parent first gives his son a gun, may I remind him that he should take out a sportsman's insurance policy for him forthwith. The premium is very low and, indeed, I can't for the life of me understand why everybody who goes shooting does not protect himself and his gun in this obvious way.

Having warned you against unsafe guns and made my comments about the age when boys should be allowed to touch guns and handle them for the first time, I feel that my last responsibility in this book is to say something on behalf of the game which provides us with so much sport and so much good food.

Let me quote to you an extract from the Report of the Government Committee on Cruelty to Wild Animals which was published in 1951:

'The shooting of wild animals of all kinds is very widely practised both as a method of control and for sport. If the animal fired at were always killed outright, shooting would be one of the most humane methods of control, but this is by no

* Again!

means always the case and there can be no doubt that it may involve great suffering if the animal is wounded and escapes, particularly if it is not followed up and killed. This happens less frequently with experienced shots, but we think that a great deal of shooting is done by people who lack the necessary skill and experience. Despite the high cost of cartridges, many people who lack the necessary skill are accustomed to try their hand with a gun from time to time, and there is a tendency for these people, and also for some who shoot more frequently, to fire at too great a range or to use the wrong type of cartridge. At present anyone who takes out a gun licence can use a gun no matter how un-skilled he may be, and some witnesses have suggested that nobody should be allowed to shoot until he has passed the shooting test. This suggestion is in our view impractical.

'Most of the opponents of field sports advocate shooting as an alternative method of control and consider it to be more satis-factory and more humane than hunting or any other method. We agree that, in many circumstances, shooting is a very impor-tant valuable method of controlling a number of animals such as the fox, but at the same time we are convinced that for the reasons we have given inexpert shooting causes a great deal of unnecessary suffering. Also we do not accept the view which was expressed to us by some witnesses that a normal animal does not normally suffer from its wounds to any appreciable extent. . . . We realize, however, that shooting is a convenient method of control on which farmers, gamekeepers and others concerned with the control of pests depend to a great extent. It is a common practice for farmers to walk round their land with a gun and to shoot any rabbits or other pests as the opportunity arises, and this helps considerably to keep the land free from pests and conse-quently to safeguard food. Because of this it is clearly contrary to the national interest for us to recommend that shooting should be prohibited, nor has any witness proposed this. As it would be quite impossible to attempt to regulate shooting by laying down minimum ranges and other details of that sort, there is no recom-mendation for legislation that we can usefully make, but we think that more should be done to instruct people in the use of guns. We suggest, therefore, that the animal welfare organizations might give some consideration to the cruelty involved in shooting and, with the British Field Sports Society, might compile a pamphlet on the proper use of guns and the avoidance of cruelty arising from their use. It might be possible for such a pamphlet to be issued with gun licences.'

I hope that the advice I have given in this book will do something to implement the wishes of the Government Committee; but it is interesting that the report falls into the common error which will be immediately recognized by readers of this book. The idea that somebody who is completely inexperienced in the use of guns is likely to cause unnecessary suffering to the game he shoots at is a fallacy. The man who is completely inexperienced can, generally speaking, be relied upon to miss altogether. All he is likely to hurt is his own shoulder, or mouth, through bad gunmounting.

The special problem that shooting presents as a sport is that the man who is most likely to wound an animal is the experienced shot who is off his day. If you don't know how to shoot, you'll never be within ten yards, for example, of a driven pheasant. If you're a shot on the top of your form, you will consistently kill him in the air. But if you are an experienced shot who is not on the top of form, then you will again and again wound pheasants without killing them by hitting them behind. There is no solution that I know of to this problem, except to shoot better.

On occasions, I have known an experienced shot who realized that he was off form put down his gun. On others, I have known men ask their host to put a keeper or a reliable shot behind to clean up any birds which they had the misfortune to tail. On most well-organized shoots, the dogs are there to pick up runners as quickly as possible.

Apart from these precautions, there is a responsibility on every man who goes shooting to see to it that for the sake of the game, as well as his host, that he doesn't accept an invitation to shoot at all unless he is in good physical condition. In the old days of the big covert shoots, the crack shots would only drink very sparingly on the evening before they shot. They didn't sit up all night playing cards, they went to bed early, they took care of themselves; and, in many cases, they put in dry practice, or a few rounds at clay pigeons before they started out in the morning.

Shooting is indeed a great field sport and it would be a sad day for this country if it were ever interfered with. The most humane form of shooting, and the way in which the larger part of the game harvest is gathered for the food market, is driven game shooting, because most of the birds are shot in front and, if they are hit at all, they are usually picked up. The form of shooting which provides the greatest number of wounded birds is going-away shooting when a man is by himself or when he is walking-up with a line of guns. From the point of view of the man with the gun, walking-up is the easiest form of shooting. From the point of view of the game, it is the form of shooting in which the greatest care should be taken not to shoot without a fair chance and to see to it that the dogs are put on at once to any bird which is a runner.

To sum up for the last time:

1. *Keep fit.* You can't hope to shoot at your best and you have no business to accept a shooting invitation if you are tired and nervy and if you are not at the top of your form.

2. When you are shooting hare or wildfowl, remember that the natural fault is to think that the quarry is much nearer to you than it is. Better not to shoot at all than to take a chance at extreme ranges.

3. The man who wounds birds isn't the inexperienced shot who is dangerous, not to the game at all, but to the guns who have the misfortune to be out with him. The man who 'tails' birds is usually the experienced shot who is off his day. The more you study drill and practise the drill that I have given in this book, the more seldom it will be that you will have an off-day.

4. Use the best gun that you can afford and don't begrudge the extra expense of using a gun that fits you. Don't fool about with a battery of guns of one kind or another. The best gun is the one you are most used to and the gun that you yourself shoot best with.

5. Take as much trouble to wear clothes which give you maximum freedom of body movement as you do over your gun.

6. Practise . . . practise . . . practise. There is nobody in reasonable physical condition, with eyes good enough to distinguish the difference between a pheasant and a partridge at thirty yards, who can't with training become a reasonably good average shot. Further, age is not a limiting factor.

(The urban simpletons of the self-styled "anti-blood sport" societies believe that shooting destroys a species. None of them are likely to read this, but it is important that shooting men should know how to put them down. Paradoxically, shooting preserves by culling.

I remember an "anti-blood sport" journalist, named Hamilton Fyfe, who tried to tell me, over a delicious luncheon of roast pheasant which we shared, that I was a butcher for liking to shoot pheasants. I remember a nice woman who told me that, in humanity, she was a vegetarian. I pointed out to her how many creatures the farmer has to slaughter to grow cereals for her lentil steaks.

It is a fact that if birds are not shot on a partridge manor, if grouse are not shot on a moor, they will disappear. The lesson is more evident, because it is larger, in the conservation of deer. If the old stags are not shot out, they will prevent the fertile ones from breeding. So even in enclosed parks, it is a necessity to kill off the old males to preserve the health of the herd. In the wild, the job is done by predators. In a man-made world, preservation is brought about by the man with a gun.

Shooting, skilfully employed, kills off the old stock. It breaks up incestuous coveys of birds in which, as a consequence, the survivors mate healthily outside their own immediate family circle.

Defeated in argument, the "antis" will say that, even if it is necessary, there should be no pleasure in the skill of shooting. Neither should there be any pleasure for them in their own blood sport, a most unpleasant cannibalistic one of hunting their fellow human beings.

Knock them down—whatever they say, there are only a handful of them —for the ignorant troglodytes they are. Shooting, as long as there is any health in society, will go on.

The risk in the future is too many people on the ground. The environment of natural life is already in formidable threat, not merely from building development and pollution, but from a ruthless agricultural system which requires the ripping of hedges and the chemical sterilisation of the land. With less and less land available, intensive farming is seeking a solution to feed people in cities. There is no doubt that people, at a price, will be fed.

The price is likely to be the sacrifice of much of our natural herritage. Already, the hawks—noblest of birds—have been virtually wiped out. Partridges, in spite of the skill of the conservationists, are in decline. The little brown birds, the squirearchy of the countryside, are unable to compete in weed-emptied fields with no hedgerow cover.

Peter Scott has rightly said that, if a wild species is destroyed, it can have no regrets for its own loss. The loss is ours. It is pleasant to tell that the conservation of wildfowl is now controlled very largely by sportsmen. Paradoxically, shooting men afford the best protection our natural life has.)

Index

Accessories, 105 *et seq.*
Accidents, 76, 87, 90, 96, 120, 122
Aim, first, 56
Aiming points, 119
Allowance, 60, 61; tables, 63, 137, 139, 156
Angle shots, 61
Arms, 48, 50
Away birds, 51, 54, 56, 61, 122

'Back gun,' 94
Bad shooting, onus, 87
Ballistics, 65
Barrels, 183
  Burst, 238
  Cut down, 188
  Dented, 110, 237
  Long, 85, 183 *et seq.*
  Short, 185 *et seq.*, 204
Beaters, 57, 75, 93, 97, 112, 148
Beresford, Hon. Robt., 201
Blue, looking into, 117, 126, 127
Body movement, 38, 40, 61, 224
Borrowed gun, 206
Butts, 112, 113, 115, 119–21
  Butt shy, 123
  Movement in, 121

Camouflage, 106, 109, 160
Carrying gun, 33, 34, 105
  In covert, 36
  Walking-up, 33
Cartridges, 209 *et seq.*
  Bag, 71, 81, 109
  Balling, 92
  Belt, 110
  Cartwheeling, 91
  Cases, 212
  Cheap, 91, 236
  Corrosive effect, 234
  Dangers, 94 *et seq.*
  Defects, 212
  Fouling, 103
  Getting at, 71
  Hand-loaded, 211
  Jammed, 238
  Magazine, 110
  New crimped, 212

Cartridges—*continued*
  Swollen, 212, 240
  Testing, 211
  Tracer, 222
Children and guns, 243 *et seq.*
Choke, 188, 192 *et seq.*
  Pattern tables, 214, 215
Clay pigeons, 42, 172 *et seq.*, 213, 222
  Don'ts, 174
Cleaning, 96, 159, 160, 233 *et seq.*
Clothes, 50, 70, 79, 104 *et seq.*, 160, 247
Components, 192 *et seq.*
Confidence, 45, 226, 228
Consistency, 35, 225
Covert shooting, 110, 115, 152
Crossing shots, 61, 63, 118, 156, 225
Crows, 85, 90
Cruelty to Wild Animals Report, 244 *et seq.*

Dangers, 36, 72, 87 *et seq.*, 96, 117, 147 *et seq.*, 189
Danger Zones, 75
Descending bird, 140
Discharge, timing of, 52
Discipline, 97
Discomforts and cures—
  Bruised arm, 70
    cheek, 70
    chest, 70
    finger, 71
    mouth, 70
    shoulder, 70
Disease, 114
Distance judging, 65, 66, 134, 160
Dogs, 110, 131, 132
Doubtful birds, 74
Driving, 73, 130
Duck, 112, 161

Etiquette, 73 *et seq.*, 85, 101, 161
'Eye,' 61 *et seq.*
  Master, 227
Eyes, 53, 57, 61, 174, 207, 218
Extractors, 111

Fast birds, 123, 141
Feet, 38, 39
  Correct position, 38
  Faults, 39
  Stance, 39
Fields of Fire, 75, 99, 121
Field sense, 168
Following on, 117
Following through, 120, 148
Footgear, 108
Footwork, 21, 38, 50
Forefinger, 95

Game bag, 111
Game hanging, 111
Gates, 87, 88, 94
Gloves, 95, 198
Golden Rules, 57, 123, 145, 155, 161,
  247
Gough, Lord, 230
Grip, 43, 44, 45, 49, 204
  Shape of, 44
  Slack, 48
Ground Game, 69, 90 147 et seq.
Grouse, 111 et seq., 123, 135, 226
  Flights, 114, 115
  Missing, 57, 123
Gun actions, 92
  Assembly, 232
  Bores of, 194 et seq.
  Choke, 103, 192 et seq.
  Cleaning, 96, 159, 160, 233 et seq.
  Fitting, 43, 52
  Fore-end, 197, 205, 225
  Foresight, 201
  Locks, 195
  Muzzle blast, 219
  Patterns, 215, 216
  Proofmarks, 242
  Pulls, 48, 58, 143, 199
  Shapes of grip, 44
  Springs, 196, 233
  Testing, 207
  Top Rib, 202
  Triggers, 199
Guns, 183 et seq.
  Cheap, 190, 240
  Easy opening, 196
  For clay pigeons, 175
  Measurements of, 204 et seq.
  One arm, 230, 231
  Over-and-under, 183
  Secondhand, 44, 52

Guns—*continued*
  Single trigger, 238
  Too heavy, 54
  Unsafe, 31, 239 et seq.
  Weight, 199, 206
  Wildfowl, 38, 157
  Women's, 79

Handguard, 94, 198, 225
Hands, 35, 43, 153
  Grip, 43
  Left, 34, 35, 44, 47, 204, 228
  Right, 35, 36, 37, 43, 47, 145
Hangar, General, 210
Hares, 89, 101, 111, 147 et seq., 154,
  247
  Killing, 148
  Missing, 148
  Rules, 149, 151
Hawker, Colonel, 31, 105
Head, 36 et seq., 55, 127, 143, 157
Headache, 55, 56, 228
Headgear, 104, 106
Hedges, 76, 88, 92, 97, 125, 146
Height, judging, 66
Herbert, A. P., 242
Hides, 157, 158
High birds, 139, 146, 225
Hurry, don't, 122

Illusion, optical, 66, 127, 186, 187
Incoming birds, 60, 61
Inconsistency, 224
Indoor drill (see Dry Practice)
Injuries caused by faults, 67 et seq.
Insurance, 92

Jays, 90, 163

Keepers, 75, 94, 113 et seq.
King George V, H.M., 206

Leconfield, Lord, 86
Leicester, Lord, 86
Line, down the, 174
  Guns keeping, 89
  Passing, 123
Loaders, 80, 94, 119, 219
  In butts, 122
Loading and unloading, 71, 72, 82
Loads, 56, 139
Low, shooting, 40, 54, 89, 97
  Shots, 66, 89, 122, 134, 225

Magpies, 90
Manners, bad, 115
  Good, 94, 98
Marking, 74, 100, 131
Maunder, Alec, 175
Misfires, 95
Mishaps, field Curing, 239 *et seq.*
Missing, 35, 49, 56, 58
  Behind, 58
  Grouse, 57, 120
  Hares, 148
  Partridge, 57, 124
  Pheasant, 59
  Rabbits, 57, 152
Mittens, 59
Mounting, 35 *et seq.*, 41, 48–50, 55,
  61, 122, 141, 142, 153, 156, 159
  Don'ts, 41
Muzzle-loaders, dangers, 31, 96

Neck, 54, 56, 228
Nerves, 58, 127, 142, 228
'Norfolk Liar,' 111
Novices, 90, 95, 173
Numbering, 73

Over, shooting, 57
Overhead shots, 61, 66
Over-keenness, 76
Overthrow, 143

Partridge, 41, 53, 57, 75, 86, 99, 100,
  111, 114, 121–5, 226, 230
  Importance of silence, 130
  Missing, 57, 136
Percentages, 102
Pheasants, 58, 63, 73, 85, 89, 98–100,
  111, 115, 126, 130, 134 *et seq.*,
  226, 231
  Missing, 59
Physical disability, overcoming, 228
  et seq.
Pigeon, 106, 109, 165 *et seq.*
  Missing, 165
Poacher's pocket, 111
Pointing gun, danger of, 32
Poking, 99, 118, 129, 158
Position, altering, 98
Practice, dry, 36, 42, 51, 68, 135,
  141, 153, 157, 247
Precautions, 32, 116
Prematures, causes of, 32
Pump guns, 80, 190 *et seq.*

Rabbits, 57, 90, 93, 97, 101, 147
  et seq.
  Missing, 57, 152, 167
Range, 61, 190, 193
  Effective, 91
  Judging, 66
Ready position, 61
Recoil, 36, 39, 62, 69, 77, 203
Ricochets, 91, 94, 147
Rides, shooting in, 89
Ripon, Marquis, 86, 99
Raising birds, 136
Routine movements, bad, 89
Runners, 100

Safety catch, 31, 37, 76, 94
Safety Zone, 74
Seasonal overhaul, 237
Shoots, farmers, 93
  Rough, 98
  Syndicate, 89
Shot, indication by clays, 202
  Balling, 92
  Cartwheeling, 91
  Charges, table, 215
  Size, 209
  Speed, 60, 62, 141
  Spread, 145, 193, 194
  Square, 194
  Testing, 212
  Visible in flight, 216, 220
Shoulders, 39, 45, 48, 60, 78
  Looseness, 46
Skeet, 175 *et seq.*
  Ground, 177
Slow birds, 63
'Snap caps,' 51, 227
Snatching, 51
Snipe, 51, 163, 164
Speed of birds, 61, 63
Squirrels, 163
Stance, 38, 39, 45, 125, 136, 143, 149,
  172, 173, 206
  Straight arm, 206
Stands, 97, 137
Stick seat, 110
Sticking point, 136
Stocks, 204 *et seq.*
  Bend and length, 204 *et seq.*
  Cast-off, 52, 206
  Shape of the butt, 203
  Too short, 206
Stop sticks, 116

Straight on shots, 156
Straightaway shots, 60
Street, A. G., 230
Swing, 58, 61, 126, 156

Tailing, 247
Taking time, 127
Targets, clay, 171, 173
  Errors, cause of, 175, 208
Temperament, curing, 58
'Tip-catting,' 51
Tipping, 102
Traps, makeshift, 179
Traversing, 123
Trees, actual height, 66
Troeh, Frank, 175, 200
 Tromboning,' 225

Unloading, 94

Vulnerability of game 158, 164
  Grouse, 119
  Pheasant, 137, 144
  Pigeons, 165
  Wildfowl, 158

Walking-up, 37, 41, 75, 93, 124, 131
  247
Walsingham, Lord, 86, 99, 102
Wildfowl, 109, 155 *et seq.*, 160, 24
  Shorter stocked gun, 109
Wind, 98, 123
Wire, 88
Woodcock, 93, 99, 163
Wounded game, 100, 247